WITHDRAWN
UTSA L

MANAGING PROJECTS IN THE REAL WORLD

THE TIPS AND TRICKS NO ONE TELLS YOU ABOUT WHEN YOU START

Melanie McBride

Apress·

Managing Projects in the Real World: The Tips and Tricks No One Tells You About When You Start

Copyright © 2013 by Melanie McBride

This work is subject to copyright. All rights are reserved by the Publisher, whether the whole or part of the material is concerned, specifically the rights of translation, reprinting, reuse of illustrations, recitation, broadcasting, reproduction on microfilms or in any other physical way, and transmission or information storage and retrieval, electronic adaptation, computer software, or by similar or dissimilar methodology now known or hereafter developed. Exempted from this legal reservation are brief excerpts in connection with reviews or scholarly analysis or material supplied specifically for the purpose of being entered and executed on a computer system, for exclusive use by the purchaser of the work. Duplication of this publication or parts thereof is permitted only under the provisions of the Copyright Law of the Publisher's location, in its current version, and permission for use must always be obtained from Springer. Permissions for use may be obtained through RightsLink at the Copyright Clearance Center. Violations are liable to prosecution under the respective Copyright Law.

ISBN-13 (pbk): 978-1-4302-6511-5

ISBN-13 (electronic): 978-1-4302-6512-2

Trademarked names, logos, and images may appear in this book. Rather than use a trademark symbol with every occurrence of a trademarked name, logo, or image we use the names, logos, and images only in an editorial fashion and to the benefit of the trademark owner, with no intention of infringement of the trademark.

The use in this publication of trade names, trademarks, service marks, and similar terms, even if they are not identified as such, is not to be taken as an expression of opinion as to whether or not they are subject to proprietary rights.

While the advice and information in this book are believed to be true and accurate at the date of publication, neither the authors nor the editors nor the publisher can accept any legal responsibility for any errors or omissions that may be made. The publisher makes no warranty, express or implied, with respect to the material contained herein.

President and Publisher: Paul Manning
Acquisitions Editor: Robert Hutchinson
Editorial Board: Steve Anglin, Mark Beckner, Ewan Buckingham, Gary Cornell,
    Louise Corrigan, James DeWolf, Jonathan Gennick, Jonathan Hassell, Robert Hutchinson,
    Michelle Lowman, James Markham, Matthew Moodie, Jeff Olson, Jeffrey Pepper,
    Douglas Pundick, Ben Renow-Clarke, Dominic Shakeshaft, Gwenan Spearing,
    Matt Wade, Steve Weiss, Tom Welsh
Coordinating Editor: Rita Fernando
Copy Editor: Kezia Endsley
Compositor: SPi Global
Indexer: SPi Global
Cover Designer: Anna Ishchenko

Distributed to the book trade worldwide by Springer Science+Business Media New York, 233 Spring Street, 6th Floor, New York, NY 10013. Phone 1-800-SPRINGER, fax (201) 348-4505, e-mail orders-ny@springer-sbm.com, or visit www.springeronline.com. Apress Media, LLC is a California LLC and the sole member (owner) is Springer Science + Business Media Finance Inc (SSBM Finance Inc). SSBM Finance Inc is a Delaware corporation.

For information on translations, please e-mail rights@apress.com, or visit www.apress.com.

Apress and friends of ED books may be purchased in bulk for academic, corporate, or promotional use. eBook versions and licenses are also available for most titles. For more information, reference our Special Bulk Sales–eBook Licensing web page at www.apress.com/bulk-sales.

Any source code or other supplementary materials referenced by the author in this text is available to readers at www.apress.com. For detailed information about how to locate your book's source code, go to www.apress.com/source-code/.

Apress Business: The Unbiased Source of Business Information

Apress business books provide essential information and practical advice, each written for practitioners by recognized experts. Busy managers and professionals in all areas of the business world—and at all levels of technical sophistication—look to our books for the actionable ideas and tools they need to solve problems, update and enhance their professional skills, make their work lives easier, and capitalize on opportunity.

Whatever the topic on the business spectrum—entrepreneurship, finance, sales, marketing, management, regulation, information technology, among others—Apress has been praised for providing the objective information and unbiased advice you need to excel in your daily work life. Our authors have no axes to grind; they understand they have one job only—to deliver up-to-date, accurate information simply, concisely, and with deep insight that addresses the real needs of our readers.

It is increasingly hard to find information—whether in the news media, on the Internet, and now all too often in books—that is even-handed and has your best interests at heart. We therefore hope that you enjoy this book, which has been carefully crafted to meet our standards of quality and unbiased coverage.

We are always interested in your feedback or ideas for new titles. Perhaps you'd even like to write a book yourself. Whatever the case, reach out to us at editorial@apress.com and an editor will respond swiftly. Incidentally, at the back of this book, you will find a list of useful related titles. Please visit us at www.apress.com to sign up for newsletters and discounts on future purchases.

The Apress Business Team

This work is dedicated to all of the project teams I've led over the years—especially to those of you who ended up working long into the night, putting out raging fires, and otherwise cleaning up my messes as I was learning my craft. Thanks for making me look good!

Contents

About the Author

Melanie McBride PMP, is a Technical Project Manager at Intel Corporation. With over 15 years' experience managing projects in the semiconductor industry, she has worked variously as product development project manager, operations project manager, and vendor development manager. McBride is a recognized subject matter expert at Intel, where she writes a weekly blog on project management best practices. She speaks regularly at such professional conferences as PMI's Global Congress. She holds an MS in physics from Texas Tech University.

Acknowledgments

As with any large endeavor, this book could not have been developed without the assistance of a large team of people. Although it's truly impossible to thank each and every person who has contributed to my understanding of project management and influenced the content of this book, I'd like to take this opportunity to thank some of the key contributors to this work.

Because the heart and soul of this material stems from the internal blog I write at Intel, *The Accidental Profession*, I'd first like to thank the thousands of folks who read and comment on this blog every week, without whom the book could not have been written. I'd like to thank Paulette Moore for being the first to comment and spreading the word far and wide; Russel Zauner, Nancy Winter, Nisha Desai, and Sharon Shindel for being long-time supporters; Jeremy Schultz for more technical support than any friend should have to provide; and Jeff Moriatry for motivating me to write a blog in the first place.

Much of what I write about I've refined over the years through brainstorming and in-depth conversations with my peers. I'd like to thank Jennifer O'Farrell and Scott Stanko for their help in demystifying MS Project and for teaching me how to level resources the proper way. I'd like to thank Tom Stokes and the Chandler Breakfast PDM crew for their insights and ideas, all shared over many cups of coffee. I'd like to thank the Arizona chapter of PMI for their support and the many opportunities to speak at their events. Thanks to Steve Bell, Tiffany Sargent, and Shannon Hart for showing me just what really good leadership looks like. For helping me refine how to explain and master those mysterious soft skills, I'd like to thank Nazia Khan, Ed Garcia, Monica Solera Alfaro, and Chris Mendoza.

I'd be remiss if I neglected to thank my family, who have become an outstanding resource for my project management practice. I'd like to thank Christy Odom for teaching me how to communicate effectively with irate customers; Stormy McBride and Katrina and Allen Odom for schooling me on how you really motivate a team; and Jerry McBride for all those vent sessions and for helping me see that project management really is a universal skill. For her constant support and instilling in me the "go-figure-it-out" mentality, I thank my mother, Carol McBride.

For constantly making me look good and for following wherever I lead, I'd like to thank the Intel Key Generation Team. In particular, I'd like to thank Chris McConnell for countless brainstorming sessions, many of which have ended up on the blog and in this book For letting me try out this blogging thing, the freedom to pursue it wherever it has led, and unwavering support, I'd like to thank my manager, Masud Chowdhury.

Finally, I'd like to thank all those folks who worked with me to get this baby out the door—Stuart Douglas and the Intel Press guys as well as all the fine folks at Apress, including Robert Hutchinson and Rita Fernando.

Preface

I've heard it said many times that project management is the "accidental profession." Somehow people across the land have stumbled into this massively challenging, sometimes frustrating career, and no one is really sure how it happened to them. That's how it worked for me. One day I'm a fairly successful engineer who was slowly getting sucked into more and more "management" activities instead of pure engineering. The next thing I know I'm handed a project and told, "You own it!". . . Uh, okay, thanks . . . this is a good thing, right? By the way, what exactly do I "own"?

Most veteran project managers (PMs) out there came up through the ranks just as I did. We were recognized as people who got things done in a dynamic matrixed environment and were given increasing amounts of responsibility as we got more things done. This was during the Dot-Com Boom and everyone was working like dogs to get cutting-edge technology out the door within companies that were growing by leaps and bounds. Most of us didn't have a clue about project management best practices when we started, and frankly I didn't hear about the Project Management Institute (PMI) until I'd been a practicing PM for several years. All of my early PM training came from the company's training arm and on-the-job rough and tumble. Needless to say, I made a lot of mistakes and mostly learned by doing.

Today there is a superabundance of quality resources out there for new project managers. There are advanced degrees in project management, sophisticated training available within most companies, and innumerable books on the topic for those so inclined. PMI is a treasure trove of best known methods (BKMs) and resources, with local chapters that make it easy to network with other professionals in your field. But for me, project management will always be essentially and irreducibly a learn-by-doing endeavor in which genuine capability improvements come only with experience.

Sure, there are a lot of project management-oriented books available today, and for the most part they are very good—very good, that is, at breaking down the mechanics of the job. Trying to figure out how to put together a comprehensive risk management plan? There's a book for that. How about how to build a dynamically linked schedule in Microsoft Project? Yep, there are more than a few books out there that talk about it. But what if you want to figure out how to get a really complex project kicked off? How about ways to get into that information loop outside of the formal communication channel? What if you're looking for a discussion on how to avoid getting grilled at your next project review meeting?

Well, those things are much harder to come across, so this book attempts to shed some light on those dark, dusty places that fall between the cracks of theory and best practice out in the real world where irate colleagues, unrealistic product launch dates, and virtual meetings reign supreme. Here you'll find targeted discussions on the common challenges project managers face every day, broken out by project phases to help you jump quickly to solutions for the challenges you have today and can expect to run up against tomorrow.

The strategies, tips, and tricks discussed in this book are all proven techniques. I know because I use them all the time! These are the things I had to figure out the hard way . . . by screwing it up, breaking things, pissing people off, and mismanaging my stakeholders and deliverables. In short, they're what I learned along the way to becoming a competent PM.

I hope they help!

Initiating Phase

How to Figure Out What's Really Going On

One common challenge all project managers (PMs) face is just how to figure out what's really going on. I'm not talking about the politically correct spin the marketing representative is putting on for her boss. I'm talking about the real deal—the lay of the land, if you will. How comprehensive is the project plan? Is work really preceding at a fast enough pace? What does the Engineering Manager think of this latest feature? Will anyone be working this weekend?

All of these bits of information flotsam and jetsam are available if you know how to go about finding them. What about that *backchannel* of information you can sense out of the corner of your eye but have no clue about the information that's actually exchanged there? Inserting yourself into the back-channel information flow is tricky and not everyone understands just how to do this.

What about stakeholders? Just how do you go about figuring out who the important ones are? It turns out that there's a systematic way to figure that out.

Oh, and let's not forget about requirements! Are they frozen solid, slightly slushy, or viscous and loose? How do you figure that out, huh?

Inserting Yourself into the Backchannel

Okay, have you ever gotten the feeling that everyone knows what's going on before you do? How about that niggling feeling that you're somehow out of step with everyone else on the program? Key decisions get kicked around and decided upon in hallway conversations by an in-crowd that you're not a part of? Yeah, me too, and it feels like a bad high school flashback, doesn't it? Whenever I get that feeling, it's a sure sign that there's a backchannel information flow that I'm not a part of. In a perfect world all I would have to do is walk up and say, "Hey, I need to know that information too! Can we have a formal meeting with minutes, agendas, action items, and everyone in the organization to discuss these very important issues?" However, here in my reality that never works and in fact that strategy usually makes the situation worse. Whatever your reality is, you have to be successful in your current environment. And in this type of environment, you have to figure out how to insert yourself into that backchannel information flow as smoothly and as silently as possible.

Many folks are honestly intimidated by that in-crowd and uncertain of just how you get yourself into that backchannel. But here's the thing, when we're stuck and can't figure out how to move forward, we often want to change the environment when it would be more productive to change ourselves. Trust me, when faced with this situation, the most productive thing you can do is change your tactics. To be honest, it's really not that hard to get into that hidden information flow, but there are a few dos and don'ts...

DO

- **Read Susan RoAne's book, *How to Work a Room*.**[1] This little gem will give you the specific strategies for worming your way into any conversation. She gives you step-by-step instructions for inserting yourself into a group discussion—and this stuff really works. Practice her techniques a few times and being ignored in the hallway will be a thing of the past.

- **Bait the lure.** Publish data the decision makers care about. Advertise the work your team does so that when impacts to potential strategies are being kicked around, your name comes up as the subject matter expert (SME) for your area. Basically what I'm saying here is—throw out tantalizing tidbits of information those decision makers need and before you know it, you'll be pulled into those backchannel conversations.

---

[1]Susan RoAne. *How to Work a Room: Your Essential Guide to Savvy Socializing*. William Morrow, 2007.

- **Give off a friendly and collaborative vibe.** You want to be seen as a collaborative problem solver not as someone who has to be "convinced." Instead of saying, "Are you on crack? No, we can't do that!"—try something like this: "Sure that sounds interesting. Let me do some research and get back to you." In this way, you are aligning yourself with the in-crowd instead of setting yourself up as a roadblock, all without being a yes-man.

- **Demonstrate your integrity to build trust.** Don't gossip or spread rumors about decisions that are not done deals; likewise do not divulge confidential information. How many times have you heard rumors about a strategic decision being made that in the end was not true? If you want to stay in the backchannel then you need to pay attention and use some discretion.

DON'T

- **Make a lot of noise and demand to be included.** This is a situation where a little stealth and emotional maturity are needed. People get to choose whom they interact with, so become someone they want to collaborate with, not someone they are actively avoiding. Obviously I'm not advocating perfecting your toadying behavior; instead try for friendly and avoid any hint of an emotional rollercoaster. You can scream your little heart out on the drive home.

- **Think more meetings and minutes are the answer.** Meetings are great for getting work done, but demanding additional meetings to get information will not endear you to those already inhabiting the backchannel. Think about this for a minute. How willing am I going to be to share information with you if I've got to attend yet another meeting with a weak agenda and nothing in it for me? Not very, right? And when you factor in the likelihood that these additional meetings are going to fall over my lunch hour or my commute, then you really have a snowball's chance of getting me to voluntarily include you in the backchannel. Same goes for asking me to write up minutes from a casual conversation I just had with the graphic designer. I've got plenty to do and drafting more documentation that only a handful of folks need is not high on my personal "to do" list. Remember, no hallway meeting produces minutes. See what I mean?

- **Be a suck-up.** That's right, you won't get the right kind of respect if you're always agreeing and gushing with praise. Be sincere and if you don't think the decision being kicked around is a good one, then challenge it constructively.

▓ **Extra-points hint**   Never, never, never try to bring in tasty treats as a way to bribe your way into the backchannel…That never works and it completely undermines what little authority you might have.

And finally, the MacDaddy of all don'ts…

- **Don't make this situation into more than it is.** I'm betting that you have plenty of stuff to work on without worrying about what's being decided in those hallway conversations. Stay focused on what you have to do and don't worry so much about being out of the loop. In the end, if your input is critical to the decision, then they will come to you. If you're input isn't critical to the decision, then, frankly, it's time to just get over yourself and get some other work done.

There you have it: a few tips to get you started. If you're following them, then eventually you will wake up one day and find yourself in that backchannel. This kind of thing takes time and can't really be forced, so relax and just give it your best shot. The benefits of being in that backchannel of information will be worth the extra effort you put in to get there—and remember, when you finally get there, be open to pulling others into that backchannel. I hope this has given you some actionable ideas for how to get into that hidden information stream that flourishes from time to time in any large organization.

Figuring Out Who Your Stakeholders Are

The term *stakeholder management* is one of those insider jokes, right? I mean, you understand what each individual word means and you have a sense of what the other person is talking about, but you still don't have a clue how to go about it. You hear that it's a critical thing to do all the time, right? But here's the kicker—does anyone ever tell you how you're supposed to do it? Nope!

I finally figured out that most people talk a good game when it comes to stakeholder management but frankly don't know what they are doing or why they are doing it. I used to consider an email from a stakeholder acknowledging the requirements, test criteria, functional requirements, and so forth as sufficient to "manage" them. This is sadly not the case. I've since come to realize that true stakeholder management is a constant and generally fruitful activity, not unlike sustaining your network. Oh, and you can't really "manage" their expectations until you figure out just who they are. So, in an effort to clue everyone in on the joke (which isn't really a joke at all), here's how you get started. There's a very simple method for determining who your stakeholders are and, as long as you go about it in a systematic way, you should have no trouble at all.

Melanie's Stakeholder Identification Method:

1. Fire up Excel and create a new workbook (Figure 1-1). Add the following headers:

   - *Key Stakeholder?*

   - *Name*

   - *Role on the Project*

   - *Org*

   - *Location/Timezone*

   - *Official Project Team Member?*

   - *Resource Manager?*

   - *Budget Owner?*

   - *Influencer and/or Technical Expert?*

   - *Deliverable Provider?*

   - *Deliverable Customer?*

   - *Final Release Approver?*

	A	B	C	D	E	F	G	H	I	J	K	L	M
	Key Stakeholder?	Name	Role on the Project	Organization	Location/Timezone	Official Project Team Member?	Resource Manager?	Budget Owner?	Influencer and/or Technical Expert?	Deliverable Provider?	Deliverable Customer?	Final Release Approver?	Unofficial Release Approver?
2		Richard Feynman	Platform Architect	R&D	OR/PST	X			X	X			X
3		Whitfield Diffie	SW Engineer	PBG	DC/EST	X				X			
4		Thomas Edison	HW Engineer	PBG	DC/EST	X				X			
5		Alan Turing	Validation Engineer	Q&R	UK					X			
6	X	Edward Tufte	Operations Manager	Mfg	CH/MST				X	X			X
7		Martin Hellman	IT Rep	IT	MS/EST	X			X	X	X		
8	X	Neil Armstrong	Sponsor	COO	AU/CDT		X	X	X		X		X
9		Melanie McBride	Project Manager	PBG	CH/MST	X	X	X	X	X		X	
10	X	Steve Jobs	Customer	Corp Mktg	WA/PST		X	X	X	X	X	X	X

Figure I-I. Melanie's Stakeholder Identification Method

2. List everyone who is officially assigned to the project or attends any meetings associated with your project under the *Name* column. Also include anyone you suspect might be a stakeholder or who has a vested interest in your project.

Caution   Use some common sense here. The goal is to identify your stakeholders, not to drag the planning phase out to the end of the year. Yes, the CEO of your company is technically a stakeholder in your project, but I highly doubt that he's even aware of your project, much less interested in your team's progress.

---

3. Take the time to fill in the Role on the Project, the Org, and Location/Timezone columns. If you don't explicitly know this information, then go find it or just ask the person directly. Don't skip this step!

4. Now, place an "X" in each of the columns as applies to each person, except *Key Stakeholder?*

5. Next, add a column for the *Unofficial Release Approver.* This is a special category for people who have the ability to stop a project release regardless of their position in the organization. There shouldn't be more than a few of these people, but they are incredibly important from a stakeholder management standpoint—so take the time to figure out who they are if you don't already know.

6. Last, analyze the table and pick out the Key Stakeholders. To get you started, here are a few people who are almost always Key Stakeholders:

   a. Anyone with an "X" in the *Unofficial Release Approver?* column

   b. Anyone who controls the overall project budget

   c. Anyone who is a consumer of your project's output—that is, your customers

   d. Influencers/Technical Experts may be, but are not always, Key Stakeholders

There you go—a systematic way to identify who your stakeholders are and their relative importance. It's worth noting that this is a critical exercise to go through anytime you join a new organization or take on a project staffed with people you've never worked with before. The entire effort should only take you one or two hours depending on how much information you have to research, such as Role, Org, Location, and so on. I've also found that many times I don't really understand someone's role when I attempt to summarize it to fit into that tiny cell—so again, this is a worthwhile exercise whenever you're planning a project.

But wait, there's more! Since you've got most of the data in one place, it's really easy to expand the table (or create a separate tab) and document your communication plan while you're at it. You'll notice that I've also included each person's location and timezone while I'm gathering data. While this isn't relevant to selecting stakeholders, this information is often in the same place when I'm trying to figure out where the person fits in the org structure. I then use this information to figure out optimum meeting logistics (timing, location, and so on). Three birds with one stone!

Finally, this is not data I'd post on a SharePoint team site or any other public forum. I keep this file strictly on my own hard drive and do not share it with the team. Sure, there's nothing confidential about this data, but it does include your subjective assessment of the relative importance of your stakeholders, which could be controversial. Further, I'm sure that there are people on your list who believe that they have more influence than you think they do. So, avoid the political minefield and subsequent distractions by holding your analysis confidential unless you have a very good reason not to. In the end, this isn't rocket science: it's a tool for the PM to understand who the stakeholders are and how to manage their expectations.

But What about the Customers?

Stakeholders are many, customers are few, and it's easy to confuse the two. But wait! Aren't customers stakeholders as well? Why, yes they are—but customers are unique and need to be treated differently than your average, run-o'-the-mill stakeholder. Not sure what I'm talking about? Think I've finally crossed over to management double-speak? Give me a minute, continue reading, and let me explain.

I consider anyone who has a vested interest in the project to be a stakeholder, and there's a definite "importance" level for each one. It's critical that the PM understand the "importance" level of each stakeholder. You need to clearly understand who's the final authority/the Big Decider/the Man with the Cash for the project. For product development projects, the Big "Decider" is usually the highest ranking engineering authority, and this is usually the person who's got the most positional power over the engineering community. Make sense? This does not mean that other stakeholders are not important, and often you will find another stakeholder with equal or more importance. For instance, the Program Manager is an important stakeholder for any project, but her relative importance will depend on how much influence she has over your project's destiny. Absolutely all customers are stakeholders, but their relative "importance" may not make them the most important stakeholders.

In fact, it's highly likely that your customer is not the most important stakeholder you have to deal with. I consider the person representing the functional group that will actually use the output of the project to be the most important customer. Too often PMs think of nebulous entities external to their company as their true customers. However, many times the actual customer for your project's output is probably going to be another internal group. While it's true that there can be more than one customer, based on my experience there's going to be just one that's the most important. So how should the most important customer be treated and how is that different from the way a PM should treat the most important stakeholder? More importantly, why do you care?

I treat customers quite differently from the major stakeholders in a few key ways. First, I always solicit the customer's preferences when the team is wrestling with a design implementation. In lieu of quantifiable data, I will defer to the customer's preference. Here's an example from one of my recent projects: the rep for the team who will be using the application my team is developing wants to see a specific tab order (the order in which the cursor moves across a screen as the Tab key is pushed). This isn't something the other stakeholders are going to care about, nor would I ask them for their opinion on the tab order. The development team had a definite opinion, but we implemented the tab order exactly as the customer wanted.

Another way I treat customers differently than stakeholders is that for me the customer is king. This comes from my days working at Applied Materials, Inc. There, it wasn't enough to think of the customer as always being right, because that's a lukewarm level of commitment to the customer. Instead, I treat my true customers like they are the king and as long as what they are requesting is doable within the agreed-upon scope of the project, that's what we do. From time to time, this does requires some skillful influencing and negotiation if the customer wants something that will negatively impact another customer group or that nebulous "external customer"—but that's all part of the game. At the end of the day, why would you argue with the king? Do you appreciate it when the waiter argues with you over that cold entrée they just plunked down in front of you? They why do it to your own customers?

Here's an example of what I'm talking about: A few weeks ago I got new tires for my truck. They never asked me how I wanted the tires installed; instead they noticed the way my old tires were done and duplicated it without bugging me. I walked out to the finished truck and immediately noticed that they'd installed the tires with the white print on the inside. This is exactly what I'd wanted and lest you think that's what they do as a default, I should point out that someone else had their tires installed the other direction, again without being asked. That level of attention to detail is the kind of focus PMs need to bring to bear with their customers.

About now you're probably thinking that it's a lot of effort for a minor stake-holder right? I mean, why should you work so hard to cater to your customer when they are not the "Big Decider" nor are they able to crater your project? Here's the thing about customers versus stakeholders that PMs need to keep in mind. Long after the project wraps up and is closed, those customers will still be dealing with the output of the project. Long, long, long after everyone else has gone away. If the project output doesn't meet and exceed the customer's wants and needs, then eventually your important stakeholders hear about it. In fact, this can turn what was viewed as a successful project into a candidate for the Worst Project of the Year Award...and there's nothing you can do about it! Yes, that's right, a disgruntled, dissatisfied, frustrated customer can tank the reputation of your team and the project faster than you can say "Oops." Further, all you can do is play defense and fall back on those no-win strategies of claiming the requirements were bad or dredging up old CYA emails. If you've ever been in this situation, then you know it's bad—real bad.

So there it is! Not all stakeholders are customers, and how you treat your customers can have a significant impact on the long-term success of your project. Treat your customers with care and don't fall into the trap of treating them the same way you would a stakeholder with relatively low importance.

Requirements? On the Rocks or Frozen?

It is crucial at the initiating phase for the project manager to assess just how clearly defined the requirements are. Think of this like you would order a margarita...are the requirements still a heterogeneous mixture of solid and liquid ("on the rocks"), gelling ("slushy"), or blended to actionable perfection ("frozen")? This information greatly affects the planning activities that come next, and determining this state is a crucial skill for all PMs.

Reviewing the Requirements Documentation

If you were to ask, I think most people would say that the project plan or the schedule is the most important project document. Me, I'd say it was the requirements document. For most of my career I've managed product development projects, and that means a *product requirements document* (PRD). Whether it's a PRD, contract, *service level agreement* (SLA), *marketing requirements document* (MRD), or something else—the requirements document is the one piece of information that truly defines the project. It's so important that if it's neglected by the team, then the project will more than likely be a failure.

One of the most important tasks a PM has is the review of this document. Peer reviews are critical to generating quality documentation, and I always prioritize this type of activity with the team. As the PM, I'm reviewing the document for something other than the technical aspects of the project. That's right, when I do a peer review of a requirements document, it's not focused on technical content. That's not my job; my job is to review for completeness and clarity. The technical reviewers are responsible for the technical content, and I have to trust that they will do their jobs thoroughly.

So, what are the things you need to consider when doing a peer review of a requirements document? Here are the things I focus on:

- *The Executive Overview/Summary: How clear and accurate is this section?* Obviously you want to look for poor grammar and bad punctuation, but is the meaning clear? Are there any run-on sentences or double negatives? You'd be surprised how often these things pop up and obscure the actual meaning. You should also scrutinize anything that's a direct cut-and-paste from another document. Frequently these sections are not a clean fit and need wordsmithing.

- *Are all Opens, Assumptions, and Dependencies clearly documented?* If opens are called out, do they have clear owners and timelines? At this stage of the project there will definitely be some opens, but the key thing is to make sure someone is driving closure on them by a hard date.

- *Each requirement should be clear and concise, even to a non-technical reviewer.* If you don't understand the requirement, then chances are it's not clear enough to avoid multiple interpretations. Log an issue and make sure the requirement gets clarified in the final revision of the document.

- *Beyond clarity, each requirement needs to be testable.* If your requirements document doesn't specifically address this area, then you need to add it. Never let a requirement slide through without a clear pass/fail criterion. Trust me on this one: If it's not clear what "good" looks like for the requirement, then you can bet "dollars to donuts" that your team will be hashing this out in a frantic attempt to close out the project later.

- *Are any of the requirements designated as "optional" or "low priority"?* That's a real bad sign and you should never go to a 1.0 revision on a requirements document with optional items. The requirement is either in or it's out. If no one can make a call on whether or not this item is required, then remove it from the document. These "optional" or "low" requirements can always be added back in later through the change control process if they become "must haves." Optional requirements only serve to confuse and distract the team. Don't let 'em slide.

- *Finally, I always consider where the hot button items are for the various functional areas on the team.* In the last PRD I reviewed, we are doing some major upgrades to a software application but we are not planning to do anything to improve the operating performance. The performance requirements called out in the PRD are exactly the same as they were in the original development effort. As the PM, I want to make sure that the folks responsible for operating the application are okay with no performance upgrades. Therefore when I submit my feedback there will be a question to the PRD owner asking if this requirement has been confirmed with the manufacturing team. I'll also probably ping the manufacturing rep and ask him to double-check that requirement during his own review of the document. It's these minor coordination actions that greatly improve the quality of the final requirements document.

Okay, that's what I'm focused on when I review a requirements document as the PM. If I'm also a technical expert for the project, then I'll do a second review where I only concentrate on the technical completeness of the document. Personally, I find it better to do two separate reviews because I need to look at the document from different perspectives...but that could just be me. ☺

I'd be remiss if I didn't cover one last point when it comes to doing peer reviews of requirements documents. Frequently the document owner struggles with getting the reviewers to provide feedback in the requested timeframe. In my opinion, there's nothing more important for the team to achieve at this stage of a project than completing the peer review and freezing the requirements document. If the requirements owner is having a difficult time closing the review out, then I step in and help influence the team to get the reviews done. As a last resort I set a hard date for freezing the requirements and make it clear that it's time to "speak now or forever hold your peace." At that hard date we, as a team, agree to freeze the requirements and then all other changes must go through the formal change control process. Whatever you do, do not allow this to drag on as it just pushes your schedule and really adds a lot of ambiguity for those executing the project work.

I've reviewed a lot of requirements documents in my time, and I've found that it pays to put enough attention and focus on this activity. A poorly developed requirements document spells doom and gloom for the team later during execution. As the PM, you need to review the document from a unique mindset which is sometimes hard to achieve if you're also focused on the technical completeness. Remember that no one else on your team is going to review the requirements like you will—so be sure you're paying attention to those six items I list above.

Separating the Wheat from the Chaff

Depending on the maturity and type of project management process in the organization you work in, you will be required to create and maintain any number of documents per project. Often the number of documents you have to create can be overwhelming. Ironically the subset of those documents that I actually use to manage the project is fairly small. In fact, I only regularly use five documents. Being able to sort out the documentation wheat from the chaff at this stage of a project is a skill all PMs should master, and your choices here will inform the planning work you'll tackle next.

Usually the documents you're required to produce as a PM fall into those two categories: wheat and chaff. The *chaff* are those documents you have to create per your organization's established business processes that do not help you manage the project. I also consider those documents that contribute minimally to the project as chaff. What types of documents fall into this category? They're things like safety checklists (ever notice that you never find a forgotten requirement while doing these?), approvals for every document ever considered on the project, quality assurance audit reports (the business process compliance kind), the retrospective report-out (does anyone actually use this data?), regulatory compliance checklists, and so forth and so on. In fact almost all checklists fall into this category since you're unlikely to fill it out in such a way that would cause you even more audit attention.

Most PMs know the content of these checklists cold and ensure that the proper work is incorporated into their project plan so, when it comes time to complete the checklist, it's a pencil-whipping exercise. Sure, that's not how those checklists are intended to be used, but if you've been around that particular block a time or two, then you know that that's just what they become after you've used them a few times.

Now the *wheat* is another matter. Here are the five project documents I think are critical to managing a project and why I think they should be on the list:

- **The requirements document**—by whatever name whatever you call it (PRD, MRD, contract, engagement agreement, etc.)—is the most critical document for any project. I really don't need to tell you why this one is on the "most critical" list, but I will give you an example of how critical it is. My brother is a PM in the construction industry, and for him the contract is his most important document. By the end of a project he even has some of it memorized because in his business they succeed or fail based on change requests, and he has to be able to tell quickly whether or not a customer request is included in the contract or not. He can't run his projects without thoroughly immersing himself in the requirements.

- Second only to the requirements document is **the dynamic schedule**. This is invaluable to the PM as a tool for doing "what-if" modeling, for tracking progress, and for making commitments. If the schedule is well developed, it becomes your secret weapon.

- **The change control log and the various change requests** generated throughout the project are other critical documents. You need traceability and you need to keep track of changing customer commitments. Your team also needs these documents to ensure that everyone is on the same page with respect to changes in scope. Not convinced? Just ask your Quality Assurance Engineer! These documents are vital to monitoring the project and keeping things on track.

- I consider the **risk register critical** inasmuch as I think some level of risk management is vital, and the register is the tool you use to develop your risk management plan. I frequently use a nonstandard template to do risk collection, so transferring the information into the required document template is a non-value-added task as far as managing the project is concerned…but that's my problem since I want to use a more streamlined template.

- Finally, I consider **meeting minutes** a necessary evil and am on the fence as to whether or not they are critical. You see, no matter how much effort the PM puts into generating the minutes, I get the distinct impression that almost no one refers to them later. It doesn't seem to matter what information is in the minutes either. How many times do you get pinged by teammates for a specific date or commit? It's clearly in the minutes, but it's faster to shoot the PM a quick IM or email right? Okay, that might be an oversimplification, but you get my point. My other problem with meeting minutes is that they are generally used as a CYA tactic. I've never seen a disagreement turned around because someone else pulled up meeting minutes and demonstrated where the item under contention was discussed in the past. This never ends well and mostly burns bridges. I try very hard to never pull this one…but that's me.

I hope this discussion has encouraged you to look at the documentation you have to create for each project. If it's not contributing to the management of the project, then you should definitely question why it's needed. At a minimum, you should adjust the amount of time you spend on this kind of dubiously useful documentation to reflect the subsequent value in managing the project. So, do you have to produce a lot of chaff? If so, now's the time to kick off some waiver requests to get out from under a mountain of no-value-added documentation.

Formal Change Control Doesn't Have to Hurt

I couldn't believe it when I heard it, but apparently it's true. According to several colleagues and acquaintances, there are quite a few PMs who don't utilize a formal change control process. I know this, based on the shock and awe I frequently get when I mention the latest change request for a project. It seems that the fact that I'm actually using a change control process is unusual. Apparently there are a lot of PMs out there who don't use any change control process whatsoever! Holy cow! How can anyone manage a project without change control? I'm speculating here, but I suspect that the primary reason PMs don't employ a change control process is that they believe that a formal change control is too much hassle—too bureaucratic, if you will.

This perception is entirely false. You can implement formal change control without significant expenditure of effort, focus, time, or bureaucratic hassle. More importantly a formal change control process is like Wonder Woman's bullet-deflecting bracelets—deflecting almost all scapegoating attempts later in the project when the bottom has fallen out and everyone is diving for cover. It's also unparalleled for keeping the entire team on the same page as far as the scope of work is concerned. Don't believe me? Allow me to explain what I do for change control on my projects and hopefully convince you that it's entirely doable.

Melanie's Guide to No-Hassle Change Control

1. *Ensure that the entire team reviews and approves the requirements document(s).* In the standing team meeting, ask for any and all objections, discuss anything that's brought up, and then explicitly state (and record in your minutes) that the document is now frozen at revision 1.0. All further changes to the requirements must have a formal change request submitted. This is important to do formally, as it sets the baseline for the scope of work for the project.

2. *Create a change control request (CR) form if your organization doesn't already have one.* Here are the minimum fields you need on the form: description of the change, who's requesting the change, a change request ID number (can be the same as the date), fields for all functional areas of the project team to enter their impact assessment, and approval fields for all functional areas. You can obviously expand on these but, at a minimum, this is the information you'll need to capture.

▓ **Tip**   If your org already has a CR form but it's a monster, consider making some of the fields in the form "optional." Never suffer through a bloated, time-sucking form for what should be a straightforward process.

---

3. *Every time there's a change to any requirement, insist that a change request form be submitted to the team.* This will require some diligence on your part, since most teams need to be trained to do this. Don't worry, though—after about three change requests, this will become the norm and you won't have to play the change control cop anymore.

4. *Each time a change request form is submitted, make time in your standing team meeting to review it.* Discuss, evaluate impacts, and plan for implementation in your meeting. Finally approve, reject (providing justification for the rejection), or send back to the submitter for more information. Note that this assumes that your entire team is the Change Control Board (CCB).

5. *If the change request is approved, add the work to your schedule, recommit your project deliverables if necessary, and ensure that the requirements document's content and version number are updated to reflect the change.*

6. *Lather, rinse, and repeat for all future changes to your project's scope of work.*

Done right, formal change control should take no more than a few minutes a week on average and will result in greatly improved communication across the team. Furthermore, those change request forms provide a great record of why the scope of the project was changed and when those changes occurred. These records are what I meant earlier about Wonder Woman's bracelets. The only hard part about a formal change control process is facilitating the review and impact discussions; everything else is fairly straightforward.

So, if you are not already using a formal change control process, then I strongly urge you to start. Still not convinced it's worth the hassle? Check out the post mortems for your last few projects. I'm betting one of the common threads you'll find is *scope creep*. Formal change control contains scope creep and ensures that, if the scope is growing, the implications of that growth are comprehended in the overall project plan and that the customer commits.

Effective Meetings in the Real World

People talk all the time about how much they hate meetings, how they have too many meetings, how the meetings they attend are all badly run with no outcomes, and so on. You know what I'm talking about—and face it, we've all said those things before. Worse yet, as PMs we create those crappy meetings! Today companies go to great lengths to teach all of us how to have effective meetings, but we just don't play that way. When was the last time you were in a meeting that resulted in decisions and actionable data? How about a meeting with a good agenda? I'm not talking about a static list of bullets like "status update" here, but relevant discussion topics with clear outcomes. I'm betting that it's been a while, and I'd also bet that you run some of these mind-sucking meetings.

Now here's that cold splash of reality water. Meetings are critical to getting work done. Period. As a PM, it's your responsibility to ensure that every meeting you host is well-run and adds value for the attendees. If your team meetings are not producing decisions and solutions to problems, then you're doing something wrong and you need to fix it now. As the cliché goes, be part of the solution, not the problem.

As the leader, aka the PM, the single most important thing you can do to improve your meetings is to improve your attitude about them. Remember, as the team leader your attitudes and actions set the tone for the rest of the crew. If you run around badmouthing meetings in general and complaining loudly that you have too many meetings, then don't be surprised if others view your meetings that way too. If you don't prepare ahead of time, arrive late, and don't hold yourself accountable, then why should your team do these things either? Yep, as everyone knows when they get dumped by that super-hot girl/guy—it really is you! Sorry!

Start taking meetings seriously and prioritize the preparation for them accordingly. Oh, and while we're talking about preparation, here's a hint: it's much more than sending the calendar hit and finding a conference room. You need to think about what you want the outcome of the meeting to be, what's relevant and actionable for your team, and how to build and reinforce a strong team dynamic. This isn't something you can whip up in the 10 minutes prior to the meeting. Again, if you aren't prepared, how can you expect your team to be? Seriously, it's time to start thinking about meetings differently.

The 30-Minute Meeting

Once you've mastered running your standing hour-long meetings efficiently, the next logical step is to start having shorter meetings. When I first started doing 30-minute meetings I quickly realized that they are much harder to facilitate. There's just no wiggle room for ratholes, unprepared team members, or a weak agenda. This is the major league of meeting facilitation, and you have to bring your "A" game. So how do you do that?

First things first, right? What's the agenda? For a short meeting, your agenda needs to be very tight. It should not be generic items such as "schedule review" or "team updates." I've found that for truly effective 30-minute meetings you need a dynamic agenda that is specific to that timeslot and that week. If your agenda is a placeholder for things like status updates, really think about whether or not a 30-minute meeting will work for this forum. Along with an agenda, a brief meeting like this really needs an objective. I find it best to state this clearly in the meeting invite. The most effective use of a 30-minute meeting is to drive a decision on a contentious topic.

The second thing to understand is that you must be very, very effective at facilitating the discussion. You need to quickly clue into who is/is not participating and the direction of the discussion. In a 30-minute meeting it's very easy for a few to steamroll the rest of the team into a decision that falls apart about 10 minutes after the meeting is done. It's also very easy to waste time on a rathole instead of the core discussion. Remember as the meeting facilitator, you are personally responsible for keeping the discussion on track and leading the team to complete the meeting objective. This means that you're probably going to have to interrupt people and quickly move topics offline if they are not core to the meeting objective. Remember, if the meeting is poorly facilitated and nothing is achieved, then everyone's time is wasted.

Now for the fun part! The third thing to take into consideration as you embark on shorter meetings is that you're going to need to train your team to be effective in this timeframe. You need to set the expectation that everyone come prepared to discuss the topics on the agenda (you have one of those, right?). I always make a deal with my teams that I'll ensure we stay on track and end on time as long as everyone comes prepared to participate. Then of course there's the subtle application of peer pressure to encourage everyone to be ready to rock, so as not to waste the rest of the team's time. I find that it only takes one efficient, short meeting to make believers out of the whole crew.

The fourth thing to remember is to not be a tease. If you schedule the meeting for 30 minutes then it really needs to end in 30 minutes. It's that simple. We've all been in meetings where the words—"this will be a short one"— are uttered with complete sincerity. I don't know about you but I get really testy if the meeting is poorly facilitated *and* it runs long. Don't compound the problem by teasing me that I'll actually recover some extra time in my day. Be honest about what you need to achieve in the meeting and schedule the appropriate amount of time to meet the objective.

Finally, I should point out a common pitfall when it comes to 30-minute meetings. Many of us are familiar with the standard manufacturing *stand-up* meeting where everyone gets together and shares their status in a very quick and informal manner. This works really well for some situations, but it won't work for anything that requires lots of debate and discussion. If all you're doing is sharing information such as "the tool is up and we have no issues," then by all means use the 30-minute duration. On the other hand, if you're discussing the latest engineering challenges, then you will probably find that a 30-minute meeting simply does not have enough time to share status around the room and do some debate and discussion.

You can run effective 30-minute meetings, where decisions are actually made and everyone participates. I know, 'cause I do it all the time. I just don't plan on a 30-minute meeting unless I know we can achieve the meeting objective in that timeframe. The key here is to gauge how much discussion needs to be done before a decision can be made. If your original 30 minute meeting runs 20 minutes long, then you'd have been better off treating the whole thing like an hour-meeting and just finishing early right? It really is worth mastering the 30-minute meeting because once you do, you'll find your team's participation in all meetings increases across the board. In fact, if you are particularly successful you'll find your team asking for more 30-minute meetings and fewer of the longer ones.

Meeting Facilitation: How It's Really Done

For the new PM or someone who happens to wake up one day and find themselves a full-fledged PM, meeting facilitation is a bit of a mirage. You can clearly see what 'good' looks like off in the far-distant land of Perfect World. However, you work in the Real World where things such as competing priorities, impatient teammates, and an informal workplace make formal meeting facilitation awkward, unwieldy, and unlikely. There's just something weirdly pretentious about asking someone to be the timekeeper—much more spending five minutes at the start of each meeting talking about the meeting guidelines.

Okay, so what does work in the Real World? What I've found is that no one technique or tool works all of the time. I'm constantly trying to read the situation and adjust as needed. Every time I run a bad meeting I do a mini-post mortem to figure out what to do differently. That said, here are a few of the tools I have had success with:

- **Situational awareness is key to good meeting facilitation.** This is a hard skill for a PM to develop, mostly because if feels secondary to the job you should be doing—running the meeting. You need to have a sense of whether or not the physical (or virtual) environment is supporting the purpose of the meeting. Trust me, meetings in the café are not going to be productive for more than 2 people. Does the speaker phone work adequately? How about the video? Are there enough chairs for everyone? These are the kinds of things you have to think about in order for the overall meeting to go smoothly.

- **You also need to pay attention to the team dynamics**—such as who is or isn't talking, the overall tone of the meeting (collaborative or combative?), and where the pockets of disagreement are. I have a pretty low-tech method for monitoring this kind of thing in virtual meetings. Before the meeting I'll write the name of everyone attending the meeting on a Post-it note. As the meeting progresses I'll place a mark next to each person who talks. This is a quick visual way to understand who's not participating in the meeting. Once I know who's not playing, I can address specific comments to them or ask for their opinion. You can also use this method in reverse if you have the feeling that someone is dominating the meeting.

- Another technique I've perfected over the years is to **keep the discussion on any one topic to around 10 minutes max.** No matter the topic being discussed there are always a few people on the team who aren't affected by the outcome. Be respectful of their time and either limit the discussion in the meeting or take it offline and report the outcome in the next meeting.

- **Utilize physics!** Since the speed of light is faster than the speed of sound, you can convey information more quickly if you employ a visual medium. Okay, all this means is that I type the meeting minutes real-time while the meeting is happening and project them. This actually serves two purposes: first it improves the team's understanding of whatever we're discussing; second, I really think it speeds up the discussion. It's also very helpful when your team has members for which English is not their native language. I try to limit slang and cultural references but I know I'm not successful all the time. Capturing the key points of the discussion visually, right in the meeting, greatly improves the quality of the communication for the whole team.

- And finally, here's one for your inner control freak. **Be ruthless in keeping the meeting on track.** Do not let any one person take control of the discussion. For some people this can be the hardest part of meeting facilitation. You have to interrupt people and you have to tell others to take the discussion offline, all while remaining professional about telling them to shut up! ☺ I see this most frequently when a loquacious manager attends a team meeting on an occasional basis. I used to work for a great guy who loved to talk and every time he was in a meeting with my team he tended to dominate the conversation. I was continually wresting the conversation away from him and turning it back to the agenda. He was never offended and frankly didn't realize he was doing this. I've also seen examples of managers hijacking the meeting to drive some action they want to happen now or to just pound the table. This situation sucks and there's usually no winning here, sorry to say.

So those are some of my tips and tricks to facilitate meetings. Think about your own meetings and be honest…could you do better at facilitating them? Since you are effectively commandeering people's time and attention, you need to make sure that they get something out of it by ensuring that the meeting is well-run and productive.

Don't Let Your Boss Come to the Meeting

All right, consider this fair warning—if you manage direct reports you're not gonna enjoy this bit. In fact, if you continue to read it you're going to feel all squirmy and uncomfortable because I'm tellin' it like it really is.

What's the single most effective way to undermine your authority as a PM, run a completely ineffective meeting, and totally de-focus your team? Invite your manager to the party! Yep, despite what you may have been told, it's never a good idea to bring your functional manager into a regular team meeting. Even if you work for someone who's completely reasonable and perfectly savvy about interpersonal communication skills, you're just askin' for trouble if your boss shows up to one of your meetings. Trust me on this one...there's rarely a legitimate need for the boss to show up and play in a working-group meeting.

Okay, I can hear some of you now..."But wait Melanie, my boss is so awesome and he only wants to help out. What could possibly be bad about having him participate in my team meetings?" Well let's see...there was that guy who managed the pilot line who liked to pace around the table and bang his fist in his hand to make a point, and then there was the functional manager who liked to hear himself talk...a lot! And of course who could forget the engineering manager who liked to hand down decisions without any input or comprehension of the consequences? Here I should point out that I genuinely liked all of these managers and they truly didn't mean any harm in coming to my team meetings. In the case of the pilot line manager, he just happened to love the film *Gladiator* and in his zeal he would completely freak out my project team. It would take me the better part of a week to chill them out and convince them that he didn't really mean that they would all lose their jobs if the project slipped so much as an hour. The talker? He had the best stories and was super-entertaining, so we definitely had a good time when he showed up. The problem was that absolutely nothing got accomplished in those meetings, and that's despite the fact that I was constantly wrestling the conversation away from him to get it focused back on the agenda. The engineering manager I mentioned caused me a full week of work just to get the team re-focused back on the original scope of work every time he decided to "pop in." Take it from me: Never get into a situation where a functional manager dictates how you lay out traces on a board...can you say "re-work"?

Still not convinced? Okay, consider how it looks to your team when your boss is there. Who's the leader now? When it comes time to make a decision, who gets the "Decider" card? You? Or your manager? Oh, and if you think your boss is just gonna sit there and be quiet, think again. That goes completely against human nature, and it's a rare manager who can let their direct report stumble or fail without jumping in immediately to help. Have you ever been in a meeting where the meeting organizer's boss is sitting in to "observe"?

Notice how they can't help correcting the organizer right there in front of the entire team? That's what I'm talking about here. This is probably the single most effective way to undermine your position as the team leader, bar none.

There's another issue with having your boss attend your meetings. It's almost second nature to everyone in the room to defer to the boss. So now your boss is put into a position to make decision on issues that you would normally handle. Do you really think it makes you look good for the boss to have to decide which technical solution to implement? Maybe, but what about all those mundane decisions you make in the course of a project meeting? Who's going to pick up the marketing collateral? Should the team get together for lunch on Wed or Fri? Do you need a change request for that update to the training documentation? Does the planner order a 10% buffer quantity of interposers or 25%? See where I'm goin' here? If you give your boss the impression that you and your team can't make simple decisions like those above, what confidence is he or she gonna have that you can be trusted to make much harder, more critical decisions? I know you don't intend to give that impression when the boss shows up for the meeting, but trust me, it can happen all too easily. Beware my friends, beware.

By now I hope I've convinced you that it's never a good idea for your boss to attend your team meetings, but what if you can't avoid it? What if the boss is insistent that he or she be present for some particular decision or meeting? What do you do then? In that situation the first thing I do is ask myself whether or not I can set up a one-off meeting to address the issue my boss is concerned about. This is usually the best approach, as you can limit the agenda strictly to that topic and contain the damage. If I can't set up a dedicated meeting, I ask myself what is the motivation behind the request to be at my team meeting? Often I can address this motivator separately and offline, such as when the boss is wound up about a schedule slip.

▨ **Caution**   Never, never, never let your boss come in and cudgel your team about being late. You might as well shoot yourself in your own foot!

If those two strategies won't work, then I get a bit more "creative" and strategically "forget" to send the boss the meeting calendar hit. Ironically, the more impassioned the boss is to attend a meeting, the higher the likelihood that she will completely forget about the meeting next week. Sneaky? Sure. Effective? Absolutely!

All right, I'd be remiss if I didn't mention the only time it's a good idea to bring your boss (or anyone else's boss for that matter) into your team meeting. Managers listen up! The only time you should invite your boss to a team meeting is to hand out praise for a job well done. That's it! No exceptions! Further, it's a really good idea to have the boss come at the end of a meeting or have them do their thing at the beginning and then leave. To be honest, unless the boss specifically asks to come to my team meeting to deliver the "atta boy," I prefer to have them send an email to a broad distribution as I think that's more motivating for the team…it gives them something their peers can rib them about later.

There you go—the nasty reality about having a manager attend your project meetings. Sure, it sounds like a reasonable idea on the surface, but based on many uncomfortable meetings with a stupid amount of damage control to do later, it's just not a good idea. Even today, where I like and respect my boss, I do not invite him into the team meetings as a rule. I'm really not trying to hide anything from the boss here; it's just that his very presence can under-mine my authority and de-focus the team, despite his real desire to help us out. Does he make an appearance once in a while? Sure, but it's not a regular occurrence.

Taking Minutes in the Real World

In an average week, for any given project I'm managing, I'll attend three or four meetings and I am responsible for the minutes for most of them. Even if I'm not the minute-taker, as the PM I need to facilitate getting the key points documented in the minutes. All this adds up to lots of minutes!

So this begs the question: how do you handle your minutes? I think taking good meeting minutes is a learned skill and it takes a lot of practice to get to the point where you can participate in the meeting, facilitate the meeting, and type up the minutes in real time. Don't kid yourself: this is really hard to do for a variety of reasons. Some folks never get to the point where they can do all three simultaneously. My best advice to you, if you can't do all three of those at once, is to ask for a volunteer to take the minutes. You can also ask a neu-tral party to facilitate the meeting, but frankly almost no one does that. Last you can go off and improve your typing skills. Who knew that typing would be one of those high school skills that I'd use daily as a grown-up? Heck, with the exception of the word *champagne*, I haven't uttered a word of French in twenty years, so that class wasn't as useful in retrospect! ☺

How I take minutes and what format they end up in are an area of constant innovation for me. I find a format that works well for a while, and then it seems stale and frankly underperforming. I believe that a high-performing format will increase the usability of the information captured and actually encourage participation in the meeting. I'm always on the lookout for new ideas on how to handle my minutes.

Here's an example of what I mean when I refer to a *high-performing format*. A couple of years ago I managed a project that fed up into a large product development program. The program manager was very experienced, and I learned a great deal from watching her work. One of the absolutely brilliant things she did was to not publish meeting minutes. She didn't take minutes like we take minutes. Basically she created a spreadsheet to use as a discussion guide and record for the program team meetings, which she posted in the program repository. One tab was set up to talk about whatever opens or hot topics the team needed to address. A second tab was set up to facilitate discussion on topics related to operational excellence—what was working, what wasn't working, what we should change, and so forth. The final tab was set up to record key decisions. Each week the team members were expected to open up the spreadsheet and add topics to the first two tabs that they wanted to discuss in the meeting. During the meeting we stepped through the spreadsheet tabs and any key decisions were documented. That's it! It was brilliant in its simplicity and it was incredibly functional for that team. For what it's worth, I use this same technique anytime I fast-track a project because it's more efficient than my usual method, and on a fast-track project the team is very motivated to go grab information out of the minutes if they need it.

Now in contrast, I once worked in an organization where the format of the meeting minutes was so cumbersome that the PMs would spend about an hour per meeting cleaning them up after the meeting was done. To be fair, this was also partly due to the fact that some of the PMs struggled to type and facilitate at the same time. To this day, I don't understand why they didn't ask someone else to take minutes. For my part, I had the typing down but the format was so persnickety that even I would spend a good 20-30 minutes doing clean-up for each set of minutes. That was just plain crazy, especially when you consider that we all had more project work than we could handle. In hindsight, I should have driven a change to that stinkin' minutes format... Ah, live and learn, eh?

Speaking of awkward formats—a few years ago, I worked in an organization where the preferred vehicle for documenting almost all of the project data was a web tool that had been developed in-house. It provided space/fields for documenting everything from revision changes on key documents to the risk register. One person described it to me as "PMBoK in a Box"[1] and according to my Op X rep, all I needed to do during the team meeting was step through each page and update it. The problem with that tool was that it didn't have a good way to capture key decisions or the discussions that would happen during meetings. I hated this tool and never did use it to capture "minutes." Happily I heard that it bit the dust, so that's progress from my perspective.

---

[1]PMBoK is the acronym for *A Guide to the Project Management Body of Knowledge*, the compendium of project management standards and best practices published by the Project Management Institute in its 5th edition in 2013.

Today I use MS Word or OneNote with a fairly loose format for meeting minutes and I spend about 5 minutes cleaning them up afterwards. I capture the team members' update, the schedule update, risk management activities, the change log, track-action items, and opens all in the same document. I'm constantly tweaking how I take minutes. I don't change formats mid-project, but I do switch it up for new projects, depending on the pace and team makeup.

Improving Your Virtual Meetings

Once an old friend and coworker from a previous employer commented on the fact that I seemed more animated than he remembered. "What the heck is this guy talking about?" I thought. This comment percolated in the back of my mind for a while, and it took me a few days to figure out.

I was sitting in my beached-whale-gray cubicle participating in yet another virtual meeting when it hit me. He thought I was more animated because I *sounded* more animated than he remembered. You see, when I worked with this guy virtual meetings were the new, new thing and not the pervasive SOP they are today. As I sat in that meeting, I realized that about half of the participants spoke in what can only be described as passionless, dead-zombie voices. There were virtually no subliminal cues as to what they were thinking or how strongly they felt about any particular point. To be honest, it was sleep-inducing to be a part of that meeting and, in retrospect, I probably should have excused myself and ditched the meeting.

Sadly, this happens a lot, but it's easier than you think to improve your communication skills in this area. I know this because I made it a goal to improve my facilitation of virtual meetings a few years ago. One of the key lessons I found was that I could greatly improve the overall communication just by changing the way I sounded. The goal here is to convey subliminal context with vocal intonation and word choice. Basically, you want to extend the depth of communication by layering in more meaning behind the words you use. To help you out, here are a few techniques I refined over the years:

- *Always greet each person on the conference call.* Greet some of the folks more enthusiastically than others, based on how well you know them. Trust me a cheerful and hearty "Hey Melanie! How's it goin'?" goes a long way to setting the tone of a meeting. Just be careful not to come across as an announcer at a low-rent circus.

- *Smile when you speak...if you want to convey a positive message.* Conversely frown when you need to convey some doubt or misgivings. Stand and pace around your cube if you want to convey confidence and/or urgency. I don't honestly know why this works, but I can attest to the fact that it does.

- *Practice speaking in different volumes to enhance the message.* A slightly louder "Hey Melanie! How's it goin'?" conveys something completely different if those words are spoken much more softly. Go ahead and try it right now for yourself. I'll wait! Two words of caution here: circus announcer! 'Nuff said.

- This next technique takes some practice but is very effective once you master it. *Change the cadence or pace of your words.* When I mean business and want to signal that the joking around is done, I tend to speak more briskly and use very precise wording. This is especially effective if I want to emphasize a decision the team has made or recap a meeting before breaking it up. By speaking faster and more precisely I signal that what I'm saying is important. Obviously the opposite is also true.

- Once you've mastered your vocal intonations and cadence, it's time to *try playing with your word choices.* Instead of saying, "Thanks for getting that deliverable done early," say, "Wow, two weeks early on that deliverable! You rock!"...Okay you might need to tweak that to reflect your own personality, but I think you get my drift here. Think about the adjectives you use most, and then identify alternates that convey more meaning. For instance, instead of saying that something is increasing, say that it's ramping rapidly or that it's experiencing exponential growth. Simple changes to word choice can greatly enhance the message. If this is hard for you, then rustle up a thesaurus and use it regularly...I do!

Now, I know there are some folks out there rolling their eyes about these tips and tricks. That's cool, but I'd like to challenge you to pay attention to how the other people on your next conference call sound. Pull out a scrap piece of paper and jot your observations down as the meeting progresses. Can you glean additional meaning from their intonation and word choices, or are they a blank canvas? Now think about how you spoke and what you could have done differently to enhance the communication of your key points. This stuff isn't rocket science and it's pretty easy to master, so why not give it a shot? What can it hurt? And if you're lucky you'll find your virtual meetings get a tad more productive.

The Project Kickoff Meeting

It's a tossup to me which one is more important: the *kickoff* or the *go/no-go* meeting in the lifecycle of any project. First off, what's the primary purpose of a kickoff meeting? Very good! It's to get the entire team on the same page with respect to the project. That's important, right? So why do so many PMs do a half-hearted job at them? The kickoff happens somewhere in the nebulous boundary between scoping the project and in-depth planning. This is the busiest time for a PM across the entire lifespan of the project. Somehow, 'cause you're crazy busy, the kickoff meeting gets short shrift. It seems adequate to slap a quick meeting on the team's calendar and a vague plan of "just explaining" the project to the team and getting started on the estimation work. Unfortunately, a weak kickoff meeting starts your project off at a disadvantage, and that can that make life a lot harder on the PM than it has to be.

If a weak kickoff is detrimental, what does an effective one look like? The kickoff meeting should set the vision for the project: everyone should understand what the project is expected to achieve (at a high level), why this particular project is important, where it sits on the org's overall priority list, and so forth. It's also the first time you're going to meet as an intact team, so here's where you need to setup the team dynamic. Does this team need to be nimble and fast to execute? Is this a long-haul project where collaboration across the team will make the difference? Is this a fly-under-the-radar project where innovation trumps the status quo?

That's a lot to think about so let me break down my standard kickoff meeting agenda...and yeah, I have a template I follow for every project.

Melanie's Kickoff Meeting Agenda

1. *Who's on the Team?* Here I use a simple org chart graphic and it goes without saying that you need to spell everyone's name correctly and get the name each person prefers to be called correct. Here's a hint: it's not "Mel"—it's "Melanie".

2. I call this section *The Guidelines* and it's a single slide where I talk about my expectations for how the team will work. This is where I'm setting up the team dynamics. More on this later!

3. *The Project Objective.* This is a simple, concise statement of what the project is supposed to achieve. If I can't come up with that "simple, concise statement," then I know I'm not ready to hold a kickoff meeting, because I don't understand enough about the project yet to convey it to my team.

4. *The Technical Overview.* During this part of the agenda I have the technical lead spend 5–10 minutes giving the team a high level overview of the work. This isn't meant to be a requirements session but rather a good introduction to the challenges ahead—a springboard to get everyone thinking.

5. *Next Steps and Major Milestones.* I deliberately wait until after the technical overview to throw out the milestones into play, because I want my team to focus on what we have to achieve rather than freak out 'cause we don't have enough time. If the requirements document is 80%-complete, then I'll also announce the start of the estimation process. Otherwise we talk about what work needs to happen right away.

6. *Opens and Action Items.* This last section is where we talk about meeting logistics: how often and when will we meet. Here I take the action item to set up the standing team meetings.

Okay, that's my standing agenda to kick off any project, but I want to come back to *The Guidelines* in item #2. How often do you talk explicitly about your expectations with your team? I'm talking about things like the fact that you expect them to arrive on time to meetings and come prepared. Or that everyone's opinion is valued, will be heard, and seriously considered. Sure you can just assume that everyone understands these points as they are pretty much ingrained in our culture…but wait just a minute here! If you don't *explicitly* state these expectations, aren't you leaving a door wide open for misunderstandings and frustrating behavior later on in the project? Hey, I get it! I know it's downright awkward to say, "Melanie, I expect you to be on time and prepared for all team meetings." I'm not so thrilled about having to do that one-on-one either, which is why I explicitly state these things in the kickoff meeting…for every project even if the team members have seen this stuff before. Finally, here's a fun fact for ya: after I started explicitly stating my expectations for team behavior in kickoff meetings, I saw a noticeable decrease in people ditching my team meetings and a decrease in the number of folks who didn't provide an update prior to the meeting if they had to bail. Coincidence? Possibly, but I think it's more likely that by explicitly stating those guidelines, I've reminded folks of just how they are expected to behave as part of a team.

So, I bet you didn't think I had that much to say about a kickoff meeting, huh? Again, this is one of the most important project meetings you'll host and you really need to get this one right. If you do, you start off strong with a team that has a clear vision and the framework for working together. If you slap a kickoff together, then you're going to spend bunches of time aligning all the functional areas on a common understanding of the scope of work—plus you've still got to figure out how to influence that team dynamic in the direction you want it to go. Having done just this many times, I can now say with conviction that an effective kickoff meeting makes a huge difference later on as you're trying to move your team from the "storming" phase through to the "performing" stage.

Team Building

As you kick off a project, you start with a collection of people who are only loosely connected through the objectives of the project. Your goal then is to forge a cohesive team from this collection of people as quickly as possible. Sadly, many PMs never develop that cohesive team because they aren't paying attention to the team dynamics, nor are they taking deliberate actions to define just what that dynamic will be. This chapter considers just what role the team dynamic plays in the overall success of your project. As a PM you most likely do not have direct authority over your teammates, so you need to understand how to motivate your team. How you motivate a team of drivers is very different than the techniques you would employ on a low priority project. How would you like your teammates to interact for the best results? As the team leader you need to foster an environment that's relaxed and open. How do you go about that? Well, stay tuned and I'll tell you!

Team Dynamics

I think actively managing your team dynamic is important…but how the heck do you do that? This is another one of those areas of project management where you understand the words but have no clue of their actual meaning, so I thought I'd try to shed some light on the topic.

To demonstrate the importance of understanding the team dynamic, let me tell you a story about two teams I worked with a few years ago. The two different product development teams were part of a larger group that's worked together for years. All team members are very good at their jobs and this makes it easy to manage these projects. Colocated, highly experienced team members? Can you say *PM nirvana*? ☺

I originally thought that these two teams would have similar dynamics and that I could manage the projects in similar ways. Well, it turns out I was wrong. While I'd realized that these two teams worked differently, it wasn't until we moved to a new office location that I understood what was going on.

When my group moved to a new building and into new cubicles, I noticed something interesting. Most of my group elected to change their cube layouts, but a few kept their cube designs the same. In fact, these folks who didn't change the layout also set up and decorated their cubes *exactly* the same way they were in the previous location. A few of the "changers" probably only changed due to the constraints of the new location, but still others took this opportunity to completely restructure their workspaces. Interestingly enough, one of the project teams is predominately "changers," while the other one had all the folks whose cubes remained the same. This was the key to what was going on with the team dynamics.

I now think of the people who elected to completely change their cubes as *change agents*. These are the folks who actively seek out and embrace change. The team that has a majority of change agents on it moves much faster than the other team. In the team meetings, there's usually someone proposing a new solution to a problem and it's much more interactive, with everyone chiming in on any topic under discussion. Most of the time I feel like I've barely got hold of the reins and it's all I can do to keep the horse focused on the bend before the straightaway sprint to the finish. In these meetings I rarely have to prompt anyone for their two cents and I often find myself dialing down the rhetoric so we can focus on the data. This team gets psyched by the big win such as implementing never-before-used technology faster than we estimated. I try to keep them motivated with stretch goals and provide the big picture vision.

The second team is completely different and composed mostly of those who did not change their cube layouts. This team is quieter but no less focused. In the team meetings I pay more attention to who's talking and who hasn't weighed in on the issue under discussion, ensuring that everyone's heard. This team is rock-solid and I feel more like the person with the map saying, "Head due east for 2 miles, then turn south." I'm providing the navigation and they are the steady engine getting us to the destination. This team has also pulled off some amazing engineering feats, but they are quieter about it. I need to make sure I'm advertising what they've accomplished, because they are not likely to do it themselves. These guys are motivated by recognition of their respective contributions to the team, as opposed to some fantastical technical achievement. I struggled to find ways to inspire and motivate this team, yet the end product was delivered on time and of the utmost quality.

It's fascinating how different the team dynamics are. On the surface, the teams' makeup and experience levels are very similar, but trust me—what works well with one team can have very different results for the other. For instance, I started holding the team meetings in a physical room instead of virtually.

The change-agent team almost rebelled, primarily because they had to take time to walk downstairs to the conference room. The other team seemed to welcome the change and I noticed that the flow of information in the meeting had really improved. You see, the second team really valued the opportunity to get together as a team, whereas the other team chafed at what they saw as an unnecessary hassle. Go figure. ☺

I honestly enjoyed working with both teams and they both challenged me in different ways. I hope I've convinced you to take some time and think about the dynamics of the various teams you are currently working with. Are you using the same tactics and tools for all of them? Are these tools really working across the board? Chances are the answer is no and it's time to do some tweaking. I see this tweaking of the team dynamics as part of the art of project management. It's not easy or well-defined, but the payoff when you get it right is stupendous!

If you're a little fuzzy on just what I mean by *team dynamic*, that's okay… it took me years to figure some of this stuff out and I don't think I've truly mastered it yet. This is part of the "art" of project management, and it takes a lot of practice to actively shape and control your team dynamics.

By *team dynamic* I mean the way your team members interact—what constitutes the norm for behaviors within the team. That dynamic can be collaborative, trusting, relaxed, competitive, combative, uncomfortable, dysfunctional, and so on. Each team behaves differently depending on its members. I believe that you can affect this dynamic through deliberate action. Let me give you an example. I once lead a team consisting of three highly competitive members plus two members who were motivated through their contributions to the team. To keep the highly competitive folks motivated, I set a challenging goal with a tangible reward if the team could hit one of the project milestones. The other two folks were motivated to contribute to the team goal. What this did was focus and motivate each team member on a common goal, despite having different motivators to get there. You see, by formulating a goal that required collaboration across the team, I was able to nudge that team dynamic in the direction I wanted it to go. Collaboration, not competition. Sure, I was trying to motivate the team, but I was also deliberately trying to establish collaboration as a norm for how we worked together. Make sense?

Now if you're like I was, then this whole concept of deliberately trying to shape the team dynamic takes a long time to resonate. Many folks are honestly oblivious to this whole concept. They let these things drift and if they are really good at motivating individual team members, then every so often they luck into a team that works well together. The kicker here is that this is just serendipity and not really that repeatable. Here's where you need to drink the Kool-Aid—you need to accept that you can shape the team dynamic through deliberate actions. Go ahead and take a big gulp…I'll wait!

Tastes good doesn't it? Once you accept that you can actively influence the team dynamic, just how do you go about it? Well, before you can start influencing you need to know what you have to work with. Consider your team members. What motivates them? How are they interacting today? A good way to gauge this is to pay attention at the beginning of your team meetings, as everyone is joining the meeting. What's the chitchat about? Who's talking and who are they talking to? During the meeting, pay attention to how each person interacts with others and with the group. If someone asks for help, is help offered up freely and generously? Are some of your teammates getting impatient at the pace or quality of their peers' output? Do you get a sense that everyone is engaged in the discussions? What you're looking for here are patterns of behavior and clues about ways you can motivate the team.

After you know what you've got to work with, start formulating a strategy. The idea here is that you provide an incentive to motivate the behavior you want to be part of the overall team dynamic. Here are a few ideas to get you started thinking along these lines:

- *For teams made up of highly competitive members:* I've had pretty good success with tangible rewards (such as free food) for teams with a lot of very competitive members. Broad recognition at the org level can also fill that tangible reward, but that's highly dependent on what motivates those folks.

- *For teams that haven't worked together before:* Work on deepening the relationships between members. A good way to do this is to start off a conversation at the beginning of the meeting about what everyone did over the weekend. Even getting the meeting going with some comments about the weather will encourage conversation across the team. Try asking about kids or pets because most of us have one or the other or both. The goal here is to get team members to see each other in terms of common or unique interests. It goes like this…Melanie likes to bake cakes and so do I; therefore we have a connection that goes beyond the specific project we are working on at the time.

- *For combative teams:* Focus on expanding each person's understanding of his fellow team members' priorities and points of view. Here's where you want to make sure that everyone understands just why it is that Melanie cannot add yet another I/O port to that design. See, some of your team members are going to believe at some level that I am out to spite them, whereas in fact there may not be any more physical space to put in that I/O port. Expand understanding and perspective across the team to dial down the confrontations you have to referee.

- *For teams where members act as individuals rather than as a cohesive whole:* Establish a distinct team identity. If you've got the budget, go get some T-shirts made up. Psychologically, we all want to conform to our peer group yet at the same time stand out from it. A common uniform, such as cool-looking shirts, fills both needs by allowing the team to conform amongst themselves yet stand apart from the larger organization. If you don't have a budget for shirts, you can still develop a team identity through careful wording on your regular status updates and by referring to your team as a group. Here's something I do all the time. Whenever my team and I go to an open forum, we tend to arrive en masse, and when we walk in, I'll jokingly call out, *"Project XYZ's in da house!"* That works with my personality and it always generates a chuckle but, more importantly, it reinforces that concept of team and uniqueness. Make sense?

Obviously, I could go on and on about this topic, but isn't this enough to get you started? The key here is a *deliberate* strategy, and it's an ever-evolving one at that. What works for this team today may be completely ineffective for the next one. Every team is different because this dynamic is really all about the interplay between members. Pay attention to what's going on and actively work to shape the team dynamic, and you'll find that your job gets a lot easier.

Motivating a Team

The ability to motivate others is a core skill for project managers. Let's face it—your team doesn't report to you, you don't get to approve their time off, and, in some cases, you're asking them to do stuff they'd rather not bother with. I see junior PMs struggle with this all the time. They honestly believe that people will do the work assigned to them simply because it's their job to do so. What those PMs are failing to account for is the reality of working in a matrixed organization. It's highly likely that every member on the team (including the PM!) has more work assigned than they can possibly do in a 40-hour work week. To be perfectly blunt, you need to make people *want* to work on your project, and you do that through positive motivation.

Notice that I didn't say *negative motivation* because—although that tactic will work—it is not a repeatable solution. You're probably guilty of using some negative motivation from time to time. I was a master of it in a past life, I'm sad to say. Negative motivation involves compelling someone to do something they truly don't want to do or is not in their best interests to do. Here's a good example: during the estimation meeting, the PM repeatedly and aggressively badgers the team members to provide low-ball estimates. The PM will walk away happy that the schedule meets the customer's expectations, and the team walks away pissed that the PM pushed them into unachievable commits. In the end, the project will slip and most likely miss the customer commitment—all because the PM used the wrong motivation tool during estimation.

So what does positive motivation look like? Damned if I know! Seriously, it's like that the Supreme Court standard for recognizing hardcore pornography, "I know it when I see it." I take a Thomas Edison approach to motivating my teams: I just keep trying stuff till it works. What works for you today might not work on the next project. It makes sense to build up as many different techniques for motivating people that you can. Sorry, I really haven't found any shortcuts for this. What I have discovered is a few tactics that have worked well for me, so I'm sharing them with you here.

Momentum Is Motivation

I once heard a motivational speaker who made the point that if things are moving in the direction you want them to, then you are more motivated to continue the behavior that is causing the motion. I like the idea of a link between motivation and momentum mostly because it makes sense to me. This is something I can translate to a variety of motivation techniques when I'm stuck for new ideas with a fresh team. This suggests some sneaky PM mind games...

For instance, an enterprising PM could look for opportunities to heap praise and recognition on their teammates for actions that move the project forward. I've definitely found it valuable to praise someone (okay, it's more of an email "Wahoo!" than wildly effusive praise) for turning around an action item faster than normal. The next time that person has an action item for my project, they're more likely to do it faster. Hey, everyone likes to hear that they are doing something right, and if the PM helps build up some momentum for doing things right, then motivation is sure to follow.

How about that stealthy mind game of emphasizing your team's wins during your regular project status report-outs? Your team does read those, you know. Build momentum around the idea that your team is a winner, and before you know it your team will be motivated to be winners. There's also an added bonus that the rest of the organization will start to believe it, too. Pretty soon you will have this nice feedback loop that drives the motivation engine of your team.

I've also found that it's hugely motivating for a team if the PM periodically reminds them of the hurdles they've already overcome. Keep reminding your team that they *rock* and you will find that over time they will *really rock*!

▓ **Caution**   If sincere but shrewdly calibrated praise isn't your style, then please don't try to fake it. Nothing is more demotivating than a poser PM who stands up there and says he has a "great" team while simultaneously throwing his teammates under the proverbial bus. Don't be that PM!

A Few More Motivational Strategies

Free food can be a huge motivator if it's done carefully. Here's a news flash: the days of unveiling a box of donuts to wild praise and mass gorging are over. Most of us are eating healthier, and while the occasional donut is a treat, it's just not that compelling. Heck, I could have picked one up on the way to work if I'd wanted one, right? For free food to be a motivator, it needs to be something special and it needs to be a reward for extraordinary effort, not just for showing up and breathing on the project. For instance, for one fast-track project I ran, I committed to bringing in breakfast burritos for the whole team if we could pull in the release date from Friday to Monday. In this case the customer was ready for our deliverable early and it would make a real difference to the overall program schedule if my team could deliver even a few days earlier than planned. This wasn't easy since we were already scrambling, but it gave the team a clear goal and reward to work toward. In the end, we made the pull-in, the customer was very happy, and my wallet was $30 lighter. So, for the cost of some burritos I got happy customers and a team that was just raring to tackle the next challenge.

Another excellent motivator is praise, but again you need to apply it carefully. Gushing over a teammate's mediocre performance is not motivating; it's creepy! Sending an email to someone's boss extolling his "above-and-beyond" efforts for something he did on your project is an effective way to recognize superior performance and inspire more of the same. To really knock it out of the motivational park, copy the entire team and other managers if appropriate. Also, be sure to keep copies of these emails to use as material for 360-feedback during the performance review cycle.

If you defer to someone else's professional expertise and are open about trusting their judgment, then you will find they are pretty motivated to work on your project. Everyone wants to be acknowledged for their experience and expertise, and when you couple that with trust you have a great motivational tool.

▓ **Caution**   There is a great big caveat here, and that's that the trust and deference you exhibit need to be completely sincere. If you doubt in any way that the team member in question knows what she's talking about, don't use this tactic. Misuse of this one will completely sink any future hopes of motivating this person.

Finally, here's a motivational technique I've had quite a lot of success with: I set someone up to do something novel or different. By supporting their new/different/radical idea, I convey my trust in their abilities—which can be hugely motivating. I'm not talking about asking someone to do something impossible, but rather enabling those good ideas that people already have.

What I Learned about Motivation from Teenagers

I was told that I was insane for doing it, but one summer I took my two nieces and my nephew, all teenagers, to Washington D.C. for the week of July 4th. In a last minute reality check, I also invited my mother along as adult backup. We were there for seven days and every day was an amazing adventure... for the kids and for my mother! For me it was a tactical challenge unlike anything I'd faced in recent memory. Did I mention that they were all teenagers? And that adult backup? She ended up falling into the teen camp so stealthily that I never saw it coming. So there I was camp counselor for a crew of four in the big, bad city.

Anyone who has teens, deals with them in any capacity, or has been one—in other words, everyone—knows that they are a lesson in motivation waiting to happen. If you're not their parent (and sometimes that doesn't even help), you aren't going to have much success with an authoritative approach, and if you have even a smidgen of self-respect you try to avoid the wheedling, begging, and pleading approach. To save your sanity and someone from bodily harm, you have to motivate them into playing along. Surprisingly, I found this to be a familiar challenge: those teens weren't so far from the engineers, planners, architects, and so forth whom I try to motivate in my day job as a project manager.

For the record, we all had a great time, but it did take me a day or two to get in the groove when it came to motivating my motley crew. So what did I learn on my summer vacation? Several things, actually:

- First, **consultative decision making really works**. That first day, I took the direct approach and made all the decisions without input. This led to what I now refer to as the *Smithsonian Death March*. You try leading a group of sullen teenagers through a fourth Smithsonian when they wanted to stop after the second one! Trust me, feeding them cannot reverse this situation. Being the seasoned project manager that I am, I changed tactics that evening in a desperate effort to remain in control. Each evening I'd casually drop the topic of what to do the next day into the post-dinner haze of contentedness. The kids and I would kick it around and come up with a loose plan for the next day. Teens, like your team, need to have a say in what you're going to do. In this way, they are bought into the plan and feel some ownership for the overall success. After that first day, I didn't have to deal with the "I'd-rather-pick-up-garbage-on-the-side-of-the-road-than-be-here" teen attitude that I'm sure you've seen before. Hey, I owned that attitude when I was their age!

- Second, **to motivate people, you have to empower them**. By the end of the second day, all three kids could navigate the Metro system as well as I could. They still had a little trouble with the electronic pass cards (how do they get completely wiped in a kid's pocket?), but overall I no longer had to worry about the tactical aspects of daily navigation. I only had to strategically point out where we were going on the map and they figured out how to get there. Another example of this *empower to motivate* idea was how I'd set up their expenses. Each kid had to bring enough money to pay for lunch, snacks, and any souvenirs they wanted. This turned out to be pure brilliance because they got to eat what they wanted and *never* asked me to buy them a thing! But empowerment is not just about providing opportunity; it's also about letting go. I didn't control what they ate and, surprisingly, they never once ate a lunch consisting of candy bars, Doritos, and soda… which is probably what I would have spent my money on at that age. In fact, they actually pooled their money or otherwise collaborated to get the best deal for the three of them. If I were paying, then there's no way they would have come up with creative ways to save money, right?

- Third, you have to **provide opportunities for new experiences**. I'm continually fascinated by food and how it's prepared, so I love trying out new restaurants when I travel. Each evening, we'd pick a dining destination from the slew of funky, hip, and ethnic neighborhood cafes. The first night, the kids were a little hesitant but game to try something new. Each night a new restaurant and the kids got braver with their choices until finally by the last night everyone was ordering "strange" stuff and having a blast. I'm sure my sister will be shocked when her son requests a pizza with pesto, shrimp, and chèvre! The really cool part is that he would never have tried that funky pizza if he hadn't been motivated to try new experiences. Establish the motivation to go out and grab new experiences and you will inspire innovation and risk-taking in your team.

My "team" and I wrapped up that amazing week by sitting in a schoolyard on a hill overlooking the Mall. All along the skyline from the Lincoln Memorial to the Capitol fireworks sparkled like diamonds, with the most impressive "bursting in air" by the Washington Monument. It was an amazing trip and I completely cemented my rep as the Cool Aunt. But a funny thing happened along the way. I got a crash course in motivation. That's the thing about *soft skills*: they come in handy in all kinds of places but are difficult to master. It's a good idea to keep your eyes open for opportunities to practice them, especially outside of work. You just never know where you'll find the next lesson.

The Truth Shall Set Your Team Free

Management guru Jim Collins points out four key strategies to building a team dynamic that is conducive to frank and honest discourse:[1]

1. *Lead with questions, not answers.*

2. *Engage in dialogue and debate, not coercion.*

3. *Conduct autopsies without blame.*

4. *Build "red flag" mechanisms.*

    1.   *Leading with questions, not answers* is pretty straightforward, and I'm pretty confident that I'm mastered this technique. It helps a lot to cultivate a curious nature and a desire to understand why things work the way they do. One trick I used to get better at the whole "asking-questions" thing is to try to ask the "Why?" question at least five times. Make tick marks on a Post-It note or a corner of any bit of paper to keep track of how many times you've asked, so you can tell whether or not you've probed enough to get to the heart of the matter. You will have to twist "Why?" around a bit to get to five, but it's fairly easy to do with variations such as "Why do you think that is?" or "Why is this important?" Now the

---

[1]Excerpt on Fast Company (www.fastcompany.com/1802162/how-create-business-where-truth-heard) from Jim Collins *Good To Great: Why Some Companies Make the Leap ... and Others Don't* (HarperBusiness, 2001). This book is an excellent read with lots of interesting examples of good and bad leadership. If you're interested in building your leadership skills, then you owe it to yourself to check this book out.

number of questions isn't as important as drilling down into the discussion to get to the real underlying issues. Trust me, when you actually get to the heart of the matter you'll know, and I think you'll be pleasantly surprised at the results. Oh, and one last thing—don't be a dork and let anyone know that you're counting the number of questions…that's just a mnemonic to help you get better at the drill-down technique.

2. The whole idea of *engaging in dialogue and debate versus coercion* is pretty much a no-brainer. However, it's always a good idea to do a reality check from time to time and ask a few teammates (whose opinion you respect) if they think you employ coercion and how you do when it comes to setting up the team to debate an issue. Sadly, you might get a surprise from time to time, as it's all too easy to slip into coercion when the chips are down and you can't think of any other way out of the box. This feedback is essential if you want to continue to improve as a leader and as a project manager.

3. I really like the phraseology: *Conduct autopsies without blame*. I've done a lot of retrospectives, lessons-learned sessions, post mortems, and so on over the years, and it's true that these are really hard to facilitate if the project was a disaster. Take a group of people who no longer feel like a team, all of whom feel that they will get blamed for the fiasco, throw in a perky retrospective coordinator, and you have a recipe for an Excedrin Headache. If you allow the discussion to devolve into a blamefest, then nothing constructive will come out of that session. I know it's cheesy, but I have been known to throw out the phrase—"Blame the game, not the playa!"—when things start unraveling. (Okay, you might want to be careful with that one… it works for me and my style but it's one of those tactics that could go horribly wrong if you're not careful!) This really is Leadership Showtime, so keep the discussion focused on what actually happened, why it happened, and never on the "who."

4. *Last, I have to admit that I didn't remember this whole "red flag" mechanisms bit from the book.* This ties pretty neatly into my existing risk management practice, but I think I need to develop some mechanisms for seeing those red flags on the business level—that is, what's going on in my customer's organizations and how can that clue me into a

potential failure early. This also comes into play when I'm thinking about my project budget. Come the end of the quarter, I've seen project budgets get shuffled around as the organization scrambles to balance the larger budget and meet commitments to the corporation. If the PM isn't part of this process, then you sure need to understand what's going on and how that could potentially impact your project so yeah, setting those "red flag" mechanisms in place makes a lot of sense.

Laugh It Up to Improve Your Team Dynamic

Now let's talk about some tips and tricks for effectively using humor to improve or maintain your team dynamics. Consciously using humor to achieve a specific result is tricky. Humor is subjective and not everyone will get your quirky sense of it. Further, if you are not absolutely crystal clear on the expectations of its use in the workplace, you can fall into a very bad situation. That said, humor, specifically jokes, can be a very useful tool in a PM's toolbox.

I use jokes as a way to lighten the mood and get potentially contentious meetings started off in a positive mindset. If a team is working on a difficult problem and people are putting in a lot of OT, then I pull out the "Joke of the Day" strategy. I've also used this strategy pretty successfully when the team dynamic is wavering and teammates are starting to turn on each other like inmates after a failed jail break. By kicking off the meeting in a positive mindset, you're tee-ing up the tone for the rest of the discussion, and it can even distract some team members from grinding that axe they brought to the party.

The "Joke of the Day" strategy is pretty much what it sounds like. I'll post a joke up for everyone to read as we assemble before the meeting officially starts. Everyone gets a chuckle or groan, depending on how bad the joke is, and then I move right into the agenda. Do not spend too much time on this, just jump right into the business of the meeting, and do not let the conversation veer into a joke-telling contest. You will seriously regret it if that conversation goes too far.

The key to a good "Joke of the Day" is careful selection of the joke itself. This takes a little time and effort, so don't try to pull one out of thin air five minutes before the start of a meeting. I use a children's joke book as my source, but even then I have to work for it. I discard any jokes that rely on American slang, history, or culture out of respect for my geo-dispersed team. I also avoid anything that can even remotely be inappropriate. Finally, I try my best not to use something that could be construed as culturally insensitive. This actually leaves a very small subset of children's jokes to work from.

To get you started, here are a few of my standards:

- What do you get when you cross an elephant and a skunk? ... A big stink!

- What do you call a sleeping bull? ... A bulldozer!

- When is a river like the letter "T"? ... When it must be crossed!

- Why didn't the skeleton jump off the roof? ... Because he didn't have any guts!

You get the picture here: cheesy jokes you would not mind telling your five-year-old. In fact, in a weird way this adds value to some of your team members, because they inevitably go home and tell their kids these jokes and get a much bigger laugh than you will.

Now I have to send a shout-out to my buddy Steve Bell. Steve's team used video conferencing and Steve came up with an ingenious way to bring a smile to his team and keep the team dynamic positive. He basically used a portable flip chart positioned behind him but in line with his webcam. He drew a series of "hats" to represent different emotions such as Mickey Mouse ears, devil horns, a halo, and question marks popping out of his head as the situation demanded. He also kept a selection of physical hats and one of his best tricks was to add a different hat to his head as he was given new scope to manage. If he ended up with a lot of work, then the ludicrous number of hats on his head made the point in a funny but straightforward way.

So you see, you can use humor effectively to improve your team meetings and the overall way the members interact. This is yet another example of taking deliberate actions to inform your team dynamic, and the best part about this one is that, for about an hour's work, you can generate a safety stock of jokes to see you through your next month of meetings.

The "Special" Ones

As you learn and refine your craft, one thing all PMs come to realize is that how you initiate a project can have a profound effect on its overall success or failure. In fact there are the corner cases—what I like to call the "special" ones: the high-priority and low-priority projects as well as projects that feed into chaotic programs. Get assigned a high-priority project and you've got to hit the ground running and juggle a gazillion things at once. For a low-priority project you're probably going to have to beg people to talk about it. And that project that feeds into a very chaotic program? Well, you just might pull out all of your hair trying to get that one started! Obviously your standard kickoff tactics aren't going to be all that effective when dealing with these types of projects, so let's talk about tactics that do work!

High-Priority Projects

High-priority or "hot" projects are a special case, and how they are initiated can have a huge impact on the project manager's ability to influence the work throughout the life of the project.

First, let me quantify what I mean by a *high-priority project*. These are the ones with completely new tech, broader scope, new customers/markets, and more generous budgets. Everything about these babies is bigger, more challenging, and—heck—just downright more exciting. High-priority projects also come with some hard challenges. There's usually a hyper-aggressive timeline that's primarily market-driven, so there's not much opportunity to push out or miss that market window. Miss the window and you might as well pick up your ball and find another playground. There's much more visibility, and the PM will find himself interacting with folks much higher up the food chain...Can you say *stakeholder management?* You bring your "A" game and then dive in—all the while knowing you will need some new tricks to make it to the finish line. Got the picture?

You typically see a sort of mass hysteria in the early stages of scoping these kinds of projects. There are a lot of unknowns and these are not your garden-variety unknowns—oh, no. Instead, these are the things your team has never dealt with before and, trust me, they are freaked. The trick then is to get the team focused and motivated. Here are a few ideas to get you started:

1. **Get the team focused on the requirements definition.** You do this by setting up a specific timeline with a target date to have the requirements document frozen. Make it slightly aggressive to drive a sense of urgency and focus. Oh, and don't forget to do due diligence and ensure that all affected parties review and approve of the requirements documentation.

2. **Just be cool.** I find that my teams will follow my lead. If I'm freaked out about the amount of work, then I convey a level of doubt about whether or not we can pull this one off. As the team leader, I need to remain confident and calm, steering the decisions and discussions toward data. There's always at least one individual who's wrapped around the axle a little tighter than the rest, and you need to calm that one down first. Think of what you'd do with a room full of toddlers high on birthday cake... you get them focused on a specific task right? Same logic applies here.

3. **Love the "bin" list.** Yep, that's right a "bin" list is your best friend early in the planning stages of a high-priority project. If the item under discussion is outside of your team's ability to control, toss it in the "bin". Handle that one offline, not during the team meeting. Remember, if your team can't affect the problem, then you need to transfer it to some other team who can.

4. **Lay out a preliminary timeline**...even if it's arbitrary. Figure out when you need the requirements frozen (or at least only slightly slushy), per item #1; set a goal for completing the work estimates; and schedule a planning session. In short, get the balls rolling so you don't lose more time than you can afford on the front end of the project.

5. **Define an execution strategy.** What lifecycle are you going to use? At a high level, how will the product be developed and tested? Do you need to engage Legal, HR, IT, and so forth? What collaboration is needed with other teams? Your team needs this strategy to use as a framework against which they will do the planning work. You can't skip this step without rework and miscommunication later.

6. **Play your ace-in-the-hole.** Your project is a high priority for the division, so act like it. Need lab space? Play the priority card. Need to fast-track a budget approval? Start throwing around the project's priority and escalate. In short, take ruthless advantage of the relative importance of your project versus whatever else is going on in the division. Remember, you've got to act like you have the hot one for others to believe it.

7. **Finally and most importantly, set the vision.** Make sure each and every person on your team understands the business drivers for your project and what you need to achieve. They need to understand why this one is worth more than their usual best efforts—"This one's gonna require all of us to stretch and learn new tricks."

When you manage those big audacious high-priority projects the first thing you need to do is get your team focused and motivated. Use the strategies I've mentioned above to get off to a good start and fasten your seat belts... this one's gonna be fun!

Low-Priority Projects

Okay, now let's talk about the dreaded low-priority project. This is the under-appreciated one that no one views as important and whose budget and resources are slender. In short, this is the exact opposite of that pressure-cooker, high-visibility circus you just brought in on time and under budget. You really need a break—but that low-priority project? Seriously? Can't someone else, anyone else, do it? I've been there, my friend, and over the years I've learned a thing or two about these types of projects. They can be fun and the team can really innovate while the focus is on someone else.

The first thing you need to realize is that the techniques you use for a high-priority fun ride may not work very well. First, you're going to really flex your influence skills on this one. In a low-priority project, no one cares who you are and, trust me, the mere whisper of your sponsor's name isn't going to do you a bit of good. You have to work harder to convince people to help you and your team. You will need to exercise your network in new ways, so be on the lookout for opportunities to ask for help.

Speaking of your team, you aren't going to get the SMEs for this one. Nope, instead you will have a team of less experienced but hungrier players. These people are generally out to prove what they can do, and they will bring plenty of ideas to the table if you take care to establish a team dynamic that rewards fresh thinking. This is the place to use lavish recognition to reinforce that dynamic. Another way to motivate this team is to add value by hooking them up with new mentors and contacts. I've also had great success creating opportunities for the team members to experience what life is like either upstream or downstream from their specific area of expertise. Can you send a design engineer to the vendor who will eventually manufacture their design? How about having a planner help with the assembly of prototypes? This type of thing is pretty easy to set up and the return for the team member is just amazing.

There's something else to look for on low-priority projects: your new team might not be locked into the "not-invented-here" mentality that sometimes creeps into organizations. I guarantee that they will have ideas that haven't been considered by other project teams. There's goodness here if you can tap into it. One way this comes into play is with spending. Low-priority projects just have smaller budgets and you often have to figure out how to deliver the final product on a shoestring. Challenge your team to think of more efficient ways to do things, to do smarter design, and scrutinize every feature to make sure it's really needed. I once managed a low-priority project in which we essentially made the case that we shouldn't develop the product at all! Yep, we found a way to deliver the data the customer really wanted without designing a thing. The savings from this was just slightly over a million bucks, so the company saved big and we all had a really nice accomplishment for our yearly performance review!

Another thing you will need to realize is that this baby will run at a slower pace if you let it. PMs coming off of huge projects tend to try to manage these lower-priority projects at the same pace. There's probably no need for this, so don't stay up half the night with your email account just because you've been operating at that pace for the last year. Instead, focus on improving your work habits so that you get more done in the day. Test-drive new technology for communicating with the team, such as blogs, forums, or wikis. This is your opportunity to innovate as a PM too!

I bet you're ready to go off and volunteer for one of these projects now, right? Well, before you do that, I should probably break down a few of the negatives for you. First it's highly likely that you'll be dealing with, shall we say, *undermotivated* individuals? You will need to motivate someone who's probably burnt out, bitter, or just plain difficult. This can be a real challenge, so make sure you take this person seriously and address the problem early.

Second, did I mention that no one cares? Well, they don't until things go bad, so be sure you're managing your stakeholders carefully. As always, it's critical to understand what success looks like for each stakeholder. Just don't be surprised if they don't have time for you or your project. Additionally, these projects are always the first to get raided when the higher-priority projects need more resources. As the PM, you need to be especially vigilant about the point of no return. Don't let your team flounder on a project that has been raided to the point of failure. You may need to recommend that the project be killed in order to be successful in the end.

Last, for these projects you need to accept the environment they live in. You probably aren't going to get more headcount so don't waste your energy going after it. Instead, figure out how to be successful in spite of the environment…this is where that innovation thing comes in! ☺

I've found that these low-priority projects are fun to manage. They are a chance to recharge both physically and mentally so that I'm rarin' to go for the next big one. I get a lot of personal satisfaction from managing teams in which the dynamic is collaborative and we are doing new and exciting work. I hope I've convinced you that getting that low-priority project is a good thing and that I've given you some food for thought about how to manage this type of project in the future.

Chaotic Programs

What do you do when your project feeds into a larger program that's a high-complexity, high-ambiguity environment? These programs bring to mind the tornados I've experienced back in Texas. You see, a tornado has a calm spot in the dead center where the violent chaos of swirling winds subsides—the fabled eye of the storm. Leading a team in a highly ambiguous environment is tough and most PMs struggle with this; I know I do! You can't nail your project plan due to those open requirements, low-confidence commits for dependencies your team needs, unclear expectations from your fellow program PMs, and so forth. These situations take "tolerance for ambiguity" to a whole new level, and as a PM you're going to want to minimize the impact on your team as much as possible. In short, you want to position your project team in that "eye of the storm" and have the program's chaotic ambiguity swirl around you.

Over the years, after participating in many program teams, I've developed a few tricks of the trade to deal with these situations. So, for the benefit of anyone struggling to lead a team in one of these tornados, here are a few tips and tricks I've had success with in the past:

- The first thing a PM needs to do in this type of program is **drive clarity**. Yeah, I know, like that's not obvious!

    - Here's what I do: I drive a stake in the ground by defining some key milestones. These are, coincidentally, milestones my team can definitely meet. For example, when I lead board development projects, I'd go into a planning session with a date my team could deliver boards. For the other project teams on the program who hadn't finished their planning yet, having the board dates defined helped them build a plan around my date. Bottom line: **Define key dates and then let the rest of the program spin around your dates**. Note that you will frequently have to move your date as the overall program planning matures, but at least you will be able to drive clarity in the beginning.

— **Another way to drive clarity is to be extremely clear in your communication of dates and requirements**. Use phrases like "drop-dead date" and "day-by-day slip" rather than stating that a dependency has a "need-by date". For loose or open requirements, succinctly define your team's understanding of the requirement and state that unless you hear otherwise you consider this the requirement of record and your team will proceed accordingly. Do not leave room for discussion or interpretation in the communication. If anyone disagrees with the interpretation, then they will have to speak up.

— This last tip on how to drive clarity is something I've truly learned the hard way, **and it's this: Know when to offer alternatives and when not to**. If you've ever walked out of a program planning meeting with a ton of what-if scenarios to analyze, then you know where I'm coming from. In these situations, I'll make my recommendation to the program team as a single course of action. I expect my fellow team members to question and discuss the recommendation and, if serious objections come up, I'll pull out an alternative... *but* I always open with only one choice as the official recommendation. Most of the time—always assuming I'm in sync with all stakeholders—that one recommendation is accepted much faster than if I'd thrown out a smorgasbord of options. As I see it, it's my job as a member of the program team to do the evaluation of the options—not to push that analysis onto my peers.

- The second thing a PM needs to do in these environments is to protect their team from the inevitable churn.
**Give your team clear direction and don't distract
them with the possibility of a course change until
its POR**. One of the jobs of the project manager is to
take the various discussions at the program team level
and distill them into actionable information for their project team. Don't spend a lot of energy passing through
data that your project team doesn't need to do their job.
If the program team is kicking around the idea of adding
some new requirements due to changing market conditions, don't float that down to your team until it's clear
that the program team is going to adopt them; then use the
change control process to assess the impact of adding
these requirements. Often PMs think that they are doing
their team a favor by giving them a head's-up that changes
are coming but, in fact, most of the time it's distracting to
the project team. Keep them focused on the work they
are committed to do, and then manage the change so that
the impact to your team is minimized.

- The final thing a PM has to do to protect his or her team
is **to make decisions, even though often without
enough data**. Nothing slows down or distracts a team
more than an ambiguous direction. As the PM you are
expected to lead this team and that means making some
decisions you might not be comfortable with. If the team
needs a decision on how to implement a requirement and
you're unable to get closure from the stakeholders, then
as the leader you need to make a call here. If the team
has concerns about a design, you may need to decide to
spend money on prototypes… even if you don't think you
have the authority to spend that money. The good thing
about these kinds of decisions is that the more decisions
you make, the better you get at it. You aren't always going
to make the right call, but over time you'll make more
good decisions than bad. The key here is to make clear
decisions and then be accountable for the consequences,
both good and bad. That's your job as the PM.

A lot of us work in a highly chaotic, fast-paced environment today. I remember back in the '80s when the phrase "tolerance for ambiguity" was on nearly
every job req. Who could have guessed what that looked like in the real world
of business today? This stuff is hard, very hard, and your job as the PM is to
develop some skills to help your team reach that "eye of the storm."

Planning Phase

You Have to Do the Work

Planning is perhaps the most important phase of any endeavor, and it's certainly true of all programs or projects. Sadly, the planning phase is also the least appreciated and it's not uncommon for junior PMs to cut this phase short, to produce a weak schedule and continue forward without a fully thought-out execution strategy. It's my opinion that the primary reason projects fail is that the planning was inadequate. Of course, you can't plan for every bad throw of the dice, but you definitely can ensure that you have a solid execution plan that allows enough flexibility to roll with those dice when the need arises.

Project Plans Are NOT Created in MS Project

I have a pet peeve and it's when I hear people refer to their *schedule* as a *project plan*. That's just not right, and it demonstrates that the person talking doesn't understand what a project plan should be. You see, a project plan is quite extensive and is not created in MS Project! A project plan does include the schedule, but it also includes so much more. To refer to the *schedule* as the *project plan* is sort of like referring to a piece of pepperoni as though it were the entire pizza! If all you got for dinner was the pepperoni, then you'd be mighty hungry before bedtime now, wouldn't you? Likewise, a project plan that includes only a schedule is bound to leave you scrambling later in the project.

According to the Project Management Institute (PMI), a *project plan* includes the *scope management plan*, the *work breakdown structure* (WBS), the *schedule management plan*, the *cost management plan*, the *quality management plan*, the *process improvement management plan,* the *staffing management plan*, the *communication management plan,* the *risk management plan*, and the *procurement management plan*—to name just a few. Whew, I'm tired just typing all of that! This sounds like it was developed by Dilbert's friendly management consultant doesn't it?

The problem with this smorgasbord of plans is that for smaller projects, this all-inclusive master plan is overkill. Some of the plans drop out naturally. For instance, if your project doesn't include purchasing, then you don't need a procurement management plan. Likewise, if your project is very short, then you probably don't need a process improvement plan. However, there are a few of these babies that you really should be doing even if you don't create a 100-page manifesto to document your project plan.

One of these lesser-known plans I always use is the *communication management plan*. My plans are usually one page long and capture how I plan to communicate the project status both externally and internally to the team, as well as who the stakeholders are and what their comms preferences are. Believe it or not, some people actually prefer a phone call to an email and some stakeholders will only want a monthly update. The 30 minutes that I spend thinking about and documenting this plan is always helpful when planning a project. The other upside to spending time on a communication management plan is that I can clearly let people know how and when they will get project status before they start asking for it. This helps me avoid the trap of always having to provide the same status to different stakeholders day after day on an ad hoc basis. I really hate it when that happens!

Another plan I always pay attention to is the *risk management plan*. I'll talk about my risk management technique later in more detail, but I want to mention it here as well. By identifying the big risks early and actually putting plans in place to manage them while still in planning, I find that the team is surprised less often. Having that plan in place also seems to dial down the stress when the risk is actually triggered. Everyone knows what to do, so there's less management "help" to address the risk. One of the best compliments I've ever received as a PM was when a teammate commented that he was surprised at the lack of firefighting we had to do. I attribute that 100% to our risk management plan.

Okay, true confessions time: I never do a staffing management plan, because I don't have a lot of control over who gets assigned to my projects. Nor do I do a cost management plan because, again, I have very little control over the biggest cost driver, the resources. And finally a comment about procurement plans. Yes, I've developed them when the project in question required a lot of procurement. However, I find it a bit ironic that the PMs should be responsible for tracking procurement and the associated costs, when they are not the expense approvers. It's been my experience in highly matrixed organizations that the PM does not have any formal power over the project budget and associated costs. At best, the PM must affect these areas through influence and, at worst, clearly communicate any consequences and alternatives as a result of budget decisions.

So, I hope this has helped you understand a bit more about what a project plan truly is. I highly encourage you to review the various plans that make up a comprehensive project plan and use what makes sense for each project. Remember you're developing this puppy during the planning phase, which means you really should consider these things prior to kicking off project execution.

Bad Ideas

Okay, now let's talk about some really bad ideas that can come up during the planning phase. Often, folks will sidestep the work of planning by adopting a "do-whatever-it-takes" approach or simply avoid the work altogether by replacing planning with hope. Neither of these muddle-through strategies ever works, yet you still see them in use from time to time. It's also a bad idea to fall under the spell of what quality assurance professionals call the "happy path." You know what they say about things that sound too good to be true. Finally, you see a failure in the planning when a project team is working an insane amount of overtime—failing to account for all of the work will inevitably result in unanticipated overtime. So, let's talk about these really bad ideas and what you should do instead.

Do Whatever It Takes

Every once in a while I still hear someone question the value of developing a detailed schedule or even profess to not creating one at all. Just the other day a colleague of mine mentioned that his team had given up developing detailed schedules because it was just too hard and took too much time. Not everyone sees the connection between a well-planned project and high-confidence customer commits. There's a prevailing "do-whatever-it-takes" attitude in some organizations where customer commits are made with rough top-down estimates and the rank and file scramble like mad to get the work done any way they can. The management chain holds the PM and the project team accountable for hitting those commits despite their tenuous link with reality. The PM is told (or tells their team) that they need to "do whatever it takes" to make the commit, so the entire team jumps in and starts working with only a minimal plan. I'm sure you know what I'm talking about here, right?

One of the problems with the "do-whatever-it-takes" strategy is that it completely ignores the actual work content of the project. In my experience these top-down estimates are only loosely based on historical data and they are almost never based on actual project hours or actual dollars spent on an earlier, similar project. To exacerbate the problem, if the PM doesn't take the time to build a realistic project plan then no one knows whether that "do-whatever-it-takes" commit is realistic until it's too late. The marketing team made a commitment to the customer to deliver the product at a specific time based on commits from the program team that were done before the requirements were finalized and the full scope of work realized. When this happens, "pulling in the schedule" becomes the norm instead of the exception and practically everyone in the organization is overworked because there's no such thing as pipeline management. Sound familiar? Sadly, I thought it might...

Another problem with the "do-whatever-it-takes" execution strategy is that does not take into account the real world calendar we must accommodate. Pesky things like national holidays and personal vacations all hit the chopping block as the management team struggles to find a way out of a poorly conceived customer commit. I once got burned by neglecting to account for a week-long shutdown at the end of the year. I was operating under the "do-whatever-it-takes" mindset but neglected to accommodate the fact that the entire building would be powered down for some planned facilities maintenance over the holidays. The result was that the entire team worked like mad over every weekend in January to "recover" a schedule. At the time, I was so busy trying to keep all the balls in the air that I completely missed the fact that there was no way to recover the schedule with the resources we had. Exhorting the whole team to work harder did not fix the problem because there was more work to be done than could possibly get done in the limited timeframe we had...and because I hadn't done a solid project plan I didn't even know that it was impossible. D'oh!

And finally the biggest problem I see with the whole "do-whatever-it-takes" mentality is that it completely ignores industry best practices. Would you drive your car in the opposite lane just because it's open and there's no oncoming traffic? Of course you wouldn't because that is not the best way to move the vehicle down the road—it's not the *best known method*...oh, and there's that whole legal thing as well. So if you've received your PMP, then how can you completely ignore best practices and "wing it" by blindly accepting the "do-whatever-it-takes" directive? It's your job as a professional to point out what exactly it will take to execute the project relative to the resources that are available. Throwing up your hands and saying that you and your team will get it done "somehow" because "it just needs to happen" is a cop-out and you can do better. Don't ignore your responsibility to do the work of planning the project because the organization has told you to "do whatever it takes." Whenever I hear a PM say that the team needs to "do whatever it takes" or the ever popular "it just needs to happen," I know that he doesn't have a solid project plan. Don't be that person! Do the work!

Hope Is Not a Strategy

If I had a nickel for every time I've heard it I'd ...well, I'd be able to buy a really nice handbag. I'm sure that you've heard it too. It goes something like this: "I hope to have the CAD files to you by Friday," or "We're hoping to get those actuators in on the 15th," or even "Hopefully the testing will wrap up by the end of the month." Yep, I'm talking about that four-letter word, *hope*.

Now it's not like I've got anything against the word, and in fact I think you should live a hopeful life. But the thing is: hope is not a strategy, nor is it a meaningful commitment. I'm hopeful that there's a hot fudge sundae in my immediate future, but I don't really know if I'm gonna get one. If I'm talking about a project plan, then I'd darn well better know if that sundae is waiting for me, and my team and I need to know if it's got nuts or not.

Whenever I hear colleagues use the H-word in the context of a commit or a plan, there's a blaring claxon kicking off in my head. *Hope* usually translates into something like this: "I have no clue how much more work I have to do on those CAD files," or "I seriously doubt that the vendor can deliver those actuators when they say they will," or even "I can't even guess how long the testing will take." In these situations I dial back the pressure and start asking questions. I want to help the other person understand how much work is left, how the vendor's past performance informs their commit, what our historical data predict, and so forth. I need to make it okay for my colleague to step back from a commit she thinks I want to hear and give me a realistic one instead. You see, I can't plan around a hope—what I really need is a high-confidence commit.

There's another problem with the H-word that I'd guess most people miss. When you provide a "hopeful" commit or plan of action, you are communicating your own lack of confidence. In the previous examples, using the word "hope" implies a certain amount of doubt. I can't expect anyone to take me seriously if I don't believe what I'm committing to. I need to know when I can deliver those CAD files. Although that vendor has committed to a delivery date of the 15th for those actuators, that vendor sucks—so I'll commit those bad boys for the 20th, which is a much higher-confidence commit on my part. Think of it this way: If your surgeon tells you that he hopes he can remove the correct kidney this time, are you going to let him within cutting distance of yours anytime soon? Not a chance right? So when you are delivering a commitment, just don't use the H-word. Pad your commit until it's a high-confidence one if you need to. Just don't drag *hope* into it.

A hope is nothing tangible. Basing your project plan or your execution strategy on a hope is dopey. As a PM, you should strike that word from your vocabulary when you're negotiating or providing commitments. If your colleagues use *hope* as a dodge for a high-confidence commit, then you need to dig a little deeper and probably accept a later date. Remember, you can't plan on a hope. Sometimes the fix is as simple as a word choice; other times more elbow grease is required to understand what's really going on. The next time you find yourself getting beat up for a commit, make sure you're not dragging *hope* into the picture. And as for that hot fudge sundae? Well, here's hoping there's a great big one in your future, too!

Taking the Happy Path

There's this place you might have visited lately. I call it *Happy Land* and to get there you take the *Happy Path*. When you're there, you and your team are in a blissful state of mind where anything seems possible and that big audacious project you're trying to scope—well, that's a sure thing and you can definitely knock it out in six weeks. Heck, you guys can bend the laws of physics to overcome some minor technical challenges, right? And frozen requirements? Who needs 'em? You guys are innovators! Heck, while you're here you might as well fix a couple of nasty broken business processes, too.

Thwack! That's my hand upside your head. Sorry, it just had to be done. You see I've been where you are now and I've just gotta break it to you… there ain't no way to get there from where you are now. Of course I'm talking about that point in a big project where everyone has to stop talking about the "big picture" and start planting those stakes in the ground—the point at which you really have to put pixels to work listing all of the major deliverables, the sub-tasks, the dependencies, the risks, and so on. For your teammates that happens about 20 minutes into the planning session's activities. For PMs it can come much sooner, and then you face the sometimes enormous task of moving people off the Happy Path and into the Real World.

In case you've never heard the term *Happy Path*, let me break it down for you. It's a validation/quality assurance term of derision that basically represents a test scenario where everything works as expected and any potential defects are avoided through judicious crafting of the test plans. It's a land where defects are scarce and the sun always shines. You've probably overheard some overworked QA engineer mutter something like…"Stupid happy path testing! I told them peanut butter was a real possibility! But did they listen? No-o-o." (In case you're wondering, peanut butter fills tummies just fine but never electronics—never! Just sayin'…)

So here's how it goes: You've kicked off the planning session and made sure everyone agrees on the high-level objectives and deliverables. By the way, at this point your teammates are either super-energized or they are numb with dread over the looming amount of work. Then your team starts breaking out work packages and so far so good. Everyone is still in Happy Land for the most part. You know what comes next: the estimation process. After that you fight through the Network Diagram and everyone starts to visualize the project timeline. Cue the *Jaws* music right here! Suddenly it starts sinking in for everyone that the only way this will take six weeks is with some amphetamines and a time bender. Now since you don't endorse chemical enhancements and you can't bend time with your bare hands, you've got to do something else. What, oh what, is a PM to do?

Bring on the historical data! Yep, sometimes you need to throw a bucket of cold water reality on some of your teammates who are pretty darn happy living in Happy Land. Now there's nothing wrong with being excited about a new project, and there's nothing really wrong with thinking it can be done much faster than this type of thing has ever been done before....but you really need to back it up with data. If the team has never delivered anything this complicated in under six months, then realistically six weeks ain't happening— now is it? If you can pull up some data from past projects and take a high-level look at what it took to accomplish them, then, my friends, you can interject some reality. Remember, we're supposed to be engaging in informed risk-taking, not tripping merrily down the Happy Path. Okay, I hear you: "But Melanie I don't have any historical data! What am I supposed to do now?" Well, if you can't find any performance data for projects similar to yours, start looking at industry standards. Sure, they may not be super-accurate, but they will get you where you need to go. For instance, there's a standard that says that for every month of code development you need one week of testing. Oh, and for the sake of your own sanity, start collecting some data so the next time you need historicals you've got them.

Let me be clear here. It's not so much that those plans developed in Happy Land are bad. We all need big juicy targets to strive for, and as a PM you should be setting some meaningful stretch goals for your team. I absolutely love working with a team that's innovating to hit one of these targets. It really forces you to go back to basics to look at how the work gets done and figure out how to do it differently. That's the good side of Happy Land. All I'm saying here is just make sure there's a realistic chance of achieving those targets before you commit to a timeline. Sure, the Happy Path to project success makes you feel good, but it really is the road less traveled, isn't it?

I realize that some of you are currently living in Happy Land. Enjoy it while you can. It's nice there, isn't it? Pass the sunscreen and the lasagna, would you? When you're ready to come back to the Real World, use some data to put some reality into your Happy Path plan—but try to bring some of that excitement and innovation along with you when you come back.

Overtime = Planning Failure

We all do it from time to time. We mostly hate it, but we still do it. I did it a lot early in my career when I got paid specifically for it. If you're a PM, then you've probably forced people to do it or they've had to do it because you didn't do your job. I've done it when I've failed to manage my time and/or my workload. By far the most common reason it's done, though, is because organizations fail to do due diligence when planning. What am I talking about? Overtime! If you find yourself doing a lot it, then I've got just one word for you... *fail!*

When I started working in high tech, like a lot of you I was younger and getting paid by the hour. Overtime (OT) was big money and it was motivating after coming off of years of scrimping and scraping to get through college.

In short, I worked as many hours as they'd let me and I loved it! Then came a period of time where I defined success through promotions at work, and those promos required plenty of OT. I remember working on the team that developed the first 300mm semiconductor processing equipment where we all worked 12-14 hour days all the time, but we didn't care because we were doing something important. Most of us got promoted for that work too.

Around about this time I started managing projects, so then I was the person doing such a crappy job that my team had to work OT to hit the dates I'd committed to our customers. Let's just say that I mastered the skill of strong-arming a team into working weekends. Eventually, I also mastered developing a comprehensive schedule. I started incorporating things like company holidays and team members' vacations. I started using actual Work Breakdown Structures, Network Diagrams, and resource leveling. In short I was mastering my craft and as a result my teammates and I started working a lot less OT.

As I came to realize what a solid project plan looked like, I also came to have less and less tolerance for poorly planned projects and programs. I started noticing when the org I worked in didn't manage their project pipeline. These orgs are populated with overworked folks who buy into the "do-whatever-it-takes" fantasy when it comes to planning. There's usually a prevailing culture of "gaming the system" to get projects or even programs funded, and none of them ever really get canceled. Now it's true that not all organizations roll like that, but those that do expect plenty of OT from their personnel.

These days I have a much healthier perspective on working overtime. Over the years I've developed my own personal OT litmus test. You see, I'll suck it up and do the OT if it's for a specific purpose that supports an important deliverable, and has a defined end state. I do not do OT to maintain the status quo. Further, as a general rule, I no longer work weekends or week-nights. Sure, there's the occasional thing that comes up once in a while, but for the most part I work M–F, 8–5pm. In all fairness, part of the reason I can keep my hours to 8–5 is due to the particular job I have. If I spent a lot of time working multiple geos, then I'd obviously have to work different hours. But when that happens I still keep it to 40 hrs/week. It's a matter of personal discipline for me.

So, that's my take on OT. What about you? How many hours are you throwing down these days? Are you okay with that? If not, then perhaps it's time to take a good, long look at the kind of work you really want to do. Remember, you're going to spend the majority of your waking hours at work so it ought to be something you enjoy. Oh, and OT? Well, that should be an occasional occurrence and not the status quo.

The Craftsmanship of Planning

Despite what some of your teammates might think, there's much more to planning a project than figuring out requirements and a schedule. There's an art to project management, and at first blush you probably don't see it, but trust me—a well-planned project is worth the time it takes to do the job right. I focus now on the craftsmanship of planning a project.

First up, the one element everyone associates with a project plan: the schedule. While the mechanics of building a schedule are straightforward, there's a certain craftsmanship that's needed to produce useable schedules that actually enhance the project's execution. Not all project schedules are created equal, nor do they all need to be created in specialized software. What you're after is a schedule that can be used in multiple ways to enhance clarity and drive better decisions. There's also some artistry in how you organize the information in your scheduling tool. I like to break work up into the lifecycle phases and then subdivide it into work packages (or functional groups, depending on what makes sense). I also set up my own custom views. And while we are talking about views, I like to set mine up to see SPI, % Complete, Remaining Work, Baseline Finish, and the Finish trend date. How you set up your default view in whatever application you are using is up to you and its part of this art thing I'm talking about.

A well-crafted project plan has an explicit execution strategy that's documented and bought off on by the entire team and the key stakeholders. I like to host a brainstorming session to kick around various execution strategies. What work will we do in parallel? What's the impact of reducing the scope of testing? Can we meet the business drivers some other way? What features/functions can we cut or push to a future release? Where and when do we need specialized resources? While I was a PM for a printed circuit board (PCB) development team, we came up with a viable solution for the business driver that basically negated the need for the PCB we were tasked to develop. In IT, where I currently reside, there's an almost overwhelming trend toward the Agile methodology for software development, but that doesn't mean it's a good fit for all projects. So part of the art of project management is a thoughtful selection of the execution strategy, and it's something the entire team needs to participate in.

Another piece of the overall project plan that requires some careful and creative attention is your communications plan. To be honest, it takes quite a bit of experience within an organization to understand just who the key stakeholders are and how they prefer to get their updates. Some prefer an "always-on" source of project updates, while others want you to look them in the eye when you provide your commits. There's a whole truckload of soft skills at play in this area, and one solution does not fit all. If you haven't been giving a lot of thought to this area of your overall planning, then I highly encourage you to take some time and really think about how you can do this better. So many PMs take the easy route and just shoot out a standard email update, but there's a world of creativity out there to draw on. So apply some craftsmanship here and you will definitely reap the rewards.

Now, let's not forget your team dynamic when you're in the planning phase. This is Soft Skills Central and those really good PMs craft a deliberate strategy for inspiring and nurturing the kind of team dynamic that best suits the project. Are you going to be shorthanded on this project? Then you'd darn well better start thinking about how you foster a team dynamic where everyone is willing to step up and fill a gap. Is this project extremely challenging from a technical perspective? If so, then you're going to want your team to be extremely innovative and that team's dynamic will probably look a lot different from that of your run-o'-the-mill project team. Trust me, this doesn't happen automatically nor does it solely rely on "good" people. You need to think about what team characteristics you need to foster and how you will motivate those characteristics. Oh, for the record—I never thought specifically about this stuff until I'd been managing projects for a good many years. So learn from my past and jump on this now to save yourself a lot of frustration later.

Finally, we come to what I consider the overall art of planning: that's having an intuitive feel for when you've done enough planning and it's time to get started on the work. It's been my experience that those of us in the high-tech world want to jump right into the doing and let the planning sort itself out. I've honestly never encountered a high-tech project that took way too long to plan. We just don't play that way in high tech. I've heard various rules of thumb for how long planning should take, and there seems to be some consensus around 20% of the total project time should be devoted to planning. Today my projects run around 16%. (I know my average is 16% because I analyze how the project work breaks out across phases at the end of every project.)

The bottom line is that the PM needs to make sure that everyone fully understands the project objectives and knows what work they need to do and by when—all before they get too far down the execution road. It might be helpful to look at a few of your past projects and see just how much time you're spending in the planning phase. Bounce that data against your performance schedule metrics, the total number of change requests, and your defect data to get a feel for whether you're spending enough time planning. It can be tough to hold the team to the planning when they are chomping at the bit to get to the "real" work. I'm sure you don't need to think too hard to come up with some examples of projects that floundered because the planning was inadequate. Stand your ground and put enough time and craftsmanship into planning all your projects. Trust me, the execution will go a lot smoother if you do.

Old School Planning

There's a pitfall waiting to trap those of us who operate with a continuous improvement mindset. We get so wrapped up in doing things faster and cheaper, all in a continual race to do things better, that we can lose track of some really fine tools and strategies. I was reminded of this a few years ago as I helped facilitate a planning session for the New Business Initiative (NBI) guys at Intel Corporation.

At the time I worked for an internal consulting group, so I worked with various groups across the company. I often had to morph techniques to fit a specific customer's requests. Working with the NBI folks is like jumping into the rollercoaster seat without seeing where the track is going. It's gonna be a thrill-packed ride and it sure won't be slow. In this particular case, we were scoping out a plan to develop a *proof of concept* to demonstrate feasibility and provide a basis for future funding. The requirements were a *work in progress* (WIP) but we needed to nail down a project plan and schedule quickly. Further, while the customer needed a detailed schedule, they could live with *order-of-magnitude* duration estimates. They also requested that we model different resource levels to see what their options were. So, here you have a situation where the *triple constraint* (Chapter 7) is made of spaghetti and you need to bring some structure to those wiggly, loose legs of the triangle.

When confronted with a highly ambiguous environment, a solid tactic is to start putting stakes in the ground and let the rest of the plan spin out from there. I'll talk about this in more detail later in Chapter 6. It turns out that, in this type of environment, Intel had a great tool for planning that was considered archaic and inefficient but still works really well. That old-school technique is called a *Make a Project Plan* (MAPP) *Day*.

At Intel, the MAPP Day is a venerable old tradition that's not used much anymore. During a MAPP Day (which can last several days, by the way), the team uses sticky notes to write down all of the project work packages. They capture dependencies, resource requirements, work estimates, duration, and so forth on these sticky notes. Then the team uses a blank wall covered in a large sheet of paper to construct the WBS and network diagram using the sticky notes. Notes are moved around and adjusted as the team progresses through the planning. This is a highly interactive process that involves the entire team. Of course I've simplified the process a bit here, but it's sufficient to say that after a team completes a MAPP Day exercise they have a solid basis for a project plan and they've captured a draft schedule, risks, assumptions, opens, and so on. The big problem with a MAPP Day process is that it's slow if you have a large team. It's also highly dependent on all participants preparing their specific material ahead of time.

So, for this particular consult we went old school with sticky notes, flip charts, multicolored markers, and lots of tape. I don't usually do this type of planning anymore and, frankly, I'd forgotten how effective it could be. My PM colleagues were quick to mock me when I mentioned that I was setting up a sticky-note MAPP Day and every single one of them delivered earnest arguments against conducting a planning session that way. The arguments were consistent: it takes too long, it's inefficient, and no one will be prepared. These are all valid arguments and I've made them a time or two myself. There was something, however, we were all forgetting about the old school MAPP Day technique —it works!

Let me be clear here—the old school approach works very well in certain situations, but it can be a disaster in others. If you have a relatively small team and highly variable or ambiguous requirements, and if time is of the essence, then you just can't beat a sticky-note MAPP Day. If you have a large, geo-dispersed team with multiple requirements documents, then yes, there are more efficient ways to generate a complex schedule and bring the whole team into a common understanding of the project plan.

For this MAPP Day we spent an entire day reviewing the technical and business aspects of this project. We did a deep dive review of the use cases, the proposed SW architecture schemes, and kicked around project execution options. On the surface it looked like we didn't get a lot accomplished, but by the end of the day we all had a very solid understanding of the scope of the POC and lots of flip charts of data. That's not something you can do with a large team on a high-complexity project... trust me, just don't go there!

The second day was devoted entirely to developing the network diagram and here's where those sticky notes came in. There's a flexibility to brain-storming and collaborating when you write tasks on sticky notes that no amount of software can duplicate. When you move them around until they all work together, there comes a point when the entire team is collaborating and focused on a common goal. I'd forgotten how effective this technique is when planning a project and how good it is for building a solid team dynamic.

In the end, we didn't walk out of the MAPP Day with that "detailed schedule," but what we did walk away with was pretty cool nonetheless. We started as a collection of people assigned to work on a project and left as a cohesive team focused on a clear objective. There was still some work to be done to finalize the schedule and the overall project plan. In fact, the rest of the planning went pretty smoothly because we also left the MAPP Day event with a solid list of risks, assumptions, and opens. Sure, there were some things we missed and had to go back to. But overall I'd say it was a very successful planning session and I'm glad I got tagged to facilitate that MAPP Day, because it reminded me that sometimes those techniques you've discarded in the name of continuous improvement really can be the best tool for the job.

The next time you start a new project, please consider whether or not an old-school technique can do the job faster and with better team buy-in. Don't assume that the tool du jour is the best way to proceed. Each project is different, as is each team, so consider all the tools in your personal toolbox and pick the best one for the job.

What's in a Name?

There's an interesting dilemma I run across from time to time when scoping a new project. The dilemma is at first glance a wimpy one and you wouldn't be blamed for rolling your eyes. You see I sometimes struggle with what to call a new project. So what's in a name, you ask? According to Shakespeare not much, as a rose is always a rose no matter what you call it. However, many cultures believe that a name has power and invoking that name marshals that power. Okay, yeah—that's a bit too metaphysical for me, too. But I do believe that what you call a new project is important for several reasons.

First, and most importantly, the name of a project should clearly convey what the project is about, especially if it's part of a larger program. We convey an enormous amount of information with the name of a project, and it should provide context for where the project fits into the overall business and program underway. A good example of this is a program I briefly worked on at Intel. The IT program name was SAP Re-Platforming. Right away you understand that the program has something to do with SAP and it's about major changes in how we used that application. If you have a bit of understanding about what SAP does and the scope with which it's used, then you understand right away that this was a significant program for Intel. You get all of that context just by the name of the program. See what I mean?

Another reason I think the name of a project is important is that you want to be associated with something that sounds significant. It's motivating to work on something that sounds important. For instance some of us worked on projects that support WiMAX development in some way or other. When you tell your friends and coworkers that you're working on a WiMAX project ,they "get it" and can relate what you do for a living to something tangible for them. I once mentioned that I was scoping a WiMAX project to my brother, and his teenage daughter said, "Oh, for hotspots like at Starbucks, right?" Yeah, something like that.

It's also motivating to work on something that sounds cool. When I first joined Intel, I managed PCB development projects in the Embedded Communications Group (ECG). My first projects had boring names based on geography. Almost every day I'd log into the document repository to upload or retrieve data stored there and on the main screen would be a folder for a project named *Devil's Bar* (okay, that may not be the exact name, as it's been a few years now). I'd frequently bemoan the fact that I was stuck working on a project called *Boring Mountain* instead of working on *Devil's Bar*. When I mentioned this over coffee one morning, one of the guys pointed out that the original name for the gaming console we now know as Wii was Revolution. Now I ask you, who wouldn't rather play a Revolution game instead of Wii-ing?

I'd like to give you some tips on selecting a good name for your project. First, pick something that conveys context and relevance. Second, pick something that's reasonable to spell and pronounce. Can you say/spell "Supercalifragilisticexpialidocious" Finally, pick a name that conveys the image you want to reinforce. If the project is a fast-track one, then choose a name that implies that speed such as the Bullet Express (I might be reaching a bit here). Think *Shock and Awe* instead of *Boring Mountain*. Get it?

I hope I've convinced you to take a few minutes to select a good name for your next project. I doubt that you'd find this discussion in the popular PM literature, but I believe the project name does matter even if it's only a subtle influence. Choose your project names wisely, my friends!

Scoping Projects

I've scoped quite a few projects in my time, and it occurs to me that this is not well defined in project management. To clarify, by *scoping* I mean doing an initial assessment of the amount of time, effort, resources, and budget a given project will require to execute. (*Triple constraint* anyone?) The thing with scoping a project is that it's done prior to the project's even becoming a project. This is high-level concept and feasibility work, not full-blown initiation or planning. You typically don't have solid requirements—heck, the customer frequently can only articulate a big-picture idea at this early stage. Further, you need to come up with high-level estimates for the project very quickly, so that your organization can make a value decision on whether or not to pursue the project.

So what have I learned about scoping projects? That good question deserves the following answers:

- First, I've learned that you really do need a detailed schedule to be able to estimate the project timeline and resources. To get to that schedule, you need a reasonably good WBS. To get that "reasonably good" WBS, you need solid requirements. Starting to see a pattern here? Yep, that's right—there are no shortcuts, and the only thing you can do if your timeline is tight is to dedicate more of your time to the scoping activity. Plan the rest of your work accordingly.

- The second thing I've come to realize is that the overall scoping results are only going to be as good as the schedule and requirements the scoping team develops. Split the work and have the technical lead focus on defining the requirements while you focus on the schedule. You will be using this schedule to model a variety of what-if scenarios, so make sure it's dynamic and as comprehensive as you can make it. I'm not kidding here! As a PM, this schedule is your secret weapon! Nail the detailed schedule and a lot of the negotiation of requirements and execution becomes much easier, because it's backed up by data generated from your model.

- The third major thing I've come to realize is that you have to adjust your perspective. Most project managers start working on a project after the scoping is done and the requirements and timelines are reasonably well-defined. With scoping you'll drive yourself crazy if you're expecting, or driving to, solid requirements and hard dates. The objective of scoping is to figure out feasibility and options, not necessarily to plan out the entire project. Relax and keep the big picture in mind. Trust me, you will enjoy the experience a lot more.

How to Develop a Robust Schedule

Now that I've convinced you that a project plan is much more than a project schedule and that it's a lot of hard work, let's talk about just how you go about building a robust, dynamic schedule. This is the planning activity that becomes the core of your project plans so you really must invest the time to get it done and get it done right. Many PMs hate developing a schedule because it seems like a no-win proposition. No matter how much work you put into it, your sponsor's gonna tell you to either (a) grow up and face reality or, more likely, (b) sharpen your pencils and do better. Well, before you can face "reality" or even sharpen anything, you've got to know what you have to work with. So, let's start with just how you really go about developing a dynamic schedule. Oh, and for all you folks who think you've got this? I really encourage you to read the first section, especially if you think your problem with schedules lies with the tools used to develop them!

The Problem Isn't MS Project...It's You!

If there's such a thing as pure evil in project management, then I'd bet most PMs would say it's MS Project. If you were to ask ten project managers which software they dislike using the most, hands down the answer is going to be MS Project. This software inspires more fear and frustration than just about any other. In short, for project managers, MS Project is Evil Incarnate!

MS Project is not an easy piece of code to utilize. It's complex and clunky. It looks like Excel and acts like Access...sort of. This is not software you can master on your own and the usual "pick-it-up-as-you-go-along" technique just won't be enough here. There are quagmires of options that don't really act as you'd expect them to. Can you type in your schedule tasks and add dates to each one? Absolutely! However if you do that, then you will "repent at leisure," as they say back home. The problem is that this part of setting up the schedule is deceptively easy—almost any novice user can do it. The pitfalls are things like task types, dynamically linking the tasks, proper use of milestones, resource leveling, and so on.

Note   If you have no clue what those things are, then you need to go sign up for some training immediately!

Setting up a robust, dynamic schedule is not something you can do without real experience and training.

Okay, to be fair, the problem is not all due to those guys in Redmond. In fact, most of the angst is due to either a lack of training or what I call the *GIGO theory*: garbage-in results in garbage-out. How do I know this? Well, let's just say that Project and I have had our bouts in the past and I usually lost. Did I mention that it's Evil Incarnate?

When I first started using Project, I tried to figure it out as I went along. I'm not a patient person when it comes to software and reading the instructions is for sissies! ☺ It definitely didn't work out like I'd planned. I then took a basic Introduction to Project class and, frankly, all that did was make me even more dangerous with the software. You see, I thought I knew what I was doing and I was able to cobble together crude but workable schedules. Somewhere along the way, I'd stopped using Excel to schedule projects but I wasn't yet effective with Project. At this point, I had enough training in the use of the software but I lacked a fundamental understanding of the practice of developing robust schedules. I was stuck in GIGO Land and didn't even realize it.

To get to that fundamental understanding, I had to go back to the beginning and relearn what I thought I knew about schedule development. For instance, you really do need a Work Breakdown Structure (WBS). Trying to figure out or brainstorm the project's task as you type them into Project is the road to ruin and gnawed off pencil erasers. If you are struggling with this, then I recommend taking (or re-taking, as the case may be) a project management fundamentals class and focusing on the schedule development material. You can also check out the numerous books dealing with this topic and other resources as needed. You will never get better at Project until you get better at the actual work of schedule development. So, in order for Project to work right, you have to develop the schedule right before you try to use the software.

It was only after I'd mastered the theory of schedule development that I started to realize the true value MS Project brings to the PM. You see, if you develop your schedule correctly, then getting Project to model it is much, much easier. Once you get to a robust and dynamic schedule correctly entered into Project, you unlock a veritable treasure trove of information. You can now see cause and effect for schedule push-outs, model various what-if scenarios to provide high-confidence data back to change control boards (CCBs), see the real critical path (it's not what you think it is!), and answer that dreaded question, "What would it take to pull this in a quarter?". In short, you can actually use Project as it was designed to be used.

So, if you are really struggling to use Project, then I'd suggest taking some time to do some training or self-study. Mastering schedule development and MS Project really will make your life easier. Project won't magically get easier to use but at least you will understand what it's doing—and you may even know why! ☺

Now that's out of the way, where do you start? Well, assuming you have some sort of requirements document that's reasonably frozen, you start by generating a WBS.

Breaking Down the Work Breakdown Structure

PMI breaks down a systematic way to create a project schedule, and one of the early steps in the process is to create a WBS. To create a WBS, you basically start with the expected outputs of the project and then systematically break out each sub-deliverable and the related work tasks to create said deliverable. This activity generates a list of all of the tasks that must be completed for the project, neatly bucketed into work packages that represent the tasks needed to complete each deliverable. Pretty straightforward, right?

In fact, it's so straightforward that PMs often overlook the formality of generating a WBS. Instead, we frequently just brainstorm a list of tasks with our teams and call it good enough. There's nothing wrong with this approach if you comprehend the corner you're cutting here. Don't kid yourself, though—you are adding risk to the project, because you can potentially miss some of the work that has to happen when you neglect to follow a systematic approach to identifying that final task list. I frequently won't create a WBS for a small project (~4–6 weeks, 3–4 team members, and so on), because these projects are usually fast-track-get-it-done-now kind of efforts that favor speed over formality. I know that I'll be babysitting this project pretty closely so I'm cool with cutting the WBS corner here. Another situation where I'll blow off creating the WBS is when the project is very similar to past projects the team has already tackled. For instance, in the past I've worked with teams who primarily develop a specialized type of software application. The work packages for each project are pretty much the same, with only the specifics of the coding and the work estimates varying between projects. In these instances, I've already created a schedule template from a WBS developed in the past, so building the schedule is just a matter of tweaking the template to fit the specifics of the new project. This is the most efficient way to generate a schedule for like projects.

Now if I have a completely new project or team, I'm not going to cut corners by bypassing the creation of a WBS. The same is true if the project involves an engineering discipline or technology I'm not familiar with. In these situations I find that I get the best understanding of the work needed for a particular project by facilitating the WBS generation session. If you use a systematic approach coupled with basic brainstorming techniques, the entire team will be engaged and the output will be a solid, comprehensive task list. Often PMs will tell me that they are struggling because they don't thoroughly understand the work going on in each functional area. When this happens I can't help but think that they didn't go through the work of generating a true WBS.

In the end, there's no wrong way to go about this as long as you are making some conscious decisions about which tools and techniques you will use to manage your project. Sometimes it makes sense to cut out the formal WBS creation and sometimes it doesn't. To help you figure it out, here are a few of Melanie's tricks of the trade to help you out when it comes to WBSs:

- Creating the WBS isn't that different from holding a brainstorming session to identify the tasks; it's just a more structured way to get to that final task list. Try it—you'll probably like it.

- If you don't generate a formal WBS but use MS Project to track the schedule, then you might be able to extract the WBS from the Project file. This comes in handy for those pesky PM process quality audits!

Note This functionality is highly dependent on which version of Project you are using, so you might not be able to pull this rabbit outta the hat.

- If I'm going to the trouble to do the WBS followed up by generating a network diagram, then I prefer to write out the tasks on Post-It notes so that the team can move them around during the brainstorming.

- If you are not planning to create a WBS, then save your sanity and **do not type your tasks directly into Project**! Freestyle task list generation in Project is the best way to ensure that you do not have a working schedule! Trust me, I've been there too many times to count. It's much easier to develop a task list and collect work estimates with Excel and then transfer the data into Project.

- You might not need a WBS if this is a similar project to one you've done before and you have a schedule template to use, or if it's very short and you already plan to micromanage the heck out of it.

- You *do* need a WBS if you are new to the team, technology, engineering discipline, and so forth.

- Use the WBS generation meeting as a way to build and/or reinforce your team dynamic, as this is often one of the first times the entire team gets together to work on the project.

Okay, that's my take on the always-scintillating topic of WBSs. Sure, it's not rocket science or anything that complex, but I do think it pays to spend some time thinking about these things and understanding when it makes sense to follow PMI's best practices and when it makes sense to cut some corners. I hope you found this interesting and maybe even got a few ideas to use the next time you need to build a schedule.

Networking… and Not the Fun Kind

Now that you've got your tasks broken down, you need to take that information and create a network diagram. Basically a *network diagram* is a visual representation of the project's workflow. Which task goes first? What task is dependent on the material arriving in-house? Can you create the Marketing collateral while the Quality Assurance guys are doing their thing? Following me?

Pretty much everything I've said about the WBS applies to the network diagram—they are best buds, salt and pepper, Liz Taylor and white diamonds, Willie Nelson and Trigger. (Yes, Willie really did name his guitar that! I couldn't make that up if I tried. ☺), coffee and cream, french fries and ketchup…you get the picture. Bottom line? If you're going to the trouble of creating a WBS then you gotta grind out the network diagram. If you are cutting the WBS corner, then same goes for the network diagram.

Okay, when I say that you've "gotta grind out the network diagram," I'm really making it sound harder than it is. The easiest way I know to create one is to use sticky notes. Write each task on a separate sticky note, then using a nice smooth wall covered in blank paper, start laying out the workflow. Keep moving the notes around, adding more as necessary, until your diagram…your *network* diagram, get it?…makes sense. Do this as a team if possible. At Intel this work is done during a MAPP Day, as described in Chapter 5. Once you think you've got it nailed, have each person "walk" the flow and tweak the diagram as needed. Once it's good, annotate those sticky notes with a number and make sure that you've captured the predecessor and successor for each one on the note. Take a nice digital picture with your phone and then tape down the diagram. Pull off the paper, roll it up, and you've got a hardcopy of your network diagram. How easy is that?

By the way, have you noticed that we've done all of this work without MS Project getting fired up once? There's a reason for that—so step away from that laptop, mister!

Estimation: It's Trickier Than You Thought

Now that you've got your WBS and before the network diagram, you can start estimating the work. I'm not going to regale you with a blow-by-blow account of all of the fabulous estimation techniques out there. Trust me, there are tons of resources on that kind of thing and you won't have much trouble understanding the techniques. I mean, you did pass basic math back in high school right? Despite all the fancy-pants terminology, estimation processes are pretty straightforward and don't use a lot of painful math. The pitfall for PMs isn't the techniques or the math. It's something else entirely.

Thinking about the estimation process led me to thinking about just how critical the main estimation meeting can be. I think this is one of the choke points a PM must navigate very carefully. The estimating is done early in the project so the team dynamic is probably somewhere in the storming phase. The primary estimation meeting happens after the team has had a chance to review and think about the work content. Each member has a solid idea of how long it will take to complete his or her portion of the work…and each probably has a good idea of how long he or she thinks it should take everyone else to complete their work. Throw in a sense of unease about committing to work and a timeline you can't hit and you have a volatile situation. If the PM doesn't step up and lead here, the team will devolve into a disjointed group of individuals each completing his or her assigned work with little commitment to the overall deliverable.

So what do I mean by "step up and lead"? First as the PM, you have to do some legwork before the meeting. Each team member needs to complete his or her part of the estimation process prior to the meeting. If you find that some folks haven't done the pre-work, then reschedule the meeting and remove any roadblocks. Second, it's critical to explicitly spell out the expectations for this meeting. Yes, you really do need a slide that addresses confidentiality, respect for everyone's opinions, full participation, and so on. Now the fun really begins! As you move into the discussion of estimates for specific tasks or work packages, the PM must actively facilitate the discussion. Everyone needs to participate and all opinions need to be heard and considered. Inevitably there will be some disagreements where strong opinions are held. When this happens,

I have the team drill down into all of the assumptions that were made for that particular estimate. The discussion that follows may still be heated, but at the end everyone is on the same page about the work content. Other team members may have strong opinions but ultimately I defer to the estimate of the person who will actually have to do the work. It's important to understand that how you orchestrate these difficult discussions will be a huge factor in your ability to motivate and influence the team going forward. Do not alienate someone by forcing an estimate they are uncomfortable committing to.

Finally, I can't emphasize enough how important it is get the estimate right. At this point in the planning process, how long it takes to do the work is irrelevant to the customer's expected completion date. Drive an open discussion by making it clear that the goal is to understand what it takes to do the work and that schedule optimization will come later. People are often surprised in estimation meetings I run because I don't put a lot of energy into hassling people about their estimates. Frankly, at this point I don't care what your estimate is as long as you can commit to completing the work in that amount of time. I'm a strong believer that the first step in schedule optimization is to truly understand what it takes to do the job. Too often in the past I was caught flat-footed late in a project because the estimates were gamed to fit the expected customer commit. My primary goal at estimation is to understand my baseline so that I have a solid basis for optimization later. My secondary goal is to establish a solid team dynamic that is collaborative and not combative.

The Easy Way

Building a schedule can often be the hardest part of the mechanics of project management. Frequently, there's an expectation for the project duration that's based on a lot of speculation and previous experience. Some of the work will just be difficult to estimate, and let's not forget about the funfest that is MS Project. Still, a strong, dynamic schedule can be your best ally as you navigate the lifespan of the project. There's a lot out there about how to develop a schedule and for the most part, it's all very good. The problem is that all those best practices for generating strong schedules take time…lots of it! I don't know about you, but many times I don't have that kind of time. I need a schedule good enough to commit deliverables from in a week. Heck, sometimes it's a matter of days! That's just the way this project management gig happens sometimes. The real trick isn't meeting that target date but infusing the final committed date with enough reality to make the target reasonable. So how do you go about building a schedule that supports this reality? Oh and how do you do it *fast*??? In short, how do you do this in the real world?

To be honest, you'd want to do a full planning session before opening Project. The truth is that I've found that most PMs for small projects or less formal teams tend to jump right into Project after nailing the comprehensive task list and the work estimates. Sure, it's not the best way to go, but it can work for you if you pay attention to the details and develop a dynamic schedule.

As with my take on risk management, this process isn't pretty and it's not a strict implementation of the PMBoK, but it will get the job done if you mind your p's and q's, as follows:

1. Type or copy and paste the task list into Project. **Do not enter any dates at this point!**

2. Add a milestone task at the very top of your project called Project Start. Add a similar one at the end called Project Complete. Again, do not enter any dates in the Start or Finish fields.

3. For every task on the list, populate the predecessor field and your work estimates to the Work field in Project. I'm sorry to be a nag, but again: **do not enter any dates at this point!**

▓ **Tip**   It helps a lot to just hide the Start and Finish columns at this point . . . trust me, it saves a lot of time and helps everyone focus on the logic of the schedule versus the dates.

---

4. Add resources to each task, but be very careful here. In the previous scenarios I talk about above, it's unlikely that you are going to be tracking actual hours, and that's okay. The rub is that you are still going to need to look at how the work is distributed across the resources and make sure it's reasonable. This is called resource leveling and it's hard, nasty work. If you're unfamiliar with doing this, then I'd suggest checking out the many project resources available on this topic.

5. Add meaningful milestones by inserting a line item for each one. You can add as many as you want just don't forget to populate the predecessor field. Be sure to include any critical deliverables your team is expecting from another team, be it hardware, software, testing, or Twinkies. Again: **do not enter any dates at this point!**

6. Toggle the view in Project so that you can see the Relationship Diagram. This is a block diagram of how each task connects to the others in the schedule. Now step through each line item making sure that there are predecessors and successors for each task. It's worth

noting that some milestones will not have both, but every line item in your schedule will have at least one. Lather, rinse, repeat until you have a schedule that's linked from Project Start to Project Close.

7. At this point, **you still haven't entered in any dates**! Now's the time to double-check your work. Toggle the view in Project to view the Critical Path. Does it make sense? Are there enough tasks on the list?

Tip   If the answer is no, then you don't have all of your tasks linked dynamically through the predecessor/successor logic. Go back and repeat Step 6.

---

8. Okay, take a big breath and get ready to enter actual dates. Melanie's rule of thumb is this: hard-coded dates are bad, dates Project generates on its own are good. If you see a small square icon on in the Indicator column of any task, then you know you've got a hard-coded date for that task. Now go ahead and enter the Start date for your milestone, Project Start. Enter hard-coded dates for any milestones that represent deliverables to your team (this is your committed date to receive the deliverable). Hit Enter and watch the magic happen.

9. At this point your schedule should be 80% complete. You will need to clean it up a bit by tweaking some of the predecessor/successor logic and eliminating as many hard-coded dates as possible.

10. Gut check time. Ask the team members if the timeline makes sense. Break it into logical chunks such as, "Does it seem like this project should take six weeks for testing?". Refine your schedule as necessary.

11. Once you're satisfied with the schedule, baseline it. These are the dates you can commit to your customers.

Tip   I find it helpful to add the Baseline Start and Baseline Finish columns so that I can see at a glance how far the project is drifting from the committed baseline dates.

As I said, this isn't the best practices poster child for schedule development. It's my method for getting the work done as quickly as possible. It involves a lot of PM time—hours of it—so plan accordingly. In the end, you will use that schedule every week of the project and, if it's not complete or otherwise jacked up, your life will be a misery until the darn thing is over. Spend as much time up front as you can and get it right the first time. I hope this has helped you think about how you develop schedules and gives you a repeatable process.

Optimizing the Schedule

Okay, now that you have your "best case" schedule developed, let's cover how to optimize it. If you've followed my previous advice about how to build a schedule, you will end up with the most likely scenario assuming that nothing goes catastrophically wrong. Unfortunately, unless you just get lucky, that final project release date won't be good enough and you're going to need to optimize. Yep, it's time to "pull in the schedule." Cue the *Jaws* music!

Now any PM with a whip and a chair can perform a pull-in...at least on paper or in MS Project. However, it takes a bit more skill to actually optimize your schedule. To optimize a schedule, I go back to the venerable *triple constraint*: **schedule**, **scope**, and **resources**. Think of these as the legs of an equilateral triangle; affect any one leg of that triangle and you will cause a corresponding change in at least one other leg. With a schedule pull-in, you are essentially shrinking that schedule leg and holding it fixed. What this means is that you can't change one of the three without affecting the others. There's no such thing as a free lunch, remember? Okay, if you want to pull in your schedule, then you really only have two knobs to turn: *scope* and *resources*.

By far **the easiest way to pull in a schedule is to reduce the scope of work**, so you should start here when you are attempting to pull in a schedule. Go through the requirements document with your team to identify likely features or functionality you can either cut or push to a later release. Also, carefully review the test plan to see if you can reduce scope there. After you have identified some candidates for the ol' scope-chopping block, run them by your stakeholders to see if you can come up with a compromise on the reduced scope of work. Often, breaking the deliverables up and releasing them in phases is a workable solution.

▓ **Caution** Be very careful that you do not alienate your stakeholders when challenging the necessity of functions or features. It's very easy to give aggressive stakeholders the impression that your team is trying to weasel out of work at this stage, so make extra efforts to keep the discussion collaborative.

If you can't cut scope or release in phases, then **the next thing you want to look at is how the work is synchronized**. First, start by examining the critical path—or critical chain if you're following the *theory of constraints* (TOC). These tasks are the ones you need to address if you want to pull in your overall finish date. Don't waste your time trying to pull in any task not on the path, as it won't affect your end date. Here's where the *optimization* comes in. Scrutinize the critical path to determine if any of the work can be done in parallel. In my experience, there are usually some opportunities here and, if you want to get really crazy, you can consider employing Agile development concepts. One of the advantages of using the Agile methodology for your execution phase is that you can pull your testing work up in parallel with your development work…sort of.

Okay, let's say that you can't reduce or phase out the scope and you can't do any more work in parallel—what do you do next? It's time to make like a teenager with her momma's BMW and **crash the schedule**! In case you haven't been brainwashed by PMI yet, *crashing the schedule* is the term used when you add more resources to the project. So, go through your critical path tasks and determine if adding more bodies would help those specific tasks. Be aware of the fact that not every task benefits from more hands, but chances are you will have some opportunities for crashing the schedule. The end result of your crashing experiment is that you should have a list of specific tasks with associated start/finish dates and the necessary skill set needed. This is your *ask* list and, because it's really specific, your chances of actually getting extra resources increases dramatically. A resource owner is much more likely to cough up that extra head if he knows it's for a set period of time with a very specific task or deliverable rather than an ambiguous request for help.

There's one more tactic to try when you are optimizing your schedule and—fair warning—it's not a popular one. For a time, PMI defined a fourth component to the triple constraint: **quality**. (How a *triple* entity could have a fourth component has never made sense to me but, hey, I'm not PMI am I?) It's commonplace to define the quality metrics/requirements that need to be met for your project's output. One way to pull in your schedule is to **relax the quality requirements**, which in turn reduces the overall scope of work. The thing is, though, this is a really tough row to hoe and, while it should be considered as a matter of due diligence, it's rare that all stakeholders agree to a lesser quality level for a product. It does happen, and of course it carries its own risks, so you and your team should consider reduced quality as part of your analysis to pull in the schedule.

Once you've ground through the tactics discussed above, you should have several what-if optimization scenarios defined with associated risks, impacts to the end date, and resources needed to execute them. These are the basis for any negotiation with your customers and key stakeholders on pulling in the schedule. In my experience, this data goes a long way to convincing your stakeholders that your team can or cannot pull in a schedule. At some point the work "is what it is" and there's not much more you can do, especially if you want to keep the scope of work fixed while reducing the schedule. Remember that equilateral triangle? As I never tire of repeating, there's no such thing as a free lunch!

So there it is. To optimize a schedule, try to reduce the scope of work, look at how the work is synchronized, crash the schedule, and/or consider relaxing the quality requirements. Do these things, and you will have enough pull-in options to make a solid business decision.

The Proper Care and Feeding of Your Baseline

There was a time when I thought a *baseline* was pretty useless, if I even gave the concept any thought at all. I was young then and often too busy trying to stay on top of the actual project work to worry much about my schedule. Sure, I understood the concept of a baseline but, frankly, that understanding was rooted in design of experiments and measuring tangible things like current or voltage. It had little to do with scheduling. If I gave a baseline any thought at all, it was because I had to capture it on a PowerPoint slide somewhere, and even then it masqueraded under the title, "Plan Dates." Truly, it didn't play much of a role in my project management.

Fast-forward to today's projects and I'm all about the baselines. In fact, I view my current schedule baseline as so important that it's got a permanent home on my custom/default MS Project view. Nowadays instead of referring to these dates as "Plan Dates," they go by the name "Customer Commits"! To cut to the chase here, I baseline my schedule when I'm ready to give the customer commit for the project deliverables. Performing the "baseline" action in MS Project saves a baseline start and finish date for every line item on the schedule. Therefore, by comparing the Baseline Start date of a task with the Start date at some point in the future, I can tell immediately if that task is in alignment with the committed customer dates. I can't imagine managing a project without having a baseline front and center all the time.

Another point I should make is that your project baseline will evolve as the project progresses through its lifecycle. Your first baseline is still the basis for all measurements of performance against schedule and you should never discard it. However, the reality of project management is that things change and your customer commits will change as a result. Anytime my team approves a change request of measureable schedule impact, I add that work to the project schedule and re-baseline. This new baseline becomes the new and current customer commit. Lather, rinse, repeat. It's not unusual to re-baseline your schedule a couple of times during a project, so be sure you keep track of what each baseline represents.

▓ **Tip**   I do this by adding notes to my Project Start task.

Okay, so re-baselining is a perfectly legit activity most of the time—*but* it's also one of the most misused schedule maintenance practices around. If your project's schedule is rolled up to a dashboard, then chances are any variance from the originally committed dates is noted. I've observed PMs re-baseline willy-nilly to "fix" this variance. Bad PM! Bad! If the circumstances have changed and you've legitimately re-committed the project deliverables then re-baselining is the proper activity. However, if your team is slipping the schedule then re-baselining is simply sweet frosting over a rotten cake. I've also seen re-baselining used to "fix" a bad *schedule performance index/cost performance index* (SPI/CPI) metric as well . . . Bad PM! 'Nuff said, right?

Here's the thing: re-baselining to make things appear better in MS Project when in fact the train is jumpin' the tracks is wrong. It's the MS Project equivalent of lyin' through your teeth, and you know it as well as I do. I once worked in an organization where it was common practice to re-baseline the Plan Dates whenever the project team was behind. Sadly, the senior management sitting in those Ops Reviews never noticed this tactic but they did have low confidence in the PMs because those projects were always late. And those PMs? Well, they defended their re-baselining practice as the only way they could avoid getting raked over the coals whenever their projects were behind schedule. What a dysfunctional group all the way around!

There you have it—the proper care and feeding of your schedule baselines. If you haven't really used them, then now's the time to start! Baseline your current schedules today and then start paying attention to those tasks that start varying from your baseline start and/or finish dates. It's easy to do and the information you get is immediately actionable. I hope I've convinced you to pay attention to your baselines and steer clear of re-baselining to fix a slipping schedule.

The Dark Art of Leveling Resources

Just to get started, raise your hand if you *level the resources* on all of your projects? In MS Project? Using the Level All button? Okay, for those of you with your hands still up, I have just one thing to say—"Much respect!" Seriously, I bow down to your superior skills! For me at least, resource leveling has always seemed like the Dark Art of Project Management. I'm not sure if it's a failure to fully understand what Project is doing—that creepy feeling you get when something "auto-calculates" for a really long time as you watch your dates bounce around—or the inevitable bad news that results from leveling resources, but for many PMs it's just plain scary. Think of this as a root canal for PMs. (Yeah, it really is that bad! I'm not kidding here! Seriously!)

Now after that ominous buildup, I know what you're thinking: "Why would I invite that much pain? Why should I even bother with the auto-leveling capability in Project?" The short answer is that, by leveling your resources, you're identifying risks and potential problems before they become Excedrin Headaches. Even if you only have five people on your project, there's just no good way to pinpoint specific weeks in which resource utilization breaks above 100% in Excel, especially when you try to factor in holidays, individual vacations, sabbaticals, and so on. It's a complex world out there, and you really need some help from a tool to get a quick snapshot of the individual work-loads for the resources on your project. Oh, and as long as you've built a careful schedule, the leveling process goes pretty quickly.

So how do you level your resource? Well, first you need to do a good job of developing the schedule. Follow the step-by-step process outlined above. At Step 9, you level them. To level your resources, go to the Resource tab:

Here you have two options: Level Resource will allow you to level an individual resource and Level All will do all of your resources at once. Click Level Now and off MS Project goes, tweaking your task dates willy-nilly. Okay, it's not quite that bad, but it really is a one-step process if you decide to level all resources at the same time.

Sounds pretty straightforward, doesn't it? Well, for the most part that's because it is! Now for a couple of tips and tricks to help you over the bumps. First, before I do any leveling I toggle to the Resource Usage view and check out all those resources in red. As I scroll the right-side window, I can see how much any given resource is over-allocated in any given week. If the over-allocation is minimal (say <20%) then I don't bother leveling that one, because I'm assuming that the margin of error in my work estimates will take care of the over-allocation over time. Also, I don't think it's unreasonable to expect a resource to put in a little overtime once in a while. This is a quick way to gauge how much resource leveling you need to do. If I have primarily one resource that's over-allocated, then I prefer to level the schedule one resource at a time. If most of the resources are over-allocated, then I level all of them at the same time. Last, it's absolutely vital that you level the resources before you add any actual hours. For some reason trying to level a resource on a task with actual hours assigned freaks Project out. (Okay, that's my interpretation of what happens and a Project expert can probably tell you what's really going on—but not me. ☹)

So, the resources are leveled and the project milestone dates align with the customer's expectation. What's the point and was it worth the extra "drama" of leveling the resources? The point is that you now have a well-developed schedule that does not assume that any of your resources are working insane hours. You have a crystal clear idea of how much work is planned per resource per week. When you're looking at ways to pull in a schedule, this is a great tool to help you see where you can backend-load work into weeks when there's not 100% utilization. Further, if you've got to over-allocate resources to pull in a schedule, then you can clearly state that you need someone to put in OT in specific weeks. This can be very helpful in motivating someone to work more hours, because you can make it clear that it's a finite effort, not something that will become the status quo.

So there you go—a little light on the Dark Art of Project Management! I hope this has been helpful and at least convinced you to give automated resource leveling another look.

Buffer? What Buffer? Surely You Jest!

Now I thought I'd talk about what is essentially a taboo PM topic: *buffering the schedule*. As experienced PMs, we know that we should utilize buffers in our schedules to undercommit and overdeliver right? It's just good risk management to have buffers, isn't it? Okay, I want to try something here, so please bear with me. Raise your hands if you have buffers built into your schedules. Okay, now lower your hands if you've got those buffers hidden, obscured, or otherwise buried in the schedule. If you are utilizing TOC you get to put your hands down now too. Who's left holding up their hands? Bueller? Bueller? Bueller? Yeah, that's what I thought...none of us.

Here's the thing: we know we need 'em, but it's pretty much "frowned upon" to explicitly utilize a buffer. The primary exception to this is those of you using TOC, which embraces the buffering economy. I'm betting that most of you, like me, have worked in organizations where every program and project must be pulled in. You know what I'm talking about here. You show up at the planning session with a high-confidence schedule only to get it picked apart, knocked around, and otherwise violated—all in some frantic attempt to pull in the dates to meet an arbitrary deadline. Somewhere in this process the real magnitude of the work packages gets lost and risks are introduced into the plan. This is the real world you work in, and that's how a lot of program/ project plans fall out. So what do you do? You bake in some buffer as risk contingency so that your team has a hope of delivering on time. (Ever notice that we do this with budgets too?) The really ridiculous thing about this is that each project that supports a larger program is going to do this and so is the program manager. Sounds a lot like tolerance-stacking doesn't it?

Over time this attitude becomes so ingrained in our PM psyche that we don't even notice it. This is just crazy! One time I was wrapping up a huge program that lasted 22 months and, as I was pulling together some data for the retrospective, I discovered that we had come in only 4% over our planned work (the actual man hours). That's phenomenal performance and yes, my team rocks, but that data point did spark a good question. One of the new guys asked how we did it—not so subtly implying that I'd padded the heck out of the underlying project schedules. No padding was employed and we did do a fantastic job executing the plan. But the truth of the matter is that I should have been using explicit buffers. At that time I worked in a team where I was allowed to do the job the right way to get results. My boss didn't care if I buffered a schedule as long as I did it the correct way for the right reasons. (For some reason, he didn't buy my argument that we should have a buffer for the month of July so that we can go hang at the lake though…go figure!)

Now here comes the weird part. I had to ping a fellow PM to figure out how to explicitly use buffers in Project. I'm not sure I've done it in recent memory. She didn't know how to do it either, and trust me she can make Project do some pretty impressive tricks! We'd both become so accustomed to hiding buffers we had to scratch our heads to figure out how to do it openly. Even weirder was the fact that I've been managing projects for this team for over two years now and I was still hiding those buffers for no good reason! It had become so deeply embedded in my thought processes that I just assumed that I couldn't use an explicit buffer. D'oh!

I used to believe that the use of explicit schedule buffers was a non-starter. Ironically, if you want to be successful project after project, then you need to use schedule buffers, so you hide them. You probably work in organizations that are expecting you to hide them—hence the ridiculous scrutiny of your project schedules during those planning sessions. I think it's time we all got off this particular crazy train. The next time you use buffers, do it openly and tie them to the risks you're really worried about. Do I think this will change the way your organization works? Not really—but who knows, you just might educate someone and convince them to get off the train, too, and isn't that worth the effort? Good luck out there!

How to Say No to Unrealistic Target Dates

It's a fact of life that PMs will be given unrealistic target dates for their projects. Sometimes these crazy dates are driven by real-world constraints such as market windows or large corporate initiatives, but they are just as often based on wild speculation—a management team with a Magic 8 Ball and a handful of optimistic dates. This is your reality and to be successful you need a slew of tricks up your sleeve to inject some reality into those pipe dreams. Let me share some of my tricks of the trade.

Triple Constraint Junkie

First, let's go back to basics and talk about one of the most powerful constructs in project management, the *triple constraint*. If you pick up a recent edition of the PMBoK, then you won't find this idea at all! Instead you find a laundry list of factors that affect the overall project. Sure, each of these factors is important but, to be honest, this long list of items obscures the constraining elements of any project: the scope of work, the schedule, and the resources. Yep, you guessed it! I'm an old-school PM and a triple constraint junkie!

Okay, for those of you who have no clue what I'm talking about, let me break down the triple constraint concept for you. Basically, the idea is that any project is bounded by three equally important and interrelated factors. First is the *scope* of work the project is tasked with completing. Second is the committed *schedule* and its associated milestones. Third come the *resources* that are assigned to the project. Everything else can be associated back to these three factors. This concept is typically represented by an equilateral triangle where each leg represents the scope, the schedule, and the resources. The integrity of the triangle must be maintained—so once you baseline your plan, think of these legs as fixed. If at some point you want to *pull in* the schedule—that is, shorten that leg of the triangle—then you must either cut the scope of work or extend the amount of resources available. Likewise, if you need to increase the scope of the project, then you have to either extend the schedule leg or the resources leg. See how this works?

As I mentioned, PMI has pretty much done away with the triple constraint, and I'm honestly not sure why they did this because it's such a useful construct. I guess part of the reason is that we humans have a really hard time leaving good enough alone…there's always a way to make something better. PMI first improved the idea to emphasize the important role quality played in projects by encircling the triple constraint triangle with a *quality* circle. The idea here was the quality constraint spanned all aspects of a project. Yep, I get that and am totally on board, only…isn't quality intrinsically related to the scope of work? As time went by, more and more "important" factors were emphasized and the good ol' triangle graphic inevitably gave way to a laundry list. Well, that's progress, I guess.

I'm not sure that's progress at all, because I use that triangle construct to develop, explain, and negotiate every project plan I create. This is why I'm a triple constraint junkie! I can easily sketch the idea out on a whiteboard to help explain just why my team can't deliver five new features with a fixed schedule and no additional resources to the extreme driver who calls herself the engineering manager. I've used the graphic to help focus teams on brainstorming ideas for how we will execute the project. Whenever I'm working on optimizing a schedule, I start with the scope of work and available resources. See how this simple triangle construct helps focus my thinking?

When I was just starting out as a PM, I didn't understand the triple constraint idea and, looking back, I can see that my efforts were more along the lines of coordinating the work than actually managing the project. It was only when I started studying for the Project Management Professional (PMP) exam that I actually encountered the triple constraint. For me as a PM, it was a pivotal moment—so yeah, I'm totally a triple constraint junkie and darn proud of it! How 'bout you? (Geez, I really think I need to get a T-shirt with "Triple Constraint Junkie" emblazoned across the chest, don't you?)

Hard Dates = Negotiable Targets

Okay, now we're getting to the good stuff! What do you do when a project deliverable date is dictated to you? First let me say that this is the reality of project management: a place where theory and the real world collide on an epic scale. I have very little input into the target date that's dictated to the project team, unless I'm the PM doing the scoping work prior to a program or project kicking off. This is my reality and I'm pretty sure it's the reality most PMs live with. To be fair, often these dates are based on market windows, and if you miss the window then you might as well pack up your toys and go home. Unfortunately, there are also those times when these dates are set by upper management based on their own personal assessments of how long the project should take. Hey, these folks were once engineers and they know how long it takes to do this work…back in the day, within the business environment that bears little resemblance to what project teams endure today. It really doesn't matter why a project end date gets dictated to the project team; it's enough to realize that it's going to happen regularly. To be successful in this environment, it makes sense to figure out how to manage that hard deliverable date.

To be successful in this environment, I think the key is to do solid planning. The depth and thoroughness of the planning separates the project coordinators from the project managers. What do I mean by this? Well, for me the main output of planning is a project plan that includes a strong, dynamic schedule and a risk register. With the work done to develop the plan and the schedule, I can model all kinds of what-if scenarios. I can pull together scenarios for my customers that offer realistic options for meeting the actual goal of the program and not necessarily the originally dictated deliverable. I consider things like parallel development paths, phased development to cut in scope as it's realistic to achieve, crashing the schedule with specific resources, and so forth. It's true that some of these scenarios never make it to the final set of options, but what I've found is that going through this what-if exercise can often spur ideas your team would not have otherwise come up with. For instance, when I was working on a particular Intel program, the board development team came up with the radical recommendation to drop the development of the planned second validation board. This idea would never have surfaced if we hadn't been running what-if scenarios to figure out how to develop the second board within very challenging triple constraints. You see, there just wasn't enough budget or resources to fulfill this mandated deliverable. Our solid planning allowed us to generate a very workable option that fulfilled the program's overall objectives but not in the mandated way. Make no mistake, this is hard work, and I think it's where the PM really needs to be on her "A" game.

In the past, I'd view these dictated dates as locked in stone and I had this attitude of "we just have to do whatever it takes." In some ways, having the end date mandated was a "get-out-of-jail-free" card for me. I knew that if the project was not successful, it wasn't because I'd done a bad job but because the end date wasn't realistic in the first place. However, this line of logic doesn't take into account the fact that the company is paying all of us to develop product and make money. We have a responsibility to challenge those unrealistic mandates and provide realistic options to meet the end goals, such as time to market or product features. Can you say *constructive confrontation?*

Let me be very clear here: I think giving the impression to your customer and/or management that you are committing to a date, when you know you can't hit it, is unprofessional and dishonest. I don't do that anymore. Sure, I did it earlier in my PM career—and every single time the project failed or was such a fire drill that everyone was toasted by the time it was over. What I learned from all those hard knocks is that thinking that "we'll just do whatever it takes" or that "it's just got to happen" doesn't work. Resources don't magically fall from the sky, no one's willing to sleep on a cot in the lab, requirements don't just drop off the scope of work, and even if—through some minor miracle—you pull it off, there's no way you're gonna get a hat trick...it's just not repeatable or sustainable. Further, no one really gets fired for pushing back with credible data.

In summary, as a PM, you're going to get "hard" dates and requirements handed to you. In order to influence those hard dates and requirements you have to have data; to get the data, you have to do the hard work of planning. There's really no shortcut here and thinking that "we'll just find a way" is just an excuse for not doing the actual planning. If I don't have a plan for how the team will hit a hard date with the desired scope, I say so up front, but I always follow that up with options and data. I realize that this isn't easy, and I'm sure every PM out there has struggled with this situation more than once. I've been fortunate that I've never been in a situation in which I felt that my job would be jeopardized by not going along with unrealistic dates. Not sure if that's due to blind luck or not. I suspect it has to do with my mindset about this. I choose to see those mandates as negotiable targets where I need actionable data to influence the outcome. I choose not to see them as set-in-stone hard dates, to achieve which the team must do "whatever it takes." "Whatever it takes" is a train wreck waiting to happen. "Negotiable targets" are the way off that train.

Saying Yes to Say No

Now let's talk about one of the tricks of the trade of project management; saying yes instead of no. Consider this scenario:

You're in the weekly program team meeting and the marketing rep proposes that you change the color of the control box chassis your team is developing. Instead of the brushed metal finish your team designed, she'd like you to just paint it Intel Blue. There are some reasonable marketing arguments for this change and the program team is looking for your buy-in. You know that the design for the chassis is completed and your team just finished the fit check. Orders for production volumes have been placed, so changing the exterior finish requires a lot more than just a can of Krylon. At this point you have three options, and which one you choose can greatly affect the amount of hassle this change generates for you and your team.

Your first choice is to just say, "No!" I call this the "Hard No". You can use the argument that it would be too expensive and your team doesn't have time to do this along with everything else they have on their plate. The problem here is that you've shut down all avenues of negotiation. If the program team decides they really need to make this change, then the only recourse is to escalate your refusal to entertain the request. You will find yourself explaining to your boss and major stakeholders why this change can't be implemented. I see this scenario a lot with new PMs, and they truly don't understand why everything is a battle. What they don't see is that by using a "Hard No" they've boxed themselves in and the battle is inevitable.

Your second choice is what I call the "Doormat Yes" response. You agree to implement the change while you're sitting there in the meeting with no supporting data. In fact, this usually happens when the PM is inexperienced or just wants the confrontational discussion/peer pressure to go away. The problem here, of course, is that you've now committed to something you truly don't know if you can deliver. You'll spend the next week or more frantically trying to make this change happen and end up explaining over and over again why the change is necessary. Trust me, motivating a team to implement a change they aren't bought-into is an uphill slog through the mud.

Your last option—and it's the one I recommend—is to use what I call a "Conditional Yes". Here you are going to play along and say something like this: "Yes, I'd be happy to take this back to my team and look into it. I'm sure we can work something out." The slick part here is that you are agreeing to research the change but you are not agreeing to do it. This gives you time to work with your team to pull together impact statements and truly understand what it would take to implement the change: a designer or engineer needs to modify the chassis drawings for the change to the silkscreen and surface finish; someone needs to figure out the specific paint color to spec in; the total cost to rework the chassis already ordered needs to be determined; you need a schedule impact analysis; and a prototype is needed to ensure that the color and silkscreen are right. You see? There's a lot more work here than just whipping out a can of Krylon and you need to help the program team understand what's involved in making this change.

Once you have your data together, you can respond to the change request with options for the program team. Here's where the power of the "Conditional Yes" comes into play. You are now viewed as a collaborative team member willing to negotiate. Of course, you're going to propose a solution based on your impact analysis, but this time no one will feel the need to escalate your intransigence to your boss. Finally, your team isn't going to need much motivation to implement the change. They are already bought into it and understand what they need to do, because they've done the analysis and prep work. In fact, I often find that the team does most of the work to implement the change before the request is fully approved. That can be good or bad, depending on the situation.

So what's the trick? When confronted with a change request you either don't want to implement or believe is the wrong direction to take, use a "Conditional Yes" to buy you some time. Use that time to develop a comprehensive picture of the change impact and then let the data speak for itself. You may still have to implement the change, but if that happens then you will know what it takes and have a much better understanding of why it's important. It's worth noting that, many times, the data really don't support the change and it isn't implemented. The example about the control box chassis happened to me years ago, and in the end we didn't paint the chassis because we found that the paint didn't make that much of an impact when the box was fully assembled into the final product. They ended up painting some other component instead… go figure. ☺

Just Because They Ask…

Have you ever had this happen? Your team is doing pretty good and in fact your schedule is trending early. Yahoo! Then a change request comes in that seems doable but is not part of the original scope. You know the kind of request I'm talking about: change the wording on a label; change the chassis color; order another vendor's similar part to save some minor amount of money. Are these pretty easy to implement? Yep! Is it worth jeopardizing the project's timeline to fulfill these requests? Not really.

It's the little things that can sink you without you even seeing it coming. The next thing you know you find yourself trying to explain why you can't ship the product early because the new labels are late. Trust me, there's no way you can spin holding a product shipment due to the new labels being lost in shipping… it's pretty indefensible and you feel like an idiot for not saying no to the original request.

Saying no to the big things is straightforward. You're crystal clear on questions of integrity, ethics, values, and the like. You can trust your gut here, and these issues are generally easier to fight for because the stakes are high. Similarly, the big changes to your project are usually outside of your ability to veto; you just have to do them somehow.

However, saying no to the small things is much harder and much, much murkier. On the surface, the stakes are low, there's little negative impact to you or your team, and it feels good to help someone else out. (Why is it always a favor to someone else that starts this chain reaction?) The problem is that there's always the opportunity for a visit from Murphy and his infamous law. The more opportunities for things to go wrong on your project, the higher the likelihood that something will go wrong. This isn't rocket science, yet I've seen this sink some of my projects that were well on their way to a successful closure. There was the time the new valve vendor couldn't actually deliver the volume we needed, or the time I spent hours reinstalling the old bus bars 'cause the new ones were delaminating. Let's just say that I learned a really clear lesson the hard way, and it's this: **Just because they ask doesn't mean you have to say yes.**

Every time someone brings a new item to one of my project's CCB meetings, I ask myself if this is a "must-do" item or a "nice-to-have" item. The "must-do" items are easy, as those are the "big things." It's everything else that can trip you up. The closer the team is to a design freeze, the greater the scrutiny of proposed changes. This is how it should work, and that's not where the pitfalls generally lie in wait.

From my experience, the change requests that come in once you are well into execution pose the biggest risk. Engineers often confuse the ease of implementation with whether a change should be implemented. If something seems easy to do, you can bet that most of your team is going to be up for it. At this point, the PM needs to ask herself what would happen if the change isn't implemented. If the answer is "nothing," then I suggest that you not make the change. You're too close to the finish line to introduce doors for Murphy to walk in. Don't do it! Trust me on this one! Instead of saying yes here, propose that the change be integrated into the next project or product upgrade cycle. It's very easy to incorporate these types of changes into a new project and you'll save yourself the hassle of reprinting 100 copies of the user's guide because someone changed the color of a chassis and the pictures no longer match!

I'd bet good money that if you thought about it for a few minutes you could recall a project that ended badly (or just roughly) due to these kinds of changes. Did you fail to anticipate the impact of a small change that later turned into a huge hassle? I hope this convinces you to get really tough on those late change requests and never confuse "easy to implement" with "should be implemented"!

The Nastiest Word in Change Control

I don't know about you, but there's one little four-letter word that sets the sirens blaring and the lights flashing in my mind. It's the word *just* and you usually hear it thrown out in a rather cavalier manner when someone is proposing a design change. It goes something like this: "It's just a matter of wrapping the code," or "We're just moving the lab two doors down," or even

"That should be no problem; it's just adding another small power supply." Yeah, I've heard 'em all and the word *just* is a four-alarm fire for me. Can you smell the smoke yet?

First let me point out that it's never "just" anything. When that nasty word is thrown in the mix it tells you two very important things. First, the person throwing that adjective around in such a high-handed manner is not the person who will be doing the actual work. The second thing it tells you is that the person flaunting his engineering skills doesn't really understand how much work is involved. It's entirely possible that the *just*-er has done this type of thing in the past...the very distant past...back when slide rules ruled engineering, but it's highly unlikely that they've dirtied their little fingers on it anytime recently.

Another thing you should realize is that you can't argue these people away. They believe they're right and anyone with a longer duration or higher complexity for the work is just slackin'. They honestly believe the work takes a minimal amount of time/effort. Also, it's highly likely that they don't understand the business processes necessary to do the work or how long those processes take. I'm talking about those pesky things like legal reviews, regulatory compliance, documentation, the whole change control process, and all that.

Okay, so how do you deal with a change request that's "just" a "minimal" amount of work? In my experience, the only way you can win this game is to be patient and play along. Get the relevant players together to break down the work. That is, identify all the work that needs to be done and how it will slot into the exiting work the team has already committed. Once you get a comprehensive list of all the tasks that need to be done, you estimate how long each task will take and how much it will cost. At this point the person proposing the change will challenge some of the estimates and that's okay. The point here is to get all the data on the table so the team can make a solid decision based on actual data. The end result of this exercise is a common understanding of the work involved to make the change. It could be that it really is a minor change with minimal impact, but frankly in my experience it never is.

Last, if it turns out that the work is "just" a bit more effort than was originally thought, be gracious and don't rub it in. Take pride in the fact that everyone on your team learned something and that you were able to navigate this change request without calling out those big fire hoses. If you handle this type of change request well, then your stakeholder will remain an ally. If you resort to arguing the "just"-ness of the change request, you alienate the stakeholder and waste a lot of brain power on a dead end. So that's it: beware of any change request that's preceded by "just"—and if it happens, go immediately into data collection mode and sidestep the dead-end arguments.

A Special Case: Planning for the Holiday Season

Most PMs miss this: the special case of deliberately planning for the chaos that surrounds the holiday season. In the United States, that season starts around mid-November and runs through the first half of January, but the concepts discussed here are really holiday-agnostic, so they should apply to whatever holiday season you have to deal with. The critical thing, regardless of the holiday, is to deliberately plan for its challenges.

The Dead Zone

If you ask me, there's only one kind of project work that should go on during the last two weeks of December and the first week of January... the extremely urgent kind. I used to fool myself when I planned a project into thinking that meaningful amounts of work would get done during this time. I would think that since it's still officially work time, then official work would get done. Wrong! It just ain't so and woe to the PM who counts on it.

First, let me point out that everyone intends to get a lot done in December. We all honestly believe that we will have the same amount of work time that we've enjoyed all year long...then come the holiday parties, the endless round of management update forums, happy hours, team lunches, and so on. Now couple that with a more-active-than-normal social life and the various personal commitments during the holidays and you can see pretty quickly that your quality work time just evaporates. Even if you don't observe the holidays or are a conscientious objector to them, your work time is affected. E-mails are returned more slowly, deliverables slip their commits, people aren't around when you look for them, and people commit deliverables over longer than normal durations. Face it: we're all über-busy this time of year.

So what's a conscientious PM to do? Well, I always strive to make sure my project plan and schedule reflect reality. Good, bad, or ugly—reality is what it is and you have to take it into account in your planning. To do this, I modify the working days in MS Project to show these weeks to be non-working days. (You can modify the teams' utilization down to something like 40% but I find it easier just to designate those days as non-working ones.) Yep, that's right *I deliberately plan to have no work done for three weeks.* I don't exactly advertise this to the program manager—or to the functional managers either, for that matter. I'm not going to lie about it, but I'm not exactly gonna take out a billboard with this information on it either. Now, don't get me wrong, no one stops working on the project. It's just that I've planned for no work to get done. This actually gives me two strategic advantages.

The first advantage is that this time can be used as buffer to be consumed if we are falling behind on the project. In my experience, people are motivated to catch up if there's a realistic expectation that it's doable. By planning for the inevitable slowdown that occurs during holidays, you have a built-in period of time during which it's conceivable that a team can catch up without Herculean efforts. This strategy has come in very handy more than once and, while it's a bit of a shell game, it is effective.

The second advantage of planning for minimal work to be completed at the end of the year is that you don't have to drive your team like a pack of Santa's Elves on Christmas Eve to get important deliverables completed. Why expect someone to skip their team holiday lunch if you don't have to? Do you really want to tell someone that they have to miss their kid's debut as a Christmas tree in the local school play? I sure as heck don't and that's the point. If the deliverable isn't urgent, then why not give people a break? By deliberately planning the project work to accommodate the realities of this time of year, you are doing just that. Despite what you might have come to believe, this is not a bad thing. The project team doesn't have to work 24/7 to complete its work if the work is properly planned.

Okay, in opening I mentioned that I thought that only extremely urgent project work should be happening in this holiday season. Here, I have to give a shout-out to all those teams in organizations that have big market windows right after the holidays. If you do product development in these teams, then there's a strong chance you have major releases or deliverables due at the end of the year. These are the folks who care a lot about the Consumer Electronics Show (CES), which happens in early January. The holiday season for these folks inevitably involves a lot of long hours. I've been there and I've felt your pain. That's just the way that particular cookie crumbles, and solid planning will help here too but it won't completely alleviate the last-minute crunch-time, either.

There are times when it's "pedal to the metal" during the holidays—but for many of us, that's just not the case. So PMs out there, have a heart. Plan for the reality of the holiday season and stop drivin' those elves crazy this time of year! ☺

I Call BS!

So hopefully, I've convinced you to incorporate the holiday associated shut-downs, slowdowns, and vacations in your schedules. There's one more thing PMs should be doing in October to get ready for the rush to the end of the year, and that's to review your team's deliverable due dates.

I've worked my share of holidays over the years, and in that time I've seen a lot of project deliverables that had a due date in the first week in January. Sure, there are those very rare cases when your customer does actually need your piece of the pie on January 3rd, but, by and large, the real date that your customer is going to do anything with your deliverable is more like the second or even third week in January. See, they take vacations during the holidays too. So whenever I run across a "need-by date" of January 1st, I call BS!

Okay, just because my BS Meter is pegging out doesn't mean that my team and I don't have to hit that date…it's still the formal commit right? So the first thing I have to figure out is whether my team can hit that January 1st commit without working over the holidays. If we're on track and I've incorporated all of their vacations and the company non-working days into the schedule, then I challenge the team to get the deliver done early. Every team I've worked with in this scenario is more than willing to put in the OT in October to be able to take off at the end of the year with a completed project in the bag. This strategy also works if you're trending a few days behind but can recover and deliver early. It's a great feeling to be walking out the door right before the end of the year knowing that you've done good work and your team has hit that deliverable early.

Now as we all know, it's not always the case that you're on track or able to pull in the deliverable. Sometimes the team is just going to have to work through the holidays. To put it bluntly—this will kill your team's morale and it should be avoided if at all possible. So what's a PM to do? Well, the first thing you need to do is figure this out early…as in October! Now is the time to scrutinize your schedule and make the call whether the team needs to work through the holidays. Before you make that call, however, you need to go back to your customer and verify that they really do need the deliverable on

January 3rd at 8AM. Most of the time this is a bogus date and you can negotiate something later. Be up front with your customer and let them know that you and your team are willing to work through the holiday if there's a real need. What I've found, time after time, is that the customer doesn't want to force anyone to work over the holidays any more than you do. They are usually willing to work with you here. Of course, this assumes that you've built a collaborative relationship with your customer ahead of time.

What about that worst-case scenario where your customer is inflexible, your team's behind schedule, and you've got to tell them that they need to work on 12/26? I'm not going to sugar-coat this...it's hard. Really hard. The one thing that makes this bad news more palatable is that it's delivered early in October. It's much easier to get your team on board with working the last few weeks of the year if you hit them with this before they make their personal vacation plans. Ever tried convincing someone to work over the holiday after they'd purchased expensive airline tickets? 'Nuff said. It goes without saying that you're going to need some major motivational tools and probably some sort of incentive to get everyone on board. No one's gonna be happy about working over the holidays and you're going to have to pull out your "A" game here to keep the train on the rails.

So what's my main point here? Figure it out now! Scrutinize your project schedules and your customer commits. It's so much better to deal with these kinds of challenges in October versus the week before Thanksgiving. It's also important to realize that as the PM, the person responsible for the project plan, it's your job to plan the work such that no one has to work over vacations or holidays in the first place. Failing to plan the work properly means that you're letting your team down. So if you haven't already taken care of this stuff, do it now—and I really hope you don't have to ask anyone to work on December 26th.

Execution Phase

Leadership Showtime

Project management presents unique leadership challenges. You're the team leader—but no one reports to you, you probably have minimal control of the project budget, and you have multiple bosses. Sure, you can find good ideas from traditional leadership tomes, but there are some unique challenges that PMs face. I'm talking about the challenges in motivating and influencing a team because—face it—you've got to get the work done through other people without direct authority. Here are a few of the tips and tricks I've learned along the way about what it means to be an effective leader as a PM.

More Action, Less Talkin'

I'm sure you've heard the old saw about actions speaking louder than words. For a PM this can be a valuable tool in your quest to influence and motivate your team. It's perilous to forget that, as the PM, you are the leader of the team and folks will be watching what you do more closely than they will listen to what you say. This is why role-modeling desired behavior is so effective. Further, no one will follow where you lead if your actions don't match your words. So what does this look like for a PM? Let me give you some ideas for where you can use deliberate actions to reinforce a team dynamic, be more effective as a leader, and promote an atmosphere of collaboration.

PMs often fail when it comes to aligning actions to words in their meeting preparation. I can remember back to a time when I didn't pay attention to how I set up meetings and only minimally prepared for them. I'd stick a stale, standing agenda in the calendar hit and that was the extent of my meeting prep. I'd expect the team members to be prepared to discuss their work, any help they needed, plans for the next week, and so forth but I was never prepared to do the same. I didn't see this as a problem because I was so busy just keeping my head above water figuring out how to manage the project. Furthermore, because my teammates never grilled me on my own deliverables—schedule status, risk-management plans, escalation resolution, and so on—I didn't really see any disconnect between what I was doing and what I was asking the team to do. I look back on that time now and cringe. I was monitoring the project work rather than actively managing it. Ah, the follies of youth...

Speaking of meetings, PMs spend a lot of time in 'em, mostly talking. It's easy to get so caught up in that meeting mindset that you miss opportunities to do some actual work. Not to say that work doesn't happen in meetings, mind you, but often it's faster just to do the work than it is to set up the meeting to discuss the work that needs to be done. Ask yourself this: In your last team meeting did you take an action item to set up a follow-up meeting for some issue? If so, is this something you could have handled directly without the additional meeting? Could the desired outcome have been achieved by doing actual work instead holding yet another meeting? See where I'm goin' here?

Okay, here's an example from my current projects. I need to include test results/data in my weekly status updates. This data resides on a web application for which I do have an account. More than once, however, I've sent an e-mail to the QA engineer asking for the update instead of just pulling the data myself. It's "faster" for me to send the e-mail—but if you count my time plus the QA engineer's time to read my e-mail, pull the data, and then send it to me, then it's much faster if I just do the work myself! I really need to step it up and just pull the data myself. Just sayin'...

One thing I've come to realize is that if you want your team to backstop each other and help out where there's a need, then you have to role-model that behavior yourself. If you've got the time, then offer to pick up/deliver parts, review technical docs, place POs—whatever it is that someone else is struggling to get done. The help is always appreciated and it's usually a nice change of pace for you. Often we get so hung up in the "that's-not-my-job" mindset that we lose track of the fact that it's a 10-minute task. When I worked in a product group at Intel, I'd periodically deliver parts to the validation team in the next building. Sure, it wasn't my job, but it only took me 10 minutes and I got a nice break out of the deal. More importantly, it reinforced the collaborative team dynamic I was trying to build.

Today I always put thought into my meeting agendas and effort into preparing for team meetings. Further, I look for ways to help the team with the project work, especially when I'm not buried myself. Sure, I can badger someone to go audit our marketing collateral and figure out what's missing, or I could just do it myself, especially if the marketing rep for the team is buried. I like the variety, plus it reinforces a team dynamic that values team members pitching in where needed. In the end, it's often the little things we do that matter. So the next time you see a teammate struggling to get something done, ask yourself if there's an opportunity for you to pitch in and role-model the kind of behavior that supports a collaborative team dynamic. If so, then, as the Nike ad urges, "Just Do It!"

Dollar Waitin' on a Dime

One of the most important parts of managing a project is maintaining the pace of work. It's critical that work continue on the project at a predictable pace according to the plan. Sure, as the PM I have a lot of things vying for my attention, so I have to make smart choices about where I spend my time. From my own experience I know that the "biggest bang for my buck" is to make sure all of the handoffs, virtual and/or real, happen when they should, the way they were planned to happen. What you don't want to happen is a situation my dad used to refer to as "a dollar waitin' on a dime."

On a project, those "dollars" are tasks on the critical path. One of your most important tasks as a PM is to make sure that the work progresses along the critical path as efficiently and quickly as possible. Anything that slows down the pace of work on the critical path needs some immediate intervention. In the real world this means I wear a lot of hats. I'll deliver parts to the shipping dock or I'll "remind" a developer that he still needs to generate the install instructions. I might walk documents through a legal review or escalate a resource shortage. Basically, I'm plugging gaps and integrating the handoff of work into a seamless flow. Now, I know that there are PMs out there who think this stuff isn't their job. You could be right, but in these circumstances being "right" doesn't rack up the "dollars"—now does it?

The "dimes" in project management are the little, inconsequential things that can trip your team up. Communication breakdowns come to mind here as a prime source of "dimes." In fact, just the other day I was in a meeting in which two teammates were locked in a heated exchange when it dawned on me that the problem was that they were using the same word to mean different things. (Can you say *platform* here? Is there any other word that gets misunderstood more often at companies that develop products? What exactly to do you mean by the word *platform*? I'm betting it's not what I mean when I use that word. ☺) There's also the poorly written e-mail where the reader has to infer some action item or some conclusion from the morass of data. "Dimes" can also be stupid things like not having enough washers (I speak from experience here! Trust me, just order more than you think you'll need), labels, or physical space on a tester. Here's an example of what I'm talking about. Back in the day, there was the case of the missing gasline filter. There we were, unable to ship a multimillion-dollar tool on time because we "lost" a $200 gasline filter. Fun times....now that's what I call a "dollar waitin' on a dime"!

Take a minute to think about how you spent your time yesterday. Did you enable some "dollars"? Are the active tasks on your critical path progressing as quickly and efficiently as possible? If not, where are those "dimes"? The trick is to train yourself to think about and recognize the "dimes" so that you can deal with them early and not endanger your team's progress. Oh, and be sure you're not the holdup for any work either…in the words of my dad, don't be the "dime" the "dollar" is waitin on!

How to Escalate Effectively

Escalating issues is a skill most PM's think they've mastered, but I don't see it. Copying your boss on an e-mail is not effective escalation. Nor is pushing the other party into a corner where they have no choice but to give in. Effective escalation is hard to do and almost no one asks himself, "How do I escalate this?". I've said it before and it should be repeated: effective escalation is one of the primary ways a PM contributes to the team's work.

First, let's start with what effective escalation looks like. The escalation is effective when 1) the problem is addressed and something is done to resolve or reduce its impact, and 2) all parties walk away happy or at least amicable.

That's pretty straightforward right? Okay, so how do you do it? To be honest, there's no one "right" way to do it, and you will frequently have to try multiple approaches to get it right. It's not uncommon to struggle with this when you're new to an organization or program. It just takes time to know who the players are and how they play the game. In the interests of reducing that time it takes to get effective, here are some things to consider when you escalate an issue:

- Just because you *can* doesn't mean you *should*. (Yeah, I know I use this phrase a lot… probably means I need to get it tattooed on my bicep or something.) Often I find that there really isn't a problem per se; instead the team needs some clear direction. For example, once you've frozen the requirements, any change must follow the formal change control process. So if someone wants the team to do something not outlined in those requirements, she can submit a change request (and therefore kick off thorough impact analysis)—but until then, that work is *out of scope*. End of discussion, problem solved, 'nuff said. Keep the team focused on what they need to do, and don't escalate something that's not a real issue.

- Copying your boss, your antagonist's boss, or heck anyone else's boss doesn't work. CYA emails are *not* effective escalation. You know how much email you get; do you carefully read each bit of flotsam and jetsam that crosses your desk? Is your boss even going to see and comprehend the escalation? Also, consider the fact that your boss probably expects you to deal with the issue directly. In general, I find email escalations to be the least effective tool in my arsenal of awesome escalation activities. (Ha! Try saying that three times fast!)

- Now, let's say that your boss is completely ineffectual at removing roadblocks and solving problems. What should you do? If you're me, then you just go figure out who's the decision maker and escalate to them. As a rule, it's never a good idea to go over your boss's head, but sometimes this will resolve an issue quickly. I've worked for people who are happy to have me solve the problem as long as I keep them apprised of what I'm doing. I've also worked for managers who'd freak out if I so much as said "hi" to their boss—much less their boss's boss. You have to gauge your relationship with your boss and make a judgment call as to whether or not this is the right tactic to try.

- Escalate and resolve the problem in person if at all possible—even if it means you have to drive to another site. Okay, this isn't an excuse for a quick road trip to Portland and its many brewpubs, but if you can drive over to another building and talk to someone face to face, do that instead of sending an email or calling. If you can't look the other person in the eye (don't forget video conferencing), then pick up the phone and try talking to them directly. Written communication leaves too much room for misinterpretation and it's slow and static for dialogue.

- To avoid a static dialogue that resolves nothing, remember to put yourself in the other person's place. What's important to them? What's causing them the most pain? Why do they even care about the problem? Would a partial solution work just as well? The better you understand the other person's perspective, the greater the likelihood that you can work out a solution that satisfies everyone. Remember that you're going to need to collaborate with this person later, so don't light the bridge on fire as you're walkin' across it.

- Finally, perhaps the most important thing to consider is this: Don't stop until the problem is resolved. All the way! If you can't give clear direction to the team, then you aren't done escalating the problem. If anyone on your team is completely blocked and can't get anything else done, then you aren't done escalating. We all know how it feels to have someone "own" solving the problem and yet we're the ones with the mess when the problem isn't solved. Don't do that to your team. Keep at it till the problem's solved.

Let me be very clear here: I strongly believe that as the PM, part of your job is to remove roadblocks and escalate those problems you can't solve yourself. Your team is counting on you, and if you're ineffective at escalating issues, then in reality you're letting the entire team down. Figure out how to escalate effectively and don't stop until you've solved the problem all the way, even if you don't totally agree with the solution. The important thing is to get clear direction for your team and remove roadblocks.

How to Get Folks to Do Their Jobs

If everyone just did what he or she were supposed to do, then companies wouldn't need PMs right? I mean, if it's your job to develop the training material for my project, then you should just do it on time without intervention from me right? Uh-huh…how's that working for you, Sparky? Not very well? I know what you mean and, trust me, I've got a bunch of T-shirts from that hassle too. Here's the thing, though: if it really were that simple they wouldn't need us. The fact of the matter is that your peers have a lot on their plates and your project just might not be at the top of their personal priority lists. This is where that influence thing comes in. More likely you will be dealing with someone who doesn't understand how to make good commitments or who honestly struggles with time management. Those may be the root causes of people not doing their job, but as the PM you've got to deal with the symptoms as well. Just how do you get people to meet their commitments?

Meeting Commitments

There's not a PM out there who hasn't encountered the problem of getting certain team members to meet commitments. We've all been there… there're always a few holdouts on the team who are "too busy" to close action items or who keep "forgetting" them.

Your immediate response is to find out why they aren't meeting their commitments. Yes, grasshopper, in order to solve the problem, you need to understand why the problem is happening in the first place. How do you do that? Well, to be blunt, you go ask the person with the slipping commitments. The key here is to approach the conversation carefully and collaboratively. You need to understand if the person is overloaded, at an impasse, unmotivated, or just out to get you. Okay, that last one is probably not what's going on, but you get my drift. You need to plan this conversation out, even if that means jotting down some notes ahead of time.

Here are some things to consider when faced with this dilemma:

- If this is your first attempt to address the problem, then I'd suggest something like this…"Hi Melanie! Wow, you seem pretty busy these days. How's that action item coming? Need any help closing it?"

- If the teammate/stakeholder gives you the "everything's-on-track" spiel but you know it's not, then you probably need a different approach. I recommend a "show-me" approach. To be honest, I'm a pretty curious person, so it's easy for me to ask some questions that require the teammate to pull up a document and show me. This is the "trust-but-verify" axiom at work.

- If this is a repeatable pattern that you've tried to address in the past, then address it head-on. Start with something like, "You know, Melanie, you haven't been able to close an action item on time in the last month. What's going on? Is there something I can do to help?"

- Finally, if the person is downright hostile or completely unwilling to close the task, then it's time to escalate. But do yourself and your teammate a favor and let them know that's what you're going to do. Try something like, "Okay, Melanie, clearly we can't resolve this issue our-selves. However, the action item must be closed for the project work to continue. At this point I need to advise the stakeholders that we are stuck and need some help to get this work completed." Remain professional and make it clear that you are escalating the roadblock, not the teammate's performance or lack thereof.

Most of the time, just the act of figuring out why your teammate isn't meeting commitments gives you all the info you need to fix the problem. However, there's always the tricky scenario where the teammate doesn't know how to make good commitments. After you've gained some experience as a PM, you'll have a good sense of when this is happening. I'm always doubtful when a teammate tells me that they'll provide a late deliverable "by the end of the day" or even better "by the end of the week," especially when I know it's a lot of work and they haven't started on it yet. When this happens I try to coach the person to think about how much work is needed versus how much time they have to do it. Nine times out of ten, the teammate has made a knee-jerk commitment without thinking through the work and their schedule. Another thing the PM should consider in this scenario is when the deliverable is really needed. If it makes sense, then cut your teammate some slack by pushing out the due date, while helping them understand how much work they need to put into it.

Now, let's say that there's no smoking gun as to why the team member doesn't meet their commitments, nor do they make careless ones. What you probably need here is more motivation. Sometimes it's as straightforward as asking someone what turns their crank. When that doesn't work, consider how to engage the team dynamic. I've found that a team with a strong collaborative dynamic can be motivated by simple rewards. Hey, face it, we all want to win and be seen as winners. These goals are deliberately challenging and require the entire team to work together. When the entire team is bought into achieving the goal, then I find that individual contributors are in turn motivated by their team to meet or exceed their commitments. It should be noted that there's a fine line between a stretch goal reward and bribery, and you need to make sure you aren't bribing the team to do their work. Motivating a team or an individual is tricky and takes a lot of effort to master, but when you get it right, suddenly there are no more missed commitments.

Okay, these are the tips and tricks I use when faced with a team member who doesn't meet commitments. This is the application of those dreaded "soft skills" that make the project management gig so interesting. It's not easy and I'm not sure it's "art," but I know for a fact that you can turn this kind of teammate around with a bit of focused effort.

Hold 'em Accountable

Okay, now let's talk about accountability. Specifically, how do you hold someone accountable to the team?

You'd think that this idea of accountability to your work group would be a no-brainer, but it's not. If your organization has a culture that's non-confrontational, overly confrontational, low-integrity, or just plain lazy, then it's likely that no one is held accountable for their work. If you yourself are deathly afraid of coming across as a micromanager, then you could be slacking in this area. Often PMs think they are holding their teammates accountable but, in actuality, there are no consequences for failing to do the work, missing a deadline, delivering with crappy quality, and so forth. Further, depending on the team dynamic, it's often up to the PM to hold team members accountable, but they may feel that they have no authority to enforce any consequences. Just how you hold people accountable has a lot to do with how effective you are at leading that team and will greatly affect the overall project performance.

We've all worked in organizations or on teams in which being accountable for your work was as foreign a concept as Cheez Whiz in France. Sure, everyone knows about it (okay, maybe not the French) but no one actually partakes of it. It looks like this… It's Thursday and you are expecting the marketing rep on your team to have uploaded the collateral for your upcoming release to the appropriate website. You believe that the marketing rep was clear about the due date and he's been telling you for weeks that his collateral is "in progress"—yet here it is, 5 PM on the day before the release, and no collateral in sight. There could be a number of things that have contributed to the lack of collateral, but I'd bet my lunch money that this is not the first time this team member has let the team down…*and*, as in the past, there are no consequences for it! Sound familiar?

So just how do you hold someone accountable for her work? Well, the most effective strategy I've run across to do this involves a two-step approach. The first step is to be very clear about the deliverable and the due date. You really need the other person to confirm your understanding here, or you'll have different problems later. Confirm that the other person has the ability to do the work and make sure that the due date is reasonable. The second step is the follow up and it's where most of us drop the ball. To be able to hold people accountable you have to formally follow up.

What do I mean by "formally follow up"? I'm not talking about a lot of slideware; rather I'm talking about a deliberate discussion between you and your teammate. You need to put something on the calendar, and you both need to be honest about the deliverable. If it's of shoddy quality, then as the PM, you owe the other person the courtesy of explaining why the quality level is not acceptable. If the work turns out to be more complex than originally thought and the due date is no longer reasonable, then the other person needs to speak up and say so. (You need to set the expectation that if this happens your teammate will let you know as soon as possible, rather than at the last minute.) If the deliverable is not met by the due date, then you need to explain to the other person the impacts of this late deliverable—and the consequences.

Holding people accountable is intrinsically linked with those consequences. They are the stick, not the carrot. From my experience, the more tangible the consequence—for instance, missing a product launch—the less likely you are to see people dropping the ball. However, sometimes the consequences are not obvious to the other person and you're going to have to help him understand what he doesn't see. Did his failure to deliver result in a loss of trust? Did it cause a hardship for another teammate? How about some damage to his professional reputation? What has it done to the team dynamic? These are sticky topics to bring up with your teammate, and you're going to want to plan out how you confront the other person before you ever open your mouth. Make no mistake, though, as the PM it is your responsibility to have that discussion and bring those consequences to the forefront. I also happen to think it's your job to help the other person overcome whatever happened and be successful the next time.

If you fail to address a missed deadline, a crappy deliverable, a failure to act, or whatever, then you are letting your team down. In the microcosm of a project team, the PM is the leader and, as the saying goes, "The buck stops here!" Part of your value-add is this ability to hold everyone accountable to the same standard. If you have a pretty stable team that's in the "performing" stage, then it's likely that the individual team members will be the ones to step up and say, "Melanie, you completely let us down by not finishing that drawing on time. How are you going to get it done now, and how are you going to prevent it from happening again?" That's the best-case scenario—but in the real world, the PM has to model that behavior and have that discussion. Here's the thing: even if it's a small thing, a failure to hold others and yourself accountable ultimately results in a loss of respect. Think about it. If I fail to hold you to your commitments, then at least on some level you know that you can blow my deliverable off because there are no consequences. Does that make you a bad person? No, but it sure does lower your respect for me, doesn't it? Tolerate no lack of accountability!

The Art of the Nag

As a project manager you often have to remind people of their lagging commitments or get information from busy or reluctant sources. These are the people who aren't returning your phone calls and are basically ignoring your e-mails. When you do manage to corner them in person they are distracted, vague, dodgy, or otherwise evasive. The problem is that you need their information/action, but if you escalate up the managerial food chain you will do permanent damage to your relationship. What's a poor PM to do?

You need to motivate these people into action, and one way to do it is to nag them into it. Now being called a *nag* is not a good thing, as it connotes images of that ex-boyfriend/girlfriend who kept whining about the fact that you forgot to pick up beer or roses, as the case may be. (Admit it; you can hear that nasally voice whining right now, can't you? Insert bone-shaking shudder here.) It's irritating and no one wants to deal with it. Obviously, this is not the kind of nagging that will get you positive results.

There is another kind of nagging that will work. The key here is to realize that in a dynamic, highly matrixed environment, there are times when people have more work assigned than they can reasonably do. Everyone gets overloaded occasionally, and then your request for information just isn't at the top of the other person's priority list. This lack of responsiveness isn't personal and, once you accept that, I think you can be very successful at nagging without alienating anyone. This is what I refer to as *The Art of the Nag.*

First, a few disclaimers: This is not an appropriate technique for urgent issues and will not address the root cause of the dodgy behavior. What it will do is get you the result you need with minimal effort on your part and manageable frustration on the part of the person being nagged. Do not use this technique as a replacement for direct confrontation if that's what's really needed.

Your goal is to leave a voicemail for the other person. Yes, a voicemail, not an e-mail, not an IM—your actual voice talking. The tone and timing of this call will be critical. In fact, it's almost detrimental to actually speak to them. Practice the message you want to leave beforehand so that you can utter it with a friendly, positive tone. Depending on how frustrated you are, this may take some effort. (That's probably what I'm doing if you hear me muttering to myself in some deserted stairwell.) Simply state your name, that you are following up on XYZ, and that you wanted to know when you can expect it. Do not threaten dire consequences, sound angry, or give the other person any reason to become defensive.

Step 1: After a few missed commits or several days of dodgy behavior, place your first phone call. Time this call carefully so that you don't actually talk to the person. You're leaving a friendly reminder that ideally the person will hear at a natural start time for work. The best time for this first voicemail is in the morning. Time it such that he gets your message first thing after arriving in the office.

Step 2: Repeat this every morning for three days as long as you get no resolution. Note that this call shouldn't take you more than two minutes to place. Further, don't follow up in any other manner on this issue unless you just happen to luck into a natural place to do it, but if he is actively dodging you, that's unlikely to happen.

Step 3: On the third day, if you still have not received the data you're looking for, step it up to two calls a day. The best time for this second call is during the lunch hour, so that he can get the message right after returning from lunch. At this point you still need to have a positive and friendly tone. Don't refer to the fact that you've now left numerous messages. Trust me, he already knows this and is probably feeling guilty about not addressing your request.

Step 4: Continue the two calls per day for a few more days. Honestly, I rarely have to implement two calls per day and I've never had to place two calls a day more than once.

That's it! It's fast, it's easy, and it works. As long as it's done carefully, no one goes away angry and you can come back to that person again on your next project. I usually don't even have to go to Step 3, so that's a total time investment of about 10 minutes spread over three days. So, the next time you are frustrated with this kind of situation, try The Art of the Nag and see how it works for you.

Evaluating Your Teammates' Performance

If you're managing projects, then it's only a matter of time before you're asked to provide performance feedback on some (or all) of your teammates. There was a time when I was regularly writing 20+ performance reviews every year and eventually I figured out how to do it. So I'm going to break down **Melanie's Guide to Writing Performance Reviews** for you:

1. Rule #1 is to provide the same feedback in writing that you would say to the person directly. If you don't have the professional respect for your teammate to say whatever it is to her face, then don't put it in writing to her boss.

2. If you're a PM, never turn down a request for feedback on one of your teammates (except in the case of Rule 7). It also goes without saying that you need to provide the feedback by the requested due date or negotiate a better one.

3. Always, always, always include something positive. Trust me on this one, there's always something good to say about everyone. If you are struggling with this one, then take a step back and look at this person's job description. There's bound to be something he is decent at, even if it's only data entry.

4. Always, always, always include some area of improvement. Often I recommend that the person work on expanding her knowledge of the market segment and customer base, because I believe that knowledge can help you make better trade-off decisions.

5. Keep your comments brief and support them with specific examples. It's especially important to provide specifics if you are discussing areas of improvement. If your feedback is particularly negative, then make double-darn sure that the data supports this feedback.

6. Set up an Outlook folder to collect specific activities, recognition, or events that you can use when it's time to write performance reviews. Every time I submit a recognition request or send a "thank-you for-your-hard-work" e-mail, I dump it in this folder so that I have plenty of material come January.

7. If you are uncomfortable or uneasy providing feedback, then stick to the facts, such as, "Melanie attended 8 of 10 meetings and submitted all of her collateral on time." If you are particularly uncomfortable providing the feedback, then I suggest professionally declining to do so.

8. If you have a lot of people to provide feedback for, then consider swinging by your local bookstore for a performance appraisal phrase book. These books are great for getting you started and for helping you say "Melanie is an adequate employee" for the umpteenth time.

There you go: some tips for writing performance feedback for your teams. As a PM, you're going to get more than your share of requests for feedback so it makes sense to figure out how to do it effectively. Sure, you're not responsible for anyone's complete performance review, but as a team leader your input is often solicited by resource managers and it's not uncommon to find bits and pieces of your feedback copied directly into the employee's performance appraisal. Make sure that whatever you say can be backed up with data and put your best effort into it. Remember, it may not be that important to you—but it's awfully important to the person you're reviewing!

The PM as a Coach

One part of project management that you don't hear a lot about is the coaching or mentoring aspect of the job. As the PM, you are a leader of a specific team and are probably viewed as an SME within your organization. As such, you are often consulted by people with problems they need help solving. How you approach these requests can greatly affect how your teammates relate to you. A helpful, friendly coach is obviously much more appreciated than a surly, dictatorial despot, right? However, understanding what you should do in these situations is a bit murkier, so this section discusses the common coaching opportunities that come up in the course of managing a project.

Let's start off with the easiest scenario: What should you do when someone needs your help deciding whether or not a formal change request is needed? Even with my experienced team, this one comes up regularly. Often I find that the other person knows the answer—yes, they need to do a formal change request. You need to ask some basic probing questions about the pending change to help the person solidify a hunch that the change request is needed. In most cases, if the change impacts form, fit, or function, then you need to do a change request. So I'll ask the other person what's being impacted and help him understand that it's important to communicate these types of changes across the entire team.

PMs will often find themselves in the coaching role when a teammate is hesitant to go talk to someone else. In this scenario, my teammate asks me to go talk to an important stakeholder—but one who is most likely difficult for them. As a general rule, I don't do this. What I will do is coach my teammate in how to talk to that difficult person. I'll talk about what I think motivates that stakeholder, what they care about, and, most importantly, why my teammate may be failing in communicating with this difficult person. I'll also coach my teammate on what to say and how to say it. The thing to remember is that most people are not as advanced as PMs when it comes to communication skills, so often you will need to share your knowledge in this area to help someone else out. If none of these tactics work, then I will volunteer to go talk to that difficult stakeholder *with* my teammate, but for me the most important aspect of this whole scenario is that my teammate learn how to deal with difficult people.

Speaking of difficult people, perhaps the most difficult person to coach is the one who is unwilling to ask for help even if they are drowning. I once worked with this guy who was incapable of asking for help. He would come into my cube and talk around an issue he was having, but he would never actually come out and ask for my advice or help. If I tried to tell him what he should do directly, he'd immediately respond with something along the lines of, "I got this." The thing was…he didn't have anything and really needed the coaching. I finally hit on a strategy that I've since used successfully to deal with this type of coaching opportunity. I simply couch my advice like this: "Hmm, that's a tricky one isn't it? If it were me, I'd definitely take Melanie out to lunch and try to win her over with lots of chocolate cake!" Okay, I probably wouldn't be that blatant, but I've found that the "if-it-were-me-I'd-do-xyz" makes the coaching much more palatable to someone who can't ask for help. And my colleague? Well, I'd hear him in his cube later in the day executing my advice, though he'd never give me credit for it or ask for the help directly.

Finally, I'd like to point out a stumbling block a lot of PMs hit when they try to coach others. If you provide some coaching but the other person doesn't follow your advice, then what do you do? There are always plenty of reasons why someone could choose to ignore your very good advice, such as they haven't been convinced that it's the best course of action, circumstances changed (at least in their minds) and they believe your advice is no longer applicable, or frankly your advice sucked. Why someone chooses to ignore your coaching doesn't really matter in the short term. They are responsible for the consequences of their actions and after doing your best to help, you have to let go and let them succeed or fail on their own merits. This is probably the hardest part of coaching…letting go. It's a mistake to constantly go back to your teammate and badger them to follow your advice. Can you say *micromanager*? Of course you can!

So that's my take on coaching from the PM's perspective. What about yours? Have you found solid tactics for coaching the hard cases? What about those teammates who need a lot of your time…as in more than you have to spare? How do you coach them without completely tanking your own work? Thinking about these kinds of questions when you can really focus will tee you up to be the best coach possible for your teams, so take some time and get your head wrapped around the idea of the PM as a coach.

Cut Off Your Right Hand

I have a colleague who was telling me about her "Right-Hand Man" the other day. This is the person she knows she can always go to for those "have-to-be-done-right-now" kind of things she can't get to herself. This is the guy she leaves in charge of her project team whenever she's out of the office. In short, this is her unofficial "second in command." On the surface there's nothing wrong with rolling this way and, to tell the truth, I used to operate this way, too. You just drift into it, and in a fast-paced, high-pressure environment it's often the path of least resistance whenever you need a backup. However, this strategy is killing your team dynamic.

The first problem lies with the message having a "Right Hand" sends to your team. You're basically saying that the "Right Hand Man/Woman" is your favorite. I'd bet my lunch money that you won't have to think too long or too hard to recall a team you were a part of on which you weren't the "Right Hand"—and it wasn't fun. No one likes to feel like they are just one of the worker bees, and good leaders know this. That's why a good leader strives to treat all team members equally while making each one feel "special." You need a team of rock stars—not a bunch of roadies and a guy named Elvis. It's also equally uncomfortable to be that "Right Hand" whom the leader obviously defers to. No one wants to be the "teacher's pet," right?

Now, the second problem having a dedicated "Right Hand" brings is that it stifles opportunities for the rest of the team. Here's what happens: the same person, your favorite, gets the opportunity to establish his or her reputation by covering for you every time you're out of the office. No one else every gets the chance…oh, and by the way, there's someone else who really wants that opportunity, too. One of the best tools in my PM Toolbox is the ability to enable my teammates to do new and challenging work, so I look for opportunities to delegate work that I think my teammates will benefit from. If I only ever punt these kinds of opportunities to one person, what kind of message does that send to the rest of the team?

Okay, the third problem I see with this "Right-Hand Man/Woman" strategy is that, most of the time, you forget to ask that person if he actually wants to assume the extra work. Remember, even an outstanding "Right Hand" will get fed up with you if you're constantly going to that well for water. Just because someone is capable of assuming the work doesn't necessarily make her the best candidate for it. Sometimes it makes a lot more sense to ask someone less experienced to take care of an urgent task. Sure, you might have to monitor the progress more than if you'd gone straight to your "Right Hand"—but in the end you're building your team's bench strength and that's a lot stronger than a single person any day.

So let's recap. If you're feeling pretty good about your "Right-Hand Man/Woman," then it's probably time to consider an amputation. No one wants to work for a leader who plays favorites, doesn't provide opportunities to grow, or dumps on you all the time because you're the path of least resistance. Seriously, cut off your "Right Hand" and start spreading the love across your team. They are going to do a better job than you think, you'll develop a dynamic that's much more collaborative, and you won't burn out a valuable resource by using it too often. Make sense? Glad I could help!

Decision Making

Decision making is a big part of leading a project or program team. As a leader you need to understand the importance of decisive action, the pitfalls of failing to decide, and the various decision-making tools out there.

First Step? Make the Decision

In the early days of my career, I had the good fortune to hear Jim Morgan, then the CEO of Applied Materials, talk about leadership. Mr. Morgan is a very practical leader and I still draw on his points of view when it comes to leadership skills. In fact, my whole take on decision making comes straight from him. Here's his philosophy on decision making in my own words:

> **Part I: Make the decision**. *You can always deal with the consequences if you make the wrong choice, but you will do more harm if you dither around and don't make a definitive decision.*
>
> **Part II: Decision making is a skill**. *You need to practice that skill to get good at it.*

Many times I've seen PMs neglect to make the simplest decisions, and when that happens the team is stuck like hamsters on their various wheels, spinning madly. If you're the PM, then you're going to have to make decisions that you are uncomfortable making. I'm not talking about those big ethical decisions: those are pretty straightforward if you think about them long enough. Instead, I mean those decisions where you don't feel that you have the authority to make the call. In our highly ambiguous environment, this happens all the time.

For instance, I once authorized the purchase of some video cards as a backup in case the onboard chips didn't arrive in time to get assembled onto the boards. Now, when I say "authorized" what I really mean is that, in the team meeting after kicking around mitigation strategies (we were pretty sure the chip vendor wasn't going to come through in time), I made the decision to have the materials folks buy those extra video cards. Did I have the explicit authority to spend that money? Not really. Okay, in point of fact, my name wasn't on that budget—so no, I did not have the formal authority. This is called *risk mitigation* and it's something you and your project team should be doing.

So what were the consequences? Well, for starters, no one asked me about that unauthorized purchase, because the total dollar amount was so small that it just never showed up on anyone's radar. It seemed like a lot of money to me at the time, so I was sure surprised when no one challenged my decision. Go figure. The other consequence was that, although we did need about 20% of those video cards, the actual on-board video controller chips came in almost on time and we ended up scrapping the remaining 80% of the cards. Again, due to the low dollar amount, no one seemed to care. In the end, the only consequence that mattered was that my customer was happy to only have 20% of their boards with video cards and there was no impact to the overall silicon development program.

So, no negative consequences. Does that mean it was the right decision? I'd say yes, because the program was not impacted. If my team had to delay delivery of boards because we were waiting on those video chips, then it would have affected everyone from Validation to Product Marketing. The money to buy the cards was well spent; it minimized the impact of the risk. Would I make the same decision again? Absolutely!

The point I'm trying to make here is that you often need to take intelligent risks and make decisions so that your team can continue working. In this example, if I hadn't made that decision, then I'm sure we would have been discussing that issue over and over again with no real progress. The materials person would have been stuck on that proverbial hamster wheel trying to get the chip vendor to deliver, all the while believing that he was going to get his head handed to him when the vendor failed to follow through. That's no way to enable your team.

Take a few minutes to think about your last team meeting. Did you make clear decisions, or just let the team continue on their respective wheels? If you're not sure of the answer, then go ask a few of your teammates. Ask them if they know what the decision was and why it was made. This is also a good time to double-check your understanding of the team's level of buy-in for the decision. If you find out that your decisions aren't as clear as you thought, then stay tuned for the next bit—Part II if you will. ☺

Now Get Better at It

There's no denying that project work can be challenging, and PMs must often make decisions with incomplete data. No one likes to be put in that position and, because it's highly unlikely that you can change the environment, your best bet is to figure out how to make solid decisions with less than optimum data.

One good way to get comfortable making decisions in ambiguous environments is to make more of them. You see, the ability to make good decisions is a skill and, as with all skills, you can get better at it with practice. So how do you practice making decisions? (Yeah, that sounds stupid even to me, and I wrote it!☺)

A technique I've had good success with is to keep a log of decisions that I've made and felt uncomfortable about. I keep this log on the back pages of my project notebook, and for each decision I capture why I made the decision I did and what data I wished I'd had before making the call. I also capture the outcome of—or fall-out from—the decision. Then I grade my decision-making ability. Once a week I review my log, add new decisions I made that week, and document outcomes of previous decisions. I'm honestly not sure if it was the log or just the practice of review that helped, but I definitely noticed an improvement in my decision making since keeping a log.

All of that introspection about decisions I've made also led me to one of my personal best practices. I realized that some of the data I wished I'd had before making a call was actually available earlier. I'd just never gone off and acquired it. Let me give you an example here. In the previous section, I talked about an example in which I authorized a hardware purchase. What I didn't mention was that I'd already had a conversation with the budget owner about what the boundary conditions were with respect to spending. This particular manager referred to it as his *pain point*…in short, he didn't need me to ask permission under a certain dollar amount. So, when it came time to make that call to authorize spending, I already knew the budget owner would be okay with the dollar amount.

The point here is that you need to identify information you could use to make better decisions before you need it. Here are a few ideas for data you can go after now so that when you are called upon to make decisions you are well-armed with data:

- Spending constraints. Is the pain point $50,000 or $500,000?

- Relative priority of your project with respect to the organization's project/program portfolio.

- Vendor shutdown windows.

- Team members' vacation plans.

- Strategic objectives for any functional area represented on your project team.

Well, I hope this has given you some ideas about how to practice making decisions and how to get ahead of the curve so that you experience fewer decision-making scenarios in which you don't have enough information. In my experience, focusing on this skill has really paid off and I encourage you to give it a shot. I still have situations that call for a decision I'm not 100% comfortable making, but I do think it happens less frequently these days.

What to Do When You Can't Make a Decision

What do you do when you need to make a decision and there's no good answer? Do you procrastinate? Do you throw your hands up and push that decision off on someone else? Or do you let analysis paralysis suck you into a black hole of ambiguity? As a PM, I make critical decisions all the time, both with and for my team. Do we engage with a new vendor? Should we cut a PO for more brackets? Can we crash the schedule to pull in the customer commit?

By now you know that I think that it's part of your job responsibility as a PM to make decisions. However there are times when no "good" option presents itself. Unfortunately, that doesn't let you off the hook with your team. The harder the decision is to make, the more it matters that you make one. So, here I give you some strategies to help making those tough decisions easier:

- **Ask yourself what other data you need to make the decision.** Often when I find myself unable to make a decision, this trick is the ticket. I ask myself what other data I need to consider before making this decision. Would a review of the order volume trending data help? Can the supplier scorecard inform this decision? How about a deeper understanding of my customer's timeline? Whatever it is, I force myself to articulate it and then take action to go get that data. This strategy also works with teams: you broker a discussion about what other data needs to be reviewed, assign action items to get said data, and then set a date to review and to make a decision. It should be noted that often the answer is, "nothing." By that I mean there's no other data to consider, and I'm dithering because I don't like the options.

- **Don't like your options? Start thinking differently.** This is an effective strategy, but it is harder to implement. Step back from the decision and start questioning the assumptions baked into the analysis of options. Are you assuming that you can't get more headcount? What would happen if you reduced the test coverage? Does the work have to be done in house? Go back to first principles and then consider what risks you can take. In short, host a brainstorming session and get your team to really stretch their imaginations about what could be possible.

- **Is fear driving your inability to make that decision?** You'd actually be surprised how often I run across this one. Usually the decision maker has a fixed idea in his head about ugly things that will happen if the decision turns out to be a bad one. Weirdly, most people think that they will be walked out…despite plenty of evidence to the contrary. Perhaps they've worked for a screamer/ vindictive bully/crazy person in the past and have some scars. If you've experienced such a dysfunctional environment, it's common to carry that fear for a long time. I'm not trying to make light of these fears, 'cause hey—you feel what you feel, right? What I'd like to suggest, though, is that if fear of what might happen is holding you back from making decisions, then why don't you spend some time really thinking about that? Could it be that you no longer work for the crazy person and that fear is unfounded now? Here's a case where a little introspection goes a long way.

- **Push out or delay the decision.** This one is tricky as you don't want to just "kick the can down the road," if you know what I mean. It should not be a stall tactic! Instead, consider what you and your team might know at a later date. Does the decision have to be made right now? Would waiting until later to make the decision make more sense? I actually use this strategy more often when considering test data. If the data isn't conclusive and the decision to kill the effort doesn't need to be made right then, it can make more sense to wait and gather more test data.

- **Pick the least "bad" of your "bad" choices and iterate if necessary**. Yep, sometimes you just need to jump off the ledge and take an informed risk. Most of the time it's more important to keep things moving forward than it is to make the right decision. Here you're aiming for the best decision you can make given the circumstances and what you know. Is the only way the team can meet that pull-in request to work significant overtime? Is a failure to deliver not feasible given the market window? If so,

then you're probably going to have to mandate overtime...
but that doesn't mean that you can't revisit your decision
and do some course correction as things change. The
trick to making that "bad" choice palatable is monitoring.
If that decision turns out to be a bad one, recognize it
quickly and make adjustments. Sure, you don't want to
waffle back and forth on an important decision, but you
also need to keep moving forward. It's a balance.

- **Always make a decision.** The one thing you definitely
  don't want to do when faced with a bunch of bad options is
  fail to lead by not making a decision. Don't kid yourself—not
  making a decision is in fact a decision to do nothing.
  This could result in a work stoppage or slowdown—but,
  worse, it reduces the momentum of the team.

So there you have it: some strategies for making difficult decisions when no
clear answer presents itself. What about you? What do you do when you are
faced with this kind of scenario?

Decision-Making Tools

I often have peers ping me to ask for advice or just kick ideas around. I don't
mind and it's often a good opportunity for me to revisit some tried and true
techniques. Here's an example. I got a call the other day from a friend of mine
who wanted to bounce something off me. My friend leads a team that is tasked
with improving one of their organization's functional capabilities. One of the
agenda items for the weekly meeting was to recommend enhancements for a
software tool. This team is made up of quasi-volunteers, all of whom are passionate about improving the software tool, and my friend was concerned that
the meeting would become ratholed on this agenda item.

The team needed to select the best four or five enhancements out of a list of
about 25 possibilities already identified. My friend's first instinct was to have
each team member vote on their "top five" enhancements and then have the
team discuss the options with the highest number of votes to close on a final
list for the software developers.

For a project manager, leading a team to make solid decisions is a critical skill,
but how often do we stop to consider which decision-making process is the
most efficient? The conversation with my friend got me to thinking about decision making and I realized that I'm not very good at selecting the best tool
for the job when it comes to making decisions. I tend to stick to my comfort
zone and stay with the *consultative* method most of the time. So, in a continuous improvement mindset, I went off and reminded myself of the most widely

used methods. I humbly present to you the list that now hangs in my cube to remind me that there are more tools in the box:

Method	Speed	Commitment
Consultative: Group members are encouraged to contribute and discuss ideas, suggestions, and opinions freely. The decision maker makes the decision.	Fast	High
Consensus: Discussion continues until everyone's concerns and interests are addressed and incorporated. The group makes the decision and all members agree.	Slowest	Highest
Authoritative: The group leader makes the decision and announces the decision.	Fastest	Lowest
Voting: Everyone gets a vote. The group majority makes the decision.	Fast	Low

As you can see, there are plenty of decision-making tools, each of which addresses different concerns. One of these, or a combination of two of them, is likely to be the most efficient way to help your particular team make a particular decision. As for my friend, she went with a blend of *authoritative* and *consultative* by opening the agenda topic with her suggested list of the top enhancements to recommend, based on some ROI analysis that had already been done. This focused the team's discussion and they were able to quickly come up with their top five recommendations and move on to other more important agenda items. Ah, there's nothing like using the right tool to get the job done quickly!

How to Select the Best Option

I've yet to manage a project where there wasn't some sort of selection of options to make. You know what I'm talking about...select the best candidate from a slew of interviewees, pick the best vendor for the marketing campaign, decide between two competing designs, pick the best software package to use, and so on. If I'm lazy, then I'll facilitate a team discussion and use the *consensus* decision-making model. As you know, consensus-based decisions yield strongest buy-in from the team, but this method does not always generate the best decision, nor does it provide supporting documentation for why the decision was made.

To get a better, data-based decision along with strong supporting documentation, you need *selection criteria*. Once you have selection criteria, all you and your team need to do is evaluate your options against these criteria. Trust me, it really is that easy!

Okay, now let's talk about those selection criteria. I first understood the power of documented selection criteria when I did vendor selection/development work at Applied Materials. It's one of those magic bullets all PMs need to understand how to use. Your strategy here is to create a set of selection criteria and then create a *grading scale* that is relevant to the choice your team needs to make. After these two things are established, all you've got to do is the actual evaluation of your options.

To create your selection criteria, you start with the requirements for whatever it is you are trying to select. For instance, if the module must fit within a 2' x 1' x 0.5' enclosure, then either it does or doesn't fit. If you have actual, quantifiable requirements, those become your selection criteria. Not a lot of ambiguity with that, is there? These criteria are pretty cut and dried and most teams don't struggle with determining them. It gets tougher when the requirements are qualitative. This is the realm of mushy, relative measures.

If your requirements are not quantifiable (for example, will the candidate fit in well with our current team dynamic?), then you need that grading scale. To generate the grading scale you basically consider both extremes of the criteria. It's completely up to you what you use for this scale because this will be a relative measure, so you can create your scale to best fit your needs. For example, if you want to evaluate/grade a vendor's maturity with respect to product quality, then your grading scale might look something like this:

Grade/Score	Observation
1	The vendor couldn't spell the word "quality" while holding a dictionary.
2	The vendor uses final inspection of outgoing parts as the sole monitoring and control process.
3	The vendor has documented monitoring and control processes, but compliance appears to be sporadic.
4	The vendor has documented monitoring and control processes in place with supporting evidence that these processes are closely followed throughout the manufacturing process.

The thing to realize here is that what scale you use doesn't really matter. I just made that table up off the top of my head and it's perfectly usable as is. This is a relative measure, so as long as all options are evaluated against the same scale, then you're good to go. In fact, I usually develop the scale in a way that makes sense to me and then get the team's buy-off before we use it. Don't make this harder than it has to be. You should be able to come up with selection criteria and a grading scale for most decisions in thirty minutes or less. (Obviously, the more important the selection, the more time you should take in generating the criteria and scale.)

What's important to realize is that you are evaluating the options relative to each other against the selection criteria. What I mean is that all your team needs to determine is whether Candidate A will fit into the team better than Candidate B or vice versa. Exactly what a score of "4" means matters little as long as each option is scored on the same scale with the same criteria.

Tip   On any numbered grading scale, you want an *even* number of scores. If you use an odd number of scores, then it's highly likely you will end up with the majority of the scores the same, as people tend to pick the middle score when in doubt. Using an even number of scores forces everyone to make a choice about how that option scores relative to each other. Make sense?

So, the next time you and your team need to select among multiple options, create some selection criteria and a grading scale. In the real world, you will probably have a good mix of quantifiable and qualitative criteria. The quantifiable criteria are either "thumbs up" or "thumbs down"—so don't count those in an overall score. Of course, there are evaluations your team needs to do that require a lot more rigor and that's just fine. For those everyday selections, however, use this structured approach. Not only will the team make quicker decisions, but they'll also make better ones *and* you will have documented why the decision was made for future reference. Now, obviously, I've made this sound pretty simple, and that's because for most things you need it for, it is that simple. I think sometimes we make things harder than they have to be and get mired in analysis paralysis. So don't go there—just circumvent that quagmire and bust out some selection criteria! Trust me, your team's gonna thank you when they see how quickly a decision is reached.

Prioritize This!

Whenever I get stupid busy, I know one of my surefire techniques to manage the chaos is to get ruthless with prioritization. It's interesting to me that while people understand the concept of prioritization, most don't actively employ this strategy. Instead we all too often let urgent items take precedence over important items and end up frantically turnin' and burnin', while accomplishing very little.

Over the years I've figured out that for prioritization to be a real and meaningful tool, I need to wield it ruthlessly. The sad fact is that many times it's just not possible to get everything on my To-Do list done, and I need to get smart about what I work on. So in the interests of sharing, here's how I prioritize:

The first pass is to assign a relative priority to the big things. Here's where you need to decide the relative importance of whatever it is you're trying to achieve. For instance, if you're planning to drive to Grandmother's house for

Thanksgiving, then perhaps tuning up the car is more important than cleaning your house. Actually getting to Grandmother's house has a higher priority than picking up your dirty socks, which can wait until you're home again. So, of all the things you have on your plate, which is the most important? Notice that I did not say, which is the most "urgent"... we'll get to that later.

After you have a clear picture of the relative priority of the big objectives, if you will, then it's time to break down those smaller tasks that contribute to said big objectives. Here's the point where most people dump out a list of tasks and start knocking 'em off. That's okay but you're still gonna feel like you're staring down a runaway train...in the dark...in a tunnel. I bet I'm not the only one who's felt like that! What you want to do with your list is pick it apart one more time and prioritize it by breaking it into three categories: what must be done, what should be done, and what you'll do if you have extra time. Now you should have a short list of tasks that support your highest-priority objective that must be done. If you can do nothing but the items on this list, then it will at least make sure that you physically get to Grandmother's house.

Okay, now let's talk about urgency. Not everything that's urgent is important to do. On any given day I have a couple of deliverables or tasks to complete that are time-sensitive, but they may or may not support my highest priorities. In general, I try to organize my work so that no one is waiting on me for a deliverable, so that I don't have to deal with a last-minute fire drill to get something completed. I'm a PM, so I'm hyper-organized and I actually plan to do work so that I finish deliverables before they are due. It's this proactive approach that allows me to avoid that last-minute rush to finish something by 5 PM on the day before Thanksgiving. You may not be into that much organization or you may love the pressure of a deadline, and that's cool. The thing to keep in mind however is the relative priority of whatever task you're working on regardless of its urgency.

Now there's one other place where prioritization is a PM's best friend, and that's whenever you're managing multiple projects. At any given time, I have a rotating list of the projects I'm working on, with the top priority going to whichever project is at the top of that list. I've found over the years that as long as I have a clear order of priority, then I can make good tradeoff decisions between projects. If I'm at all unclear about the order of projects then I go ask for a priority call. I've found that I frequently have to drag that elephant out from under the rug kicking and screaming because, let's face it— my boss would prefer that all of the projects be the highest priority. That's just not realistic, is it? Right now, I'm actively managing five projects with overlapping team members. I need to make it clear to everyone which project gets the top priority slot, and I need to manage the morale and expectations of each team differently depending on which project they are working on. This isn't as easy as it sounds, and sometimes I write down the list on my whiteboard so everyone knows which way is up. I see it as part of my job responsibilities to manage the prioritization of work among the various projects.

Presenting Project Updates

Another critical skill for PMs to have is the ability to condense everything that's happening on a project at any given time into a concise update. You see, PMs communicate project status updates all the time, and about half of those updates are delivered verbally to a live audience. You need to be able to morph your message depending on your audience. Exactly what data and to what level of detail you present needs to be tailored to whomever it is that receives this information. It needs to be relevant and actionable to each person, and that's a bit of a challenge for PMs.

Stop Sharing Too Much Information

To start off with, let's talk about just how much information you should share. I've being grilled, flambéed, and skewered with the best of 'em over information I voluntarily provided. Information is kinda like the smoke from the genie's bottle. Once it starts slipping out, there's no stopping it, and once that particular genie is out of the bottle either your most fervent wish is granted or bad things happen despite your good intentions. Now I'm not advocating deceiving your stakeholders, but I do believe you should be very careful about what information you do share. How you determine what and how much information to share is situational and, frankly, a matter of experience. This is the kind of thing you learn as a result of making the wrong choices, so I thought I'd share my take on when and what to share.

First, let's start with the information you should always share. Changes to committed dates must always be disclosed, even if it's bad...especially if it's bad! This is a matter of integrity, since you've essentially given your word that the team can deliver to a specific date. Nothing less than complete honesty is acceptable; just make sure you have a recovery plan to share when the news is bad. Further, changes to the execution strategy that could affect the customer should be shared. If your team decides to drop a particular test to accelerate the timeline, then the customer probably cares and needs to know. Conversely, if your team decides to use a different software package to develop the code, then the customer probably doesn't care and there's no need to disclose this. Essentially any information that could be actionable to the customer should be shared.

Likewise, any information that does not inspire action on the customer's part should be withheld. Ask yourself what the customer will do with this particular information. If the answer is "nothing," then consider not bringing it up. PMs often provide their stakeholders with updates to tasks that are not on the critical path. There's nothing inherently wrong with this, but consider that the stakeholder probably doesn't care. Yes, friends, that's the harsh reality... they don't care! My customers frankly couldn't care less if I get the assembly instructions done on time because all they care about is whether or not manufacturing can deliver consistently. I have to care about those documents; they don't.

In fact, the percentage of work your team is doing that your stakeholders actually care about is surprisingly minimal. What the stakeholders really care about is whether or not your team is on track to the commits and the final quality of their deliverable. The stakeholders are expecting you, as the PM, to care about and manage the details. It's your job to ensure all of those day-to-day things turn out right and do not affect the final deliverable. One mistake I often see PMs making is to disclose this level of detail to the stakeholders. Consider this: When you tell your stakeholders that the team is behind on finishing the CAD work for the chassis assembly, what you are really saying is that the team is behind schedule. Your stakeholder hears that you're behind schedule and the implication is that this schedule slip will affect the committed delivery date. Now you and I know that that impression is most likely false. Let's say, for argument's sake, that this type of thing happens multiple times throughout the life of the project. When you continually give your stakeholders the impression that the work is out of control, you lose credibility. Once you lose credibility, it's really hard to influence those stakeholders and any negotiation becomes rather painful. In short, because you disclosed a bunch of information that's not actionable by the stakeholder, you've lost their confidence and, trust me, they will monitor your every breath going forward. If you're anything like me, then you've been in this situation before and know it sucks.

Finally, I should make a few comments about spinning your message. News flash: You are not an ad agency! Don't put unnecessary spin on a status update. Don't try to obscure the true meaning or hide a looming problem. That's just plain unethical and it's a kissin' cousin to a flat-out lie. Don't do it! On the other hand, you do need to make sure that your message is communicated at the correct level of complexity. Keep status updates to those outside your immediate team succinct and to the point. Remember that your message needs to be actionable to the stakeholders. Don't add so much detail that the person being communicated to has to spend an hour deciphering the message to figure out what actions to take. If the project is on track, then just say so. If you're trending two weeks late, state that and then follow up with your recovery plan and potential impacts to other stakeholders. Last, where at all possible, use quantitative data. It will lend instant credibility to your message.

I hope this sparks some thoughts on how to improve your stakeholder communication. It's pretty easy to share more information than is good for your team or your stakeholders. We're all busy these days, so don't make your stakeholders work for it when they get your status updates. Keep 'em short and sweet and, above all else, factual.

How to Build a Presentation

Project managers have to pull together presentations all the time, and how good you are at building a slide deck can make or break your reputation. Further, PMs are often called upon to generate a slide, or ten, for someone else such as a boss or a key stakeholder. To make it even more challenging, those key stakeholders frequently don't know what they want and rely on the PM to figure out what the key messages should be. We've all been there: the Big Kahuna says something like, "Hey Mel, give me a coupla slides on that project so I can add 'em to my quarterly review with Finance on Friday." Gee, would that be the project that's currently trending four weeks behind or the one that's trending two weeks early? Oh, and would you like me to create a one-page summary for the project, or do you want the nitty-gritty details of our schedule slip? Wait! I know, you want the budget breakdown, including that whopping NRE we just paid to that outside design house right?

Yeah, I know your pain and I too have spent long, late hours trying to shoehorn data into a PowerPoint-friendly format. Over the years, I've become much more disciplined about how I go about developing a presentation and the key for me is to follow a systematic process. (This process also helps those wily stakeholders figure out what it is they want to see in the resultant slides!)

I walk you through **Melanie's 10-Step Process for Designing a Presentation** in PowerPoint for a sample training session:

1. *What's the topic?* For this example, I'm using material I prepared for a training session I gave to some of my peers on the topic, "How to Say No."

2. *Who's the audience?* Practicing PMs, located in the Western hemisphere for the most part. This material could also be reused for the Eastern region.

   a. *Who are the decision makers?* No one in this case; this is a knowledge-sharing session only.

   b. *Does anyone in the audience have a particular ax to grind over this topic?* Not that I know of for this topic and this audience.

   c. *Why would the audience care about this topic?* All are involved in stakeholder management and executing change control for their projects, where the need to say no politically arises.

   d. *Any observations from previous experience with this audience?* They like real-world examples, so use good stories for the key points.

3. *Refine the topic based on the audience.* "How to say no while still maintaining good relations with stakeholders."

4. *What are the three key points you want to make?* (State them at the beginning and reiterate them at the end of the presentation.)

   a. Just because they ask, doesn't mean you have to say yes

   b. Say yes to say no.

   c. If you have to say no, don't beat around the bush and don't back down.

5. *What images will you need for this material?*

   a. Screenshot.

   b. Woman with laptop, perhaps images of the code of conduct, money representing bribery, and so on.

   c. Delaminated bus bars.

   d. ???

6. *How long do you have to talk?* 20-30 minutes => six content slides + fluff (agenda, intro, Q&A, and so on).

7. *What presentation style are you going to employ?* This will be part talk, part knowledge-share.

   a. *What time of day are you presenting?* Late afternoon, so I need to have plenty of energy and end early.

   b. *What tone or style are you going to use?* I want to use a friendly tone with a conversational style. Do not use an overly businesslike tone for this forum, which would come across as a lecture instead of opening up the topic for discussion.

8. *Can you reuse slides from other presentations?* Yes, most of the "fluff" slides can come from an earlier talk to this forum.

9. *Where did you get your data? Is there anyone you need to acknowledge?* No, this is all my original content, but I may end up using some photos from the corporate database and those will need to be attributed.

10. *What contact info will you provide?* My Intel e-mail only.

There you have it, my own 10-step program! ☺ Again, the key for me is to follow a systematic process that forces me to clarify and refine what it is I'm going to talk about. Hope this is useful to you on your next presentation.

The Big Bad Presentation

Have you ever felt like the main entrée at a backyard barbeque? You know what I mean, you're presenting some rather unpleasant project status and the questions are coming fast and furiously from what closely resembles a pack of hungry hyena. Yeah, I've been there and I definitely have the scars to prove it. I don't have the T-shirt though, as they don't give 'em out to the roast pig at a luau, now do they?

Delivering presentations when the message is bad, ugly, and undeniable is a big challenge for project managers. Sadly, I see a lot of PMs who never figure out how to deliver this kind of message and not get cooked. In the sadder cases, the PM starts spinning the data and adopts a deliberately vague delivery in the hopes that no one will notice that the things have gone from slightly troubling to an out-of-control forest fire.

I wish I could say that I've never done that, but I'm pretty sure I did in the early days, before I figured it out. It's taken a while and more than one flaming presentation, but I finally came up with some strategies for handling these situations. In fact, I now look at delivering bad or controversial information as a challenge. So, without further ado, here are **Melanie's Tips for a Successful BBQ aka "The Big Presentation" aka "How to Avoid Becoming the Anthropologist in the Pot"**:

- Before the meeting, meet with all of your stakeholders and make sure they support the content you intend to present. Remember, no surprises!

- Do your homework and figure out who the decision maker is and what's important to her before you have to stand up and present.

- Fake it till you make it—otherwise known as show some confidence! You are the only person in that meeting with the in-depth understanding of what's going on with the project. Act like it!

- Never shade, spin, or otherwise distort the facts. The truth can't hurt you anymore than it already has, and integrity will go further with your audience than a cheap song and dance.

- Don't fan the flames if the discussion turns aggressive. Remain calm and in control. Trust me, your professionalism and emotional maturity make the other person look childish and silly. Take the higher ground and you will come out on top, even if you lose that particular point.

- Never, never, never blame your team members or their respective organizations when things go wrong. Stick to the facts and present the data in such a way that the decision maker can act on it. Throwing someone under the proverbial bus doesn't help your cause and will definitely make it infinitely harder to motivate the team in the future.

- Answer all questions with authority and confidence. If the hyenas smell your fear or doubt, they will fall on you like a wobbly gazelle.

- It's okay to answer a question with, "I don't have an answer for you on that, but I'll follow up on it and get back to you by...." Don't punt and try to make it up as you go along—this will only make the situation worse.

- If it's a virtual meeting, stand up to sound more authoritative. I don't understand why this works, but it does. I'm also prone to pacing around my cube and waving my hands, and I think the energy and emotion come through in my voice.

I'd be lying if I told you that I never have tough presentations anymore, and I definitely still get BBQ'd once in a while. That's part of the job and as long as I learn something I'm cool with that. These days it does happen less frequently. I believe that's because I've become much more deliberate in my preparation for these events and I've just plain gotten better at it.

Stop Wasting Your Crisis

Have you heard the saying: "A crisis is a terrible thing to waste"? I hadn't heard that particular spin on "... a terrible thing to waste" until one morning driving to work. Listening to the radio, I heard a gentleman being interviewed about the recovery efforts in Haiti, and that one phrase seemed to jump out at me.

It's always tricky to present out negative project status, and if the news is really bad—that you're in a crisis—the presentation of status can be like walking through a minefield. When PMs are pulling this kind of presentation together, there's a tremendous focus on presenting the situation as accurately as possible along with realistic action plans. The objective is to give the impression that the crisis is well understood and that things are now in control... always assuming that they are in control, that is! ☺ The last thing a PM wants is additional scrutiny that masquerades as "help."

One thing I have learned, though, is that this is the best time to ask for help. Yep, when everything is in meltdown mode, you can score some assistance that moves the project forward. The trick to asking for this help is to make sure it's *realistic*. Too often, I see PMs "asking" for unreasonable amounts of extra headcount or schedule pushes that are outside the realm of customer acceptance. If I present out that my project is four weeks behind schedule and to get back on track I need an additional five heads, then I'm pretty clueless about how the org really works. I think there's this tendency of PMs to think that if they put out that kind of request, even knowing it won't be fulfilled, they will have their get-out-of-jail-free card when the project eventually fails. They can later say, "See, I told you I needed those extra heads and because I didn't get them, the project failed. It's not my fault. It's management's!" Unfortunately, the world is never this simple, and the PM will long be known for the failed project and not for the ignored request for more headcount. That's just the way it is, folks!

Okay, so what do I mean by *realistic* requests for help? First, consider who the decision maker is in the forum you're presenting to. Does she have the positional and influential power to give you five additional heads? Probably not. So consider what she can deliver. My direct manager can enable some things for my project, his manager a bit more, and eventually that head of engineering can deliver some real assistance if the request is carefully thought out. It should be noted that even the head of engineering probably lacks the ability to hire five new people and put them on your project...if she could, then it would have already happened!

The second thing to consider is what to ask for. Once you understand the budget and authority of the decision maker, you can start to look for specific help the team needs. To give you a feel for what I mean, here are a few examples of help I've successfully requested in the past:

- **An extra label printer for a pilot production line**. The team was always jockeying for time to use the label printer, so I asked for another one. This request was filled primarily because it was within the budget constraints of the decision maker, and although it wasn't as good as getting five additional heads it did help speed things up.

- **An SME to help with troubleshooting**. The primary reason this help was enabled was because I requested a specific SME for specific amount of time to help with very specific tasks. I was able to get the SME's time reprioritized to help the team find the root cause of the boot failure issue that was killing our schedule performance.

- **A dedicated reliability engineer, embedded with the team**. In this example, the reliability requirements were becoming a significant burden on the development team. By asking for and getting a reliability engineer embedded in the team, we were able to complete the reliability testing and the subsequent report much faster than if the team had had to do it themselves.

One last point to consider is that everyone wants to be part of the solution, including management. By giving management something to do, you are enabling them to actually help your project team. Ask for something realistic and you will walk away with real assistance for your team. Ask for five additional heads and not only will you be disappointed (okay, you probably didn't expect them anyway, right?) but you will feed your team's frustration by sending the message that upper management isn't paying attention to their issues. And that get-out-of-jail-free card? Well, that's just fool's gold, if you ask me. Capitalize on your next crisis by asking for specific, realistic help while presenting your project's status.

Giving a Talk

As a PM, when you are asked to deliver a talk, it's tremendously flattering since you're really being asked to provide the equivalent of an op-ed piece. More often than not, the topic will be something to do with the practice of managing projects (hey, you are an expert after all!) or a specific project, program, or product. I don't often do talks. Sure, I present all the time and I think I'm pretty good at it, but a talk is something different altogether. A *presentation* is all about conveying data and the outcomes are decisions and actions. This is the verbal equivalent of technical writing. When you deliver a *talk*, you and your material need to be entertaining—something more akin to writing fiction. The audience is very different, too. I'm not really looking for belly laughs when I present a project status…that's never a good sign! When I'm doing a talk, I'm actively trying to evoke that response. So, obviously it behooves all project managers to understand the difference between these two styles and how to be successful at both.

In 2010 I was asked to deliver a talk at the Intel IT PM Learning Forum about soft skills. I immediately said yes (duh!) and only later realized that a good talk is not something you can whip out in an hour or two—which is what I usually do for a presentation. Needless to say, I hadn't factored that into my acceptance and found myself scrambling like mad to pull a quality talk together in a few days.

I knew I had enough material to generate a respectable talk, but it turned out to be harder than I'd thought. For one thing, *soft skills* is a very broad area and, frankly, we've all heard most of these theories at one time or another. Let's face it, there's not a lot of new material here, and I was determined to give my audience something that justified their time. I decided to limit my talk to a few areas and only focus on the practical applications of soft skills. My main point was that this stuff will work for you if you are strategic and deliberate about how you use it.

To liven up the talk I had a couple of stories for each area. I told the story about literally sitting on my hands while meeting with a second-level manager who was an analytical. He thought I'd completely turned my project around just because I changed my communication style. Go figure. I spun a great yarn about how I'd managed my primary stakeholder in the epic Validation versus Platform Engineering wars. In all honesty, I think these stories made the talk, probably because they were all true and they demonstrated how to utilize soft skills in project management.

The other challenge I had to tackle was the visual material. When you give a presentation, the slide content is critical and the challenge is how to condense the data. In a perfect world, a fantastic talk would need no slides because the speaker could see and engage with the audience on a personal level. In my reality, I couldn't see how a virtual audience was going to be motivated to follow along while looking at a blank monitor...okay, truly? I didn't think I'd hold anyone's attention without some visual aids to compete with surfing the web during my talk. As I designed the slides, I deliberately kept the slide content to a minimum while writing a great deal of info in the speaker's notes section. I felt that this provided the visual aid to help people follow along, as well as providing context should they want to review the material at a later date.

Last, I practiced that sucker until I could do it blindfolded and hanging upside down. It should be noted that I do practice for big presentations, but never this much. This was probably about 50% of my preparation. There were three talks at various times to accommodate the global audience, and I knew I'd need to be really prepared to deliver the early talk and the late night one. I'm not really a night owl and I was dreading trying to sound coherent while falling asleep! I practiced the talk until I could do it with only a few sneak peeks at the slides. I practiced several stories for each slide so that I could apply whichever one fit any questions and so that each audience got a little something different.

All that preparation paid off and I think the talks went well. The audiences had great questions and seemed to enjoy the material. I learned quite a bit about how to deliver a talk versus a presentation. So if you're ever asked to do a talk, definitely say yes—but be sure you have enough time to prepare... and practice a lot!

And Now for Something Insane

I was one of five speakers using the *Ignite* style of presentation to talk about collaboration at a Women at Intel Network (WIN) conference. In case you haven't heard about this whole Ignite phenomenon, let me break it down for you. Each speaker has a measly five minutes to make their argument and only 20 slides to support it. The catch is that each slide auto-advances every 15 seconds; there's no animation or builds, and text doesn't really work because the slides change so fast. Trust me, this is like nothing you've ever seen or done, and it's way outside your comfort zone when you're up on stage doing it for the first time.

The topic I'd planned to talk about was one near and dear to my blogger's heart: collaboration through blogging. I felt like I had a good story to tell and I certainly had passion for the topic. It became obvious to me that that passion was the key to success as I worked through designing the slides and then crafting the delivery.

The design of the slides was my first task, and it turned out to be both harder and more fulfilling than I'd originally thought. Because this was clearly going to be a much more visual talk than I'd done in the past, I figured that I needed to up-level my game when it came to the slides. I basically followed the methodology outlined by Nancy Duarte, in her book *slide:ology*.[1] Yes, I really did follow this process pretty faithfully. It took hours, but the results were amazing!

I spent a solid four hours mind-mapping, brainstorming, sketching, playing word-association games, and so on to come up with content ideas. I did not start with an outline as I normally would. Much to my surprise, this idea-generation process yielded what would become the core of the talk, and it was really good content! (For the PMs in da house, this was the proof-of-concept—POC—or scoping activity.) For instance, when I was analyzing the likely audience, I realized that one of the reasons people would be interested in my story was the amazing career-advancement opportunities I've enjoyed as a result of my Intel blog. This wasn't in the original plan for the talk, but this concept clearly had to be included. The idea-generation process was so prolific that I had a tough time culling them into just 20 discrete ideas/slides. Heck, even the stuff that didn't make it into the final revision was good...real good.

Once I'd settled on the ideas and content for each slide, I had to come up with the appropriate visuals. (PM translation: "Execution Phase.") As part of the idea-generation process, I'd developed a couple of ideas for each slide, so I had a punch list of images I needed to create. To be honest, I tried my hand first at finding Creative Commons licensed images but didn't have a lot of luck. Since time was slipping away like sands through the hourglass, I decided to just take the photos I needed myself. I used my trusty iPhone, kept the images simple, and used what I had around the house for the most part. To change things up a bit, I used a couple of screenshots of viewership metrics from the blog to add credibility, one diagram inspired by Duarte's Chapter 3, and only one text slide. In the end, I think I spent about six to seven hours developing the slides, and what gorgeous slides they were!

Once I'd locked down the slides, the order in which they would flow, and a key point or two I'd make for each one, I was ready to move on to the next phase: practicing the talk. (Okay, PMs, say it with me: "Testing Phase!") The absolute hardest part of an Ignite talk is mastering the timing. It goes by so fast that if you get off your pace you have very little chance of catching up before the end of your allotted five minutes. Oh, and you can't really memorize your material because you've got a tight timeline and you have to react to/anticipate reactions from the audience. To start with, I ran through this talk enough times that I'd memorized the order and the key point I wanted to make with each slide. Next, I used the animation feature in PowerPoint to practice with

---

[1] Nancy Duarte. *slide:ology: The Art and Science of Creating Great Presentations.* (Sebastopol, CA: O'Reilly Media Inc., 2008.)

the strict 15 seconds per slide timing. This was the hardest and most time-consuming part of the whole process. Next, I practiced blending the points across slides so that I could change my pace on the fly. I spent a lot of time practicing as you'd expect, and I ended up putting something like 10 hours into this part of the process.

The culmination of all of this effort was the talk on the day of the conference. I'm told I did a credible job, but to be honest I don't remember a word I said. Oh, I can definitely tell you what points I made, what analogies I probably used; heck, I can even recite whole bits of dialogue because I practiced it so much... *but* I don't remember a darn thing about being on stage! LOL! Yep, it's true, it was a blur. Far from the euphoria I expected I'd feel when it was done, all I felt was exhaustion. I'd set myself a goal to significantly improve my presentation style and public speaking skills. Little did I realize, that the WIN conference would be a huge "opportunity to excel," as a former colleague used to say. All told I put about 20 hours into this effort and I learned an incredible amount. I've definitely improved my presenting and public speaking skills, but I know that there's always more to learn, so I'm not done yet!

Standin' on My Soapbox: PowerPoint

I once ran across an article by Elisabeth Bumiller talking about how the military struggles with what I'll call the *PowerPoint Effect* in communication.[2] This is what happens when the generation of the PPT becomes more important than the information it's meant to convey. It's not clear exactly when the format of the slides becomes the most important part of the data; you just know that's what's happened when you hit hour four of preparing the presentation. I'm sure most of us have experienced that moment of utter frustration when you realize that what you have to say is less important than the pretty picture in the slide.

The article talks about military PPT presentations to the news media called "hypnotizing chickens," the intent of which is to convey as little information as possible. At first I laughed at the clever turn of phrase, but then I recalled an operations review I attended regularly a few years ago. This ops review worked pretty much like they all do, and I often presented on project status in this forum. One of the things I quickly noticed was that while I was allocated about 30 minutes to present, in actuality I got five minutes at the end of a two-hour meeting to talk. The other thing I figured out was that those chickens were definitely hypnotized by the time I presented at the end of the meeting.

---

[2]Elisabeth Bumiller, "We Have Met the Enemy and He Is PowerPoint": *The New York Times*, April 26, 2010. http://www.nytimes.com/2010/04/27/world/27powerpoint.html?partner=rss&emc=rss&_r=0

The teams ahead of me on the agenda had upwards of 20 slides, all jam-packed with data. The kicker was that for the most part all of the slides had the same format, so it made it really challenging to discern what was different as each slide made its appearance. Further, when things weren't on track, I noticed that it was popular among the slide preparers to "adjust" the plan of record (POR) date to match the trend dates. Yep, according to those slides every major milestone was dead on track to the POR all the time. But wait, that's not the shocking part…the shocking part is that no one was ever called on it! That's right, the audience was completely hypnotized! Crazy, huh?

Another point Bumiller's article makes is that not every idea or point can be "bulletized" and, in fact, complex concepts need more discussion and explanation than is practical with PowerPoint. I know I've spent many hours over the years struggling with conveying complex scenarios and their subsequent outcomes within a PPT slide. Large amounts of numerical data do not lend themselves to a single slide and indeed usually convey no information if placed within a PPT, since the audience can't really read and digest that volume of data in such a constrained format. Despite its constraints, every day someone is shoehorning data into a PPT slide because we think that's the only way to communicate in a meeting.

My team meetings do not generally involve PowerPoint presentations. It's not as though I woke up one day and decided to ban PowerPoint. Rather, it was a gradual realization that we didn't need them. In my weekly project meeting, each team member verbally discusses what they've been up to for the previous week and any challenges or help needed. I take notes while they talk and then distribute the notes after the meeting. Sure, we could use slides, but then someone would have to create them, upload them to the project repository, and at the end of the project archive them….sounds exhausting doesn't it? To be fair, we do utilize PPTs when needed, but no one feels obligated to produce a weekly slide.

That feeling of obligation drives a lot of slides, in my opinion. I think this is partly due to the fact that we've become so accustomed to using slides that we just assume they are needed. Often the only reason we make the slides is because we think we have to. If you want to avoid hypnotizing the chickens, then you need to concentrate on using PowerPoint as a backup communication tool rather than the primary source of data.

More talk—fewer slides!

Stakeholder Management in the Real World

You know, this would be an awesome job except for those pesky stakeholders! If you ask me, managing stakeholder expectations is the hardest part of project management, and every PM I know struggles with this from time to time. The good news is that there's a lot you can do to improve your skills in this area. Simply having a well-thought-out plan and applying deliberate strategies to each stakeholder can greatly increase your effectiveness. Chapter 1 talked about how to determine who your stakeholders are and their relative importance. This chapter talks about what to do with them!

Have a Plan

It is common for junior project managers to manage their stakeholder expectations in an ad hoc manner. Sure, they are careful to be friendly and informative when the stakeholders are encountered, but there's little deliberation or strategy employed in the overall management of these critical relationships. If this project manager is personable and reasonably adept at the soft skills, then this method will work just fine for smaller projects. Where the ad hoc method falls short is with difficult stakeholders, highly matrixed organizations, and large projects. Here the results of insufficient stakeholder management closely resemble a toddler pageant complete with prima donna parents, indifferent judges, and crying kids. The project manager's reputation is diminished, the team is constantly frustrated with "bring-me-a-rock" exercises, and the overall scope of the project is inflated.

The good news is that all of this drama can be averted with a couple hours of planning. Creating a stakeholder management plan is fairly straightforward and can be accomplished with a simple spreadsheet. The key here is to come up with a specific plan for managing all of the stakeholders on your project. If you leave this thing to chance or circumstance, you will find yourself right back at that toddler pageant.

The first step then is to systematically identify and categorize all of the stakeholders on your project by using a handy-dandy spreadsheet that you generate using *Melanie's Stakeholder Identification Method* revealed in Chapter 1. Now that you understand who your stakeholders are, you can easily craft a strategy for managing their expectations. Decide how often and via what format you will communicate with each stakeholder. It helps here to break them into categories based on how you communicate with them. If this sounds suspiciously like a communication plan, that's because it is! Once you've determined when and how you will communicate with your stakeholders, you need to automate. Use your current calendaring or task-tracking system to set up reminders for yourself to contact the various categories of stakeholders. These reminders can be something as simple as, "Invite Melanie for coffee and give her an informal update on the project. Make sure to ask her about her overall satisfaction with the team's progress." This part doesn't have to be complex or overly managed; it just needs to be intentional. Once you have those automated reminders in place, all you need to do is act on them. You still need to employ your networking skills, but the automated reminders make sure that you have a consistent, focused, and deliberate strategy for managing each of your key stakeholders.

Networking for Fun and Profit

Okay, now that those reminders are popping up on your calendar, what do you do about them? The good news is that stakeholder management and maintaining your professional network are basically the same thing. As with any new contact in your professional network, you need to start by understanding the other person. What's important to them and why? What's their pain threshold when it comes to schedule, scope, and resources? What type of communicator are they? All of these are questions you need to think about when determining how best to engage with your stakeholder.

Once you understand who your stakeholders are, have a plan to manage their expectations, and have automated the process so that it happens at a repeatable cadence, it's time to think about how to engage with them. By far the most effective way to build a relationship is to break bread with the other person. Invite your key stakeholders for coffee, lunch, or drinks, and start off on a friendly note. There's just something about breaking bread together that creates an environment conducive to meeting the other person halfway. At first you might talk about your differences and hash out collaborative solutions. Later, you begin strategizing on issues affecting the project or program in general. As time goes on and the professional relationship strengthens, you will start using each other as sounding boards for other work challenges. Years later, I still meet with many of my old stakeholders for lunch or drinks every few months. They've become members of my professional network and I never hesitate to reach out to them for help or to provide help in turn.

To actively manage your stakeholders' expectations, you have to know what those expectations are in the first place. Start by simply asking your stakeholders what they expect from the project. Don't be fooled here, as what they tell you is most likely only part of the story. When you begin working with your stakeholders you can nail down the basics, such as what level of involvement they want to have with the project, the frequency and format of status updates, which decisions they want to participate in, and so forth. After you've established a relationship, you can then start asking for feedback. Is there something more you and your team can do for the stakeholder? Is the frequency and depth of the regular updates adequate? Is the stakeholder satisfied with the team's progress to date? As the relationship progresses, you can move into brainstorming strategic challenges for the entire program, but you can't get to this point without putting in the work to understand who your stakeholders are and to actively manage their expectations.

A good place to start is with a customer-oriented mindset. Deliberately refer to your key stakeholders as customers, no matter if they are the final end user or not. This makes a tremendous difference with your team and with your own point of view. You see, everyone has some understanding of what exceptional customer service looks like. Sadly, many of us aren't motivated to provide that level of service, especially if the prevailing culture is not customer-focused. Therefore, the project manager must instill a customer service orientation into their teams and themselves. A stakeholder who's viewed as an important customer by the project team interacts with a team that's bought into their mutual success. This fosters a positive and collaborative environment, which in turn keeps the stakeholder's expectations in check.

Own the Communication

One mistake I often see project managers make is to not take control of the communication to their key stakeholders. All too often those same project managers believe that a well-crafted email will suffice. They then leave it up to the stakeholder to glean meaning and intent from the message, thereby abdicating any influence over the stakeholder's expectations. To actually manage and affect your stakeholder's expectations, you have to own the conversation.

It's obvious that these conversations should be open and honest, but that's only part of the picture. You also need to actively manage the information being conveyed, applying the guidelines you read in the "Stop Sharing Too Much Information" section of the preceding chapter.

Apply Some Psychology

There is a tremendous amount of research out there regarding how the brain works, and project managers can gain useful insights into how to influence their stakeholders by studying this data. This insight is particularly useful when determining a particular strategy for conveying bad news. You know that you shouldn't go into your most important stakeholder's office and just blurt out, "We're now a month behind schedule because someone dropped the controller off the forklift...oops!"—and run out the door. Instead, you need to understand how the brain works and craft an appropriate message. What you need to do is describe just why that forklift driver dropped the controller, in detail. You see, explaining an event lessens its emotional impact. By dropping your bomb and running away, you actually enhance its emotional impact, thereby ensuring an enraged stakeholder.[1] Explaining why it happened is a critical component of delivering bad news.

Another critical component when dealing with stakeholders is their overall sense of control. It's vital that you help your stakeholders maintain a sense of control over the project and a belief that the project itself is under control. You see, it makes people happy to have a sense of control over their environment and it is gratifying to exert that control.[2] Knowing this, the astute project manager will deliberately go to her key stakeholders on a periodic basis and ask them to exert some direct control over the project. For example, I might go to the stakeholder to ask her for assistance removing a roadblock. In this instance it doesn't matter that I could have taken care of the issue myself. It will make my key stakeholder happy by giving her a sense that she's part of the team and can influence what's going on with the project. Now obviously you would not want to overuse this technique and create the impression that you're incompetent, but judicious use can be highly effective and maintain a happy and supportive stakeholder.

While a project manager may go to a stakeholder for help removing a roadblock, it's much more common to consult with a key stakeholder over a major decision about the direction or prioritization of the project. In these instances, the project manager will prepare a set of recommendations for the stakeholder to review and make a ruling on. Understanding how the brain makes

---

[1]Daniel Gilbert. *Stumbling on Happiness*. (New York, NY: Knopf, 2006. Pp. 207-8.)
[2]Ibid, p. 22.

decisions can be extremely useful in this scenario. You see, when it comes to making decisions the brain behaves a bit like that toddler in that pageant I mentioned earlier. When presented with a side-by-side comparison of data, the brain tends to zero in on the differences, even if they are not relevant to the decision that needs to be made.[3] Think of the toddler who at the start of the pageant only wants to leave with a sparkly tiara. When she does place in the contest and the MC negligently grabs the tiara with the blue stone off the judging table to plunk on her head, she's immediately starts wailing because she now passionately wants the one with the pink stone. Prior to the competition she only wanted that sparkly tiara, but when it comes time to receive it, she's making a value decision about a difference she did not even care about at the beginning. Of course your stakeholders aren't going to carry on like toddlers with blue-stone tiaras, but they will certainly focus on any comparative differences in your data, so make sure that you only include those data points that are relevant to the decision.

What makes managing stakeholders so very challenging is the people. We each have our own quirks and idiosyncrasies that require the project manager to continually build a toolbox of techniques for effective communication and influence. Developing a solid plan for regular interaction with your stakeholder, owning the conversation, and applying some experimental results from the field of psychology can move you from a good project manager to a great one.

The Tricky Bits

No matter how good you are at stakeholder management, there arc always a few special ones who require more advanced strategies. I'm talking about those tricky stakeholders, such as the bully in purchasing who uses bureaucracy to exert control over your project, the marketing representative who's always on a plane to see another customer, the R&D scientist who has a whole new paradigm in mind, the micromanaging resource manager, and the poor soul who would love a root canal so that she doesn't have to work on your project. How do you manage those tricky stakeholders?

Managing the Bully

There's one type of stakeholder who regularly hands you your hat as a project manager and that's the *Bully*. Many a project manager has fallen by the wayside, simply because they failed to address and effectively deal with the Bully. My worst nemesis was a guy whom we all called "Crazy Chris." This guy was so

---

[3]Ibid., p. 157.

tightly wound he could not accept anything less than perfection and often got so close to the edge of his temper that we worker bees would take bets on when he'd completely lose it. I can close my eyes right now I see him standing in front of me, red faced, all but bouncing up and down with aggression, screaming at me that my team could not "read the test procedure." He was completely focused on having me admit that my team and I were illiterate. Needless to say, I didn't handle that situation well and I've definitely learned a lot about dealing with bullies since then. Today, there aren't as many Crazy Chrises around, but there are still people who dominate others through aggressive force of will. To successfully lead a team, all project managers need to have strategies for dealing with this type of stakeholder.

A Bully stakeholder is frequently the most aggressive person in any confrontational discussion. They exhibit low emotional maturity, are myopic about their solutions, and are dismissive of anyone else's viewpoint. You know what I'm talking about here and I don't think I need to spell it out. I'd bet my week's lunch money that each and every one of you has an example of a Bully stakeholder, either in your current project or from one in the not-too-distant past. The thing you need to understand about bullies is that it's all about winners versus losers. If they can intimidate you (and your team by extension), then they "win." Conversely, in that scenario, you become the "loser." These folks are definitely keeping score and, trust me, that score is very important to them. The trick to effectively dealing with these stakeholders is to change the game, while refraining from putting them in the "loser" position.

So just how do you curtail a Bully and turn him or her into a collaborative stakeholder?

- The first thing you must do is establish a strong first impression. Don't give in to their intimidation, don't back down from their aggression, and avoid getting sucked into this winners-vs.-losers game they have going. Maintain your emotional maturity and strive to keep things on a professional level. Call a time-out if you think they are too close to the edge, to give them a chance to pull it back together privately.

- The next thing you have to do is actively utilize your positional authority or SME status. Remember that for the Bully it's all about winning vs. losing, so establishing yourself as a winner in their eyes instantly increases their respect for you. Try saying something like this, "Okay, Melanie, I appreciate your input, and as the Project Manager responsible for making the schedule commitments for the board team, I am holding to my earlier January 10 commit." The key point here is that you emphasize your authority to make the commit and imply that you will take full accountability for meeting that commit. Don't justify your commit; just make it clear that you and you alone own that commit.

- This next strategy aligns with the previous two, and it is to demonstrate extreme self-confidence. Speak clearly and authoritatively but not loudly. If you're on the phone with the Bully, stand up. If you're having the discussion in person, look the Bully directly in the eye. Any hesitancy on your part will be perceived as a weakness, so it's doubly important to come off as very confident in these situations.

- You must be active and aggressive in facilitating any meeting the Bully attends. This will frequently require that you interrupt the Bully and pull input from other, more subdued teammates. Make no mistake, this may be very hard for you at first, but by actively facilitating the meeting, you're sending a message to the entire team that everyone's opinion will be heard and considered, not just the Bully's.

- This last one is a bit sneaky, but I've found that it works brilliantly if done carefully. Give the Bully assignments to produce data that supports their argument. This does two things: first, it acknowledges the validity of the Bully's point, thereby allowing them to feel like they've won; second, it reinforces the concept of data-based decisions. If the Bully has a good point and the data to back it up, then you definitely want the team to execute her way. However, what often happens is that the Bully realizes the flaws in her argument via the process of data collection and the problem resolves itself. Either way, you and your team win without having to go through a death match to make a decision.

All of these strategies are well and good, but don't kid yourself—you just can't change a person that much. What you can do, however, is change the team dynamic so that the Bully wants to collaborate and in that collaboration see himself as a winner. The real trick to dealing with Bullies is to get them to respect you, and then help them get into a position to win in their own minds through effective collaboration with the rest of the team.

Managing the Ghost

Ghost stakeholders are as familiar to project managers as they are frustrating. They appear to be ambivalent to the project status, major milestones, quality standards, deliverables, and so on. They travel frequently, making it virtually impossible to connect with them live and in person, which makes it extremely difficult to meet with them. They don't return your emails in this millennium and they do not see the project as a high priority.

The big "tell" for me that I'm dealing with this type of stakeholder is my own frustration with their apparent lack of involvement in the project planning. That's when I know I've got a Ghost on my hands. In general these are nice folks who are easy to get along with...if you can capture their attention for a few precious minutes. Tie the fate of your project to their responsiveness at your peril. They mean well, but make no mistake: this is a very challenging stakeholder to manage and you need a specific strategy to deal with them.

So just how do you go about managing this type of stakeholder without irritating the you-know-what out of them? How do you keep the project execution on track if it's at all tied to this stakeholder's input? Well, here are a few strategies I have refined over the years to deal with the Ghost stakeholder:

- Provide concise, regular status updates in their preferred medium.

- Trap them in an abandoned conference room and get agreement on their "guardrails:" how far they will let you and your team run without their direct input, knowledge, or approval. Be sure that you understand the aspects of the project they care about, decisions they want in on, budget limits, and tolerance for meetings.

- Respect these "guardrails" and then leave the stakeholder alone.

- Be extremely concise in your direct communication with them.

- Double-check that this person is the right stakeholder for your project. Perhaps he can delegate that role to someone with more time to support the team.

The key thing to remember about this type of stakeholder is that he really does care about your project...just not as much as you do. Your goal is to limit your project team's dependence on this stakeholder's input, direction, and approval, all while ensuring that the stakeholder remains happy with the team's work. It's also worth noting that you might have made a mistake and this person isn't truly a stakeholder at all! When that happens, have a quick chat with them to confirm that they aren't in the game, then remove them from all meeting invites and email distribution lists.

Managing the Visionary

Another very challenging stakeholder to manage is the one I call the *Visionary*. This is a stakeholder who's got a big picture understanding of the deliverable but has difficulty communicating that vision to you and your team.

What does this look like in the real world? The requirements are typically vague and high-level. This stakeholder is frequently the primary customer who tends to talk about the importance of the project and what the project can enable in the future, rather than the specifics of the deliverables. There's a tendency to dive in and discuss how to start development, often dictating approaches or methodologies to be used. Further, there's often little or no understanding of the security, regulatory, legal, and other established business process implications. The customer clearly sees how to implement their idea and can become impatient with the project team if they don't catch on quickly. Finally, there's a tendency to want to continue playing with or tweaking the deliverables, resulting in projects that just won't end. To a lot of project managers, this sounds like a nightmare—but it doesn't have to be.

So, how do you manage key stakeholder's expectations to deliver a product that looks like their big-picture vision while balancing the triple constraint? The following table breaks out specific strategies that can be used to address these challenging stakeholders.

Challenge	Tactic
The stakeholder likes to talk about the larger impact of the project... *a lot!*	Be patient but continue to bring the discussion around to the actual requirements.
Requirements are vague, big picture, or nonexistent.	Draft a detailed requirements document to start the discussion.
The stakeholder struggles with articulating their vision.	1. Offer several options for the deliverables so that the customer can clarify their expectations early.
	2. Develop early prototypes to review with the stakeholder to further refine expectations and requirements.
The stakeholder dictates development methodologies or tools.	1. Clearly document this methodology as a requirement.
	2. Clearly document expected availability dates and capabilities for any customer-supplied tools (SW, HW, facilities, and so on).
The stakeholder is unfamiliar with, or dismissive of, legal and regulatory compliance requirements.	Educate the customer early about the amount of work and time required in these areas.
The stakeholder wants to continue playing, long after the deliverables are complete.	Hold a formal closure meeting and step through each requirement, gaining stakeholder agreement that each requirement has been satisfied.

Two years ago I worked on a POC project with a customer who was friendly, flexible, and open to my team's ideas. The challenge with this particular customer was that he was a Visionary stakeholder. He had a big-picture understanding of the project deliverables but struggled with documenting the nuts and bolts of the requirements. As a result, he wanted a very sophisticated proof of concept despite the extremely short development cycle, all while dictating the software tools that would be used for the proof of concept work. By using the techniques recommended here, I was able to successfully manage the project and deliver a tool that met the intent of my customer's big-picture vision, while adhering to a very tight schedule. Further, because my approach was collaborative and I actively worked to complement the areas he struggled with, the project was a positive experience for all involved. The customer now has a very slick POC he can troll out to future customers, and I have a very satisfied customer.

Managing the Micromanager

We've all led projects where either our direct manager or another key stakeholder has micromanagement tendencies. This is not only frustrating for the project managers; it also completely undermines their authority. You can redirect those micromanagement tendencies—defang the *Micromanager* monster, if you will—with a few carefully applied stakeholder management techniques.

First, so that we're all on the same page, let's talk about the characteristics of a Micromanaging stakeholder. If you find yourself having to provide project status often and on an ad hoc basis, then you may be the victim of a Micromanager. If you find yourself providing deep-dive-level details in your regular status updates, you might be dealing with one or more Micromanagers. You could also just be over-communicating, so see the previous discussion for some ideas on how to manage that. If you see your stakeholder providing updates on your team's commitments, then you've probably got a Micromanager on your hands. Finally, the most obvious (and destructive) sign that you are dealing with a Micromanager is when the stakeholder in question goes directly to your team members for updates rather than coming to you, the project manager.

Sound familiar? I thought it might. Luckily, there's a pretty simple solution for all of those symptoms. The absolute best way to defang the Micromanager is to provide consistent, regular status updates. This sounds a bit naïve, doesn't it? Well I'm here to testify that providing *concise* updates on a *regular* cadence will eliminate almost all of your headaches dealing with a Micromanaging stakeholder. Let me break this down a bit for you.

When I say *concise* I mean just that. Your status updates need to be at the appropriate level for the intended audience. You may even need to provide more than one format if your stakeholders have significantly different needs.

It also needs to be something that the stakeholder can skim and pick up the primary messages of "on track/not on track," "look Ma, we done good/bad," and "here's how you can help us." Personally, I prefer the format of a single summary slide per project with a nifty stoplight that tells the audience immediately if things are good/green or bad/red. At the end of the day, you want to provide information that's relevant and actionable to your stakeholders.

When I say *regular*, that's pretty obvious, right? One thing I've noticed though is that those micromanagers are also the ones who are a bit more informal and who don't have a regular forum set up to review project status. If you're dealing with this Micromanaging stakeholder scenario, then I'd guess that you aren't required to provide a regular project status. In this case, it's up to you, the project manager, to establish that project status review forum. It can be as simple as an email update you send regularly, or you can set up a standing meeting to go over project status. In general I prefer to do this on a weekly basis, at the end of the week, but the cadence and timing should really be negotiated to meet your Micromanaging stakeholder's needs.

This is exactly what happened when I started managing projects for one boss. He was constantly stopping by my desk to ask for an update or, worse yet, going directly to the team members for updates. I suggested/instituted a weekly, 30-minute meeting to go over the status of all projects in flight. Once my boss got comfortable with the quality of the updates, he stopped those micromanagement tendencies. I think what he really needed to believe was that I knew what was going on and that I was actively managing the work. Eventually we were able to knock out statuses for three projects and still have time to discuss strategic actions he wants me to take—all within a 30-minute window.

Finally, I know what you're thinking—something like this: "Melanie, I'm busy enough as it is! Why should I eke out the time to do another status update that I'm not required to provide?" Hey, I get it: you're busy and this seems like extra work right? Well, first, it won't take you much time at all. Trust me, you already know that project status off the top of your head, and it will only take you 10–15 minutes per project to update a summary slide once you have that template established. Yes, it will take an investment of about an hour or so to populate a status slide with your initial project details, but you only have to do that once for each project. When you stop to consider how much time you're wasting by responding to all of those ad hoc status requests, the investment of 10–15 minutes per week on a status slide seems much more reasonable.

How to defang the Micromanaging stakeholder? Easy, provide project status information that's actionable and at the appropriate level for that stakeholder and provide the status at a predictable cadence that the stakeholder can rely on. If you do these two things, then you can defang, tame, and rehabilitate almost any Micromanaging stakeholder.

Managing the Prisoner

Almost every project has a *Prisoner:* the person who would rather be getting a weekly root canal than sitting in your project meeting. I'm sure I don't need to explain that I'm not talking about orange jumpsuits, scary tats, and the ol' bread-and-water routine here. Instead, I'm talking about the people who are on your team who really don't want to be there.

First let's talk about the characteristics of the Prisoner. Project Prisoners are often the people least engaged in meetings. They are those silent few who sit slightly separate from the group and commune with their laptops. In virtual meetings they remain utterly silent. The truly hardcore Prisoners have given up caring and are frankly just enduring your team and your project. They don't get angry or excited because it just doesn't matter to them. A Prisoner will not volunteer for extra work, even if it's to help out a teammate. The work they do for the project will be, at best, merely adequate and, at worst, late and sloppy. You tend to see a lot of this type of stakeholder on otherwise all-volunteer teams—especially those projects that involve quasi-process improvements. Honestly, it's hard to get excited about yet another "solve-world-hunger" decision-making process even if you are willing to be part of a solution, so imagine how little the Prisoner can care about that kind of project. I'm serious here: they…just…don't…care.

So how do these project Prisoners come to your otherwise amazing team? Well, for the most part they get nominated or directed to work with you by a direct manager. No one who voluntarily signs up for a process improvement team is going to be a Prisoner; conversely, almost anyone who's told to participate has some level of Prisoner mentality going. There are also those folks who are coasting in their career and they can have that Prisoner mentality too. It doesn't really matter to the project manager what the root cause is; the reality is that you have a Prisoner on your team and you need to manage that stakeholder carefully to avoid tanking your team dynamic early in the project lifecycle.

So now that you know what a Prisoner looks like, how do you go about "managing" one?

For some teams, there's a straightforward strategy for dealing with Prisoners. At the beginning of a new project, the project manager meets with each team member and asks straight up if they see themselves as a Camper, a Tourist, or a Prisoner on the project. A Camper is someone who's settled in, committed, and ready to work. A Tourist is someone who's curious but not yet convinced that the project is worth their time and effort. Obviously, the Prisoner is someone assigned to the team who really hasn't bought into the project or who simply doesn't want to be there. I really like this approach because it drags the elephant out from under the rug in a humorous and non-threatening way. Once you get it on the table that the Prisoner would rather be working at the local stockyards than working on your project, you can work together to solve the problem.

Once you're eye-to-eye with the elephant you have to figure out what to do with it. The first and most obvious tactic to consider is whether you can get this person off your project, peaceably. Sometimes this is as simple as meeting with the Prisoner's direct manager to see if there's a different resource that's a better fit. If you can pull off getting the Prisoner reassigned without damaging his or her reputation with the manager, then you look like a hero and everyone wins, including the Prisoner.

Okay, we all know life isn't always that easy, so let's say that your Prisoners are stuck on the project. A really good tactic to employ is to assign them work they can reasonably get done. Don't even think about expecting them to do anything outside of their perceived job descriptions, because that's just asking for trouble. If at all possible, try to configure the work around the Prisoners' areas of expertise or whatever they are passionate about. For instance, if you have a Prisoner who's passionate about compliance and doing the right thing, then they might be a good candidate for coordinating the legal and security reviews that need to happen. If you can tap into something they care about and feel is important, then you have a decent chance of breaking them out of their prison.

Another tactic you should consider…and I can't believe I'm saying this…is to just let them be. If you've tried to get them reassigned to no avail and there's no way to assign them work around their passions, then your best bet might just be to let it go and focus on other more urgent things. If the Prisoner is quietly doing his work and not disrupting the team dynamic, then don't create a problem you can't solve. You're not off the hook for continuing to try to motivate and inspire them as part of your team; just realize that you might not win that one.

Some of you are probably wondering what you should do with the project Prisoner who, frankly, needs to be kicked off the team. They aren't team players and they just suck the joy out of the room every time they walk in the door. They don't want to be there and, by golly, everyone's gonna know about it. To be honest, this isn't the norm and it's rare that a PM will need to get serious about removing a resource.

If you do have to go down this road, there are a couple of things to bear in mind. First, have you done all you can to turn this person and the situation around? Second, does the Prisoner realize your next steps will involve escalations to their manager? Third, do you have specific, documented evidence that the Prisoner is not meeting her commitments? As I mentioned, this is a rare occurrence but don't take it lightly. You're messing with someone's career and livelihood, so make sure you've got the facts to back up your request that she be removed from the team. Not quite comfortable taking this step? Well, to be blunt, suck it up! The rest of your team is counting on you to address the problem in a timely manner. Remember that you are the team leader and you have a commitment to each member to provide an environment that is conducive to getting the work done. It's pretty simple to fix this problem for both your team and the Prisoner with a little effort. Just remember: the worst thing you can do is ignore the elephant under the rug and hope it will go away on its own.

Managing Up

Despite what you might think, the process for managing stakeholder expectations of those who outrank you is pretty straightforward. Over the years, I've learned a lot about this area and have come to realize that there're really two three-step processes for managing this type of stakeholder.

To Influence a Decision

Step 1: Believe that you can and should approach anyone who is higher up the food chain than yourself. This is a biggie and frankly it's where most PMs falter when it comes to managing up. I hear many people say things such as, "Oh I couldn't go talk to the VP of Engineering," or "My boss would have kittens if I went and talked to his boss!" Well, that could be, although I believe it's a biological impossibility, but, to be frank, that's almost never the case. Most people would be surprised to hear that those higher-ups actually want to hear from you. Further, if your boss is any good at all, then they should be fine with you talking to their boss. Sure, they may want to understand what you are going to propose to their boss, and if you're lucky they will give you some solid coaching on how to influence the higher-ups.

Step 2: Really understand the higher-up's point of view. What is their primary interest in your project or the topic under discussion? What are the major initiatives of the organization that this person is responsible for? What are the budget implications for this person? What are the business drivers at play here? Is there a significant political implication to the discussion and its output? Finally, what type of communicator is she? Do you need to go in armed with data or a really good story?

Step 3: Go in with multiple recommendations. It's your job as the PM to bring options to the table. The goal here is to provide alternate solutions even if they seem unrealistic to you. Provide the smorgasbord and then let the higher-ups have at it. With multiple recommendations you are doing two things. You are appealing to the higher-up's ego and you're leveraging his experience. Trust me, nothing makes a GM perk up and pay attention more than the words, "I need a priority call here"—or, even better, "We need your help making a tough business decision." Nothing makes a person's heart go pitty-pat like an appeal to their ego by verbally acknowledging their positional authority. Oh, and remember you get paid no matter which option you have to go execute. ☺

To Build a Credible Reputation

Step 1: Follow the steps in the previous section.

Step 2: Never miss an opportunity to speak to the higher-up. This is basic Stakeholder Management 101 and you know the drill: "How was your weekend?" "Did you hear? We finished the final code development yesterday!" "Got any advice about how to get that latest budget change approved?" "Gee, your lunch looks better than mine." Remember, a person isn't defined by their position on the org chart, and those same techniques you use with the recalcitrant lab tech will work just fine with the marketing manager, but you have to step up and actually approach them.

Step 3: Brag about your team's accomplishments. Okay, this really is an extension of Step 2. However, when you are trying to build a solid reputation with those higher up the ladder than you, bragging is even more critical. You see, it's entirely possible that the GM you're sharing the elevator with may not know that your team just powered on that new control module in record-breaking time. You really do need to tell them that. Remember, if the person is higher up the ladder than you, then they probably have oversight to more work than you and the depth of her understanding about what's going on for every project is probably pretty shallow. So go ahead and brag your head off.

There you have it: **Melanie's Easy a-One-and-a-Two Three-Step Program for Managing Up**. It's not that hard once you get past Step 1, so take a minute and ask yourself if you really are comfortable talking to your boss's boss. If not, what's holding you back? A real "special" kinda boss or your own perception of what would happen? Sure, I've worked for the kitten-producing boss before and that can hamper your ability to actively engage with higher-ups…but it sure doesn't stop you from working to build a credible reputation with anyone in the org.

Communicating with Difficult People

Everyone in today's work force is expected to be able to "work with difficult people." In most cases, it's possible to minimize your interaction with the difficult few and still get your job done. However if you're a PM, then you just can't avoid 'em. Nope, you've got to be the one to face down Wyatt Earp in the middle of the dusty street at high noon. Of course, what you really want to do is avoid or manage the confrontation so that it's not a shootout in front of your entire team, so to do that you need to be better than average at dealing with difficult people. It's also helpful to realize that it's not that the other person is "difficult" so much as it is that they are bad communicators.

It's Them, Not Me

The first thing you need to do when dealing with a bad communicator is to get your head right. I always assume that it's my responsibility to make myself clear enough that the other person understands the point I'm trying to make. Further, it's also my responsibility to understand the point the other person is trying to make. This is a mindset and once you start taking responsibility for the effectiveness of the communication, you will find yourself dealing with a lot fewer "bad" communicators.

Okay, okay, I know what you're thinking…on to the good stuff!

What Do You Do about a Serial Interrupter?

As I see it, you need a two-pronged approach to the *Serial Interrupter*. First, stop the interrupter directly after her first attempt to interrupt you by saying something like this: "Hold on, Melanie, I wasn't finished speaking." Don't use a whiny or pissy tone of voice; instead, use your grown-up, professional one to say this. Note that this tactic may or may not work, but it's always a good starting point. Now if your serial interrupter is unstoppable, catch her as she is leaving the meeting for a quick, private chat. Here you want to call attention to the behavior by saying something like this: "You know, Melanie, you might not realize this, but you interrupted me five times in the last meeting. I frankly do not appreciate it. In the future, can you please show me some professional respect and allow me to finish my thought without interruption?" Again, use that grown-up, professional voice and be gracious when the other person apologizes, as they most often will do, when confronted directly with the behavior. Sure, this isn't a comfortable conversation, but you owe it to your colleague to show them respect by pointing out their bad behavior.

What Do You Do about Someone Who Doesn't Actually Listen to You?

These are the folks bonded with their cell phones, laptops, tablets, anyone else walking by, and so on. By far the best tactic I've found for dealing with *Someone Who Just Doesn't Listen* to me is to just stop talking. Let that "dead air" develop and eventually the bad communicator will make eye contact with you and give you their undivided attention. Here's where you say something like this: "Look, Melanie, you seem to be pretty busy now and can't devote your attention to this topic. Why don't I reschedule for another time when you can concentrate on this?" If your bad communicator is a hard case, then they'll relent and promise to focus on your conversation...for all of five minutes and then their bad behavior will resume. This is time to get tough and say something along these lines: "Okay, Melanie, you clearly can't focus on or participate in the conversation. I'll send you an email with the pertinent data and you can let me know if you have any questions." At this point, pack up your toys and go do something productive with your time. This person is basically wasting your time, and it's up to you how long you let it go on. Take control of the communication, find a better forum for conveying your data, and move on.

What Do You Do If Someone Just Doesn't Understand Your Point?

If *someone just doesn't understand your point*, you need to step back from the act of making that point and start asking some questions. This goes something like this: "Okay, I think we aren't on the same page here. Here's what I think you meant …. Is this what you were thinking?" Also ask yourself what pertinent point the other person is missing and then see if you can figure out why that is. This is where trying to walk in the other person's shoes is invaluable. Once you understand their context, then you can help them understand yours. Remember, the responsibility for effective communication lies with you.

What Do You Do If Someone's Locked into a Weird, Repetitive Loop?

If *someone's locked into a weird, repetitive loop*, there's a simple trick for breaking it. When you get a word in edgewise, say something like this: "Okay, I think you're saying that Melanie really deserves a promo, right? Did I get the point you were trying to make there?" Basically, the person repeating the same argument ad nauseam doesn't think you understand their position. Parrot it back to them and ask for confirmation of your understanding. This one works most of the time, so if you take just one strategy away from this discussion, make it this one.

What Do You Do with Folks Who Write Really Long Emails?

For those *folks who write really long emails*, try this tactic. Reply to their message with something like this: "Melanie, what specifically do you want me to do? There's a lot of data in the email below but it's unclear to me what and when you need my support. Please clarify." Note that it's imperative here that you keep your response succinct and professional. This may not "fix" the other person, but it will send the message that their email message was too complex.

What Do You Do When Someone's Data Are Shaky?

For the *person who doesn't sound confident in their data* or the point they are making, you need to understand a bit more about what's going on. If they lack confidence in their own ability, you simply say: "You know, Melanie, I trust your judgment here. What is your professional recommendation?" If you get the feeling that they need more time (or need to do more research), then let them off the hook by saying something like this: "This seems to be more complex than we originally thought. Do you need more time to analyze the data? This is an important decision and I think we need to do due diligence and make sure we understand the data before moving forward." Note that this can be tricky because you don't want to devote a lot more time to analysis, but you do need to respect the professional judgment of your colleague.

What Do You Do about the Rambler?

Now the one you've all been waiting for…what to do about the *Rambler*? (Cue Merle Haggard's "Ramblin' Fever.") To address the rambling conversation, you need to figure out what's driving this behavior. If someone is dreading your reaction to her data, you will hear this in the "dance-around-the-topic" nature of their conversation. In short, they don't feel "safe" conveying this message. To address this, you need to re-establish that "safe" feeling. You can do this by saying something like: "You know, Melanie, while I may not like your update, I'm not going to shoot the messenger." Managing your body language and tone of voice can also go a long way to re-establishing safety. Now another reason for a rambling dissertation could be that the person doing the rambling hasn't thought through the entire point, process, or dataset. Some people process their thoughts orally and you just have to be patient and let them think out loud. This can be frustrating but, again, you need to look deeper to understand what's driving this oral road trip. Last, you might have heard (or experienced) the egg-timer method of speeding people up. Basically, the idea is that you set a time limit—say, two minutes—and then let the other person speak. Once the timer dings, it's buh-bye and on to the next topic and person. I've heard from plenty of people who've been on the wrong side of that timer and have come to the conclusion that its short-term effectiveness is negated by the long-term animosity it engenders. In short, keep those egg-timers in the kitchen and out of your colleagues' faces.

So there you have it: a few ideas for how to deal with bad communicators and move toward more effective communication.

Pass the Brie…Or How to Deal with Whiners

Now what about that most frustrating of teammates: the *Whiner*? I'm convinced that the world is made up of whiners and those who have to listen to someone else whine…and we all seem to alternate between the two as the situation warrants. It would be naïve to assume that I never whine or expect that my teams always be made up of non-whiners. There's always one (or five!) in the bunch and for PMs these folks present a unique challenge.

Here are some tips and tricks for dealing with whiners—**Melanie's "Want-Some-Cheese-with-that-Whine?" Strategies:**

- The most important thing to do when dealing with a whiner is to *stop whining yourself.* Yep, your own discontent with the situation just might be the cheese to the other person's whine.

- *Be Switzerland.* As the PM you should represent each person on your team equally, which means that you can't agree that Melanie is a super slacker. Instead, you've got to help the whiner see things from Melanie's perspective and hopefully convince him that the situation isn't as black and white as he thinks.

- *Put yourself in the whiner's shoes.* What's really going on here? From what grapes does this whine come? Is there something to be addressed that's not obviously related to the house whine?

- Now if your whiner has a *problem with a teammate* and wants you to get involved, consider a couple of strategies. First, encourage him to go talk to his nemesis directly and resolve the issue. Second, remind the whiner that you extend the same professional courtesy to his nemesis that you do to him. In short, don't take sides.

- *Just listen.* Sometimes all the whiner really needs is to be listened to. They don't expect you to solve their problem and they don't want to escalate something. Rather, what they need is a friendly face to vent to a little.

- *Don't get sucked into soap opera* à la *Days of Our Lives.* Remember, you're Switzerland.

- Throw the *TMI* card when the whiner starts going down an avenue that's too personal or makes you uncomfortable. It really is okay to stop the other person and say, "Whoa! That's more information than I need. Let's get back to the work-related discussion."

The key to dealing with a whiner is to step back and look at the discussion from a different perspective. Reframe your perspective and try to help the other person do so as well. Oh, and remember, we all whine from time to time, so cut your colleagues some slack and focus on helping them put down the glass.

Crap! It Really Is Me, Not Them

Now let's talk about the most common habits of bad communicators and what you should be doing about them…when *you* have these bad habits!

You might be a *Bad Communicator* if…

- You interrupt others.

- You don't listen to what others say.

- You don't understand the other person's point of view.

- You repeat yourself all the time—seriously, you repeat yourself.

- You sound like you don't believe your own point.

- You ramble.

Now ask yourself, "Do I do any of these things?" If you're honest with yourself and the answer is, "Yeah, I do #1 all the time. Dang it! Now how do I fix that?"—try **Melanie's Fixes for Bad Communication Habits**.

How Do You Fix It If You Interrupt Others?

You interrupt others. Let's be honest here, there are a lotta folks doing this. Yep, I'm talkin' to *you*! How do you fix this bad habit? Well, frankly, you just need to stop interrupting people. Yeah, like you didn't know that one was coming right? Okay, here are a couple of techniques I use, because this is probably my worst communication habit:

- Keep a notepad handy and jot down your thoughts as they come while the other person is speaking. When they complete their thought and it's your turn, go ahead and verbally make your points. Taking the time to actually write or type my thoughts distracts me enough that I don't jump into the conversation as soon as the idea pops in my head.

- Hold a running mantra in your mind that goes something like this: "Don't talk now, it's not your turn." Yeah, this one is dorky, but it works surprisingly well for me. ☺

How Do You Fix It If You Don't Listen to or Understand Others?

You don't listen to what others say goes hand-in-hand with *you don't understand the other person's point of view.* To fix these, try jotting down notes to yourself about what the other person is saying. Try to identify the key points. This exercise in transcribing and interpreting what the other person is saying forces you to listen to them and make sense of what they are saying. This technique is especially useful in virtual meetings.

How Do You Fix It If You Repeat Yourself?

Realizing that you've just *repeated yourself* for the nth time is the first step to fixing this problem. Once I realize that I've become a broken record, I try to step back verbally and ask for confirmation that my point is being understood. This goes something like this: "Okay, that's what I think. Did you follow my logic there? Do you have any questions?" What I'm looking for here is for the other person to reiterate my argument to confirm that they understood the point I thought I was making. For what it's worth, this tactic works in reverse if you're stuck with someone who continually repeats their points.

Do You Believe What You're Saying?

Do you *really believe what you're saying?* If so, then why doesn't anyone believe that? First, if you honestly can't get behind your point 100%, then you need to reframe your argument or point so that you can. When it comes to communication, sincerity trumps all other characteristics. If you can't say it and mean it, then don't say it or change your message. Second, you need to sound confident of your argument. If you're not sure it's right, then why should anyone else be swayed by your oration?

How Do You Fix It If You're a Rambler?

Last, we all know someone who rambles, but I suspect most of us don't realize that we do it ourselves. Obviously, the trick is to be succinct, but just how do you do that? You should also consider how much information you're trying to pass along. Does the other person need supporting data, or do they just need your conclusion or recommendation? Try to focus on what information you need to convey—what is it about your point that's actionable to the other party? Cut out all of the fluff and your own thought process so that you don't ramble. The other person can always ask for more data if they need it. Make sense?

Whew! a rather long list, I know. But I hope I've given you some good ideas for how to break some of your bad communication habits.

Closure Phase

Is Your Team Ready to Release?

All the planning that's been done and all of the execution of the plan leads to the *release*. Are you ready? How do you know? Have you and your team really done due diligence with this one?

Stop Being So Annoying

There comes a point in the project where the rubber hits the road. For most product development projects, this is the big Power-On. For software projects, it's the Release to Production environment. During this event, most of the project team is focused on executing a test plan, and there's a lot riding on the outcome. Will this project be a go? Does the design work as intended? Or will there be a catastrophic failure? Inquiring minds all want to know, they want to know ASAP, and they expect the PM to be able to answer those questions PDQ. That's a lot of pressure on the PM to be in the know and to be able to deliver the right message to anxious stakeholders.

Unfortunately, many PMs go about staying "in the know" the completely wrong way, vastly annoying their team in the process. They are constantly underfoot, crowding up the lab, offering lame suggestions for troubleshooting, making distracting chitchat with anyone around them, and just generally getting in the way of the real work. I remember having to tromp over to the stupid airlock in the cleanroom to give a PM an update on the ongoing testing, because they were too lazy to go gown-up and enter the cleanroom properly. (Gee, apparently I still have some pent-up frustration about that, huh?) I can recall PMs trying to help with troubleshooting a technical problem for which they really didn't have expertise. Worse still, there's that annoying dude in the back of the lab trying to engage someone in a blow-by-blow recount of the previous night's episode of *The Office*. Bottom line? I've been the one doing the testing while the PM hovers over me like a West Texas thundercloud and it's really annoying, so I don't do that to my teams.

That's right, during the Power-On or Production Release I try not to hover, I don't offer troubleshooting suggestions, and I work really hard at keeping the distracting chatter to a minimum. What I focus on during these events is enabling the team. You see, I think it's the PM's job to make sure that each team member has what they need to carry out the testing. It's not my job to do the testing though. So, here are a few Do's and Don'ts for PMs during those "rubber hits the road" events:

Do

- *Take care of all of the logistics.* Reserve the lab space, submit the CRs, calendar the event, line up the grub, and so on.

- *Double-check that all of the required personnel are available and are planning to be at the event.* Extra points for rounding up the stragglers and getting them to the lab by the start time. (Yeah, I know that's not technically your job but from my experience there're always a few of these folks and if you want to start on time, someone—aka you!—needs to remind them that they have somewhere to be.)

- *Pay close attention to the team dynamic.* Is everyone working well together, or are they falling on each other like a pack of wild dogs? Is there someone who's getting overly stressed out or defensive? A well-timed joke or some calm direction can go a long way to maintaining a productive work environment.

- *Watch the clock.* Is the release going well? If it's not, how late should the team work? At what point should you, as the PM, call a halt and declare this one a draw to be picked up another day?

- *Facilitate a Go/No-Go decision* as soon as possible once the testing is done.

- *Be around but invisible.* I try to be highly available to smooth the way, facilitate a decision, defuse an escalating argument, and so forth. But I know I've really got it right when my team isn't really aware of my presence.

- *Wrap up the testing event on a high note.* If the testing was particularly difficult, remind the team how important this release is and congratulating them on staying the course. If it went smoothly, congratulate the team on flawless execution.

Don't

- *Wade into the discussion if you don't have something of value to add*—but make darn sure you understand the problem the team is trying to resolve and what compromises they take to resolve it.

- *Distract the team with idle chitchat.* They are there to do a job and they really don't appreciate your loud and entirely too personal cell phone conversation.

- *Be MIA.* You need to be highly available during these activities. Telling the team to call you if they "need anything" is abdicating your responsibilities.

- *Close the release activities on a down or sour note.* Do not tell them they could have done better or that the design was crap. Most importantly, don't single out an individual or functional group as the cause of a No-Go.

- *Hover!* You should be available and around, but you should not resemble a vulture waiting for roadkill to get still.

- *Make a production out of lunch.* Folks want to grab a quick bite and then get back to work. Also, be mindful of the food you're serving. For a release earlier this year I brought in Chicago-style pizza. Sure it was yummy, but then the guys started complaining about being really sleepy about 2 o'clock. D'oh!

So there you have it: some dos and don'ts for facilitating that big event. Just remember that it's no longer your job to do the testing. Instead, you are there as a sort of fixer to make sure everything goes smoothly so the team can focus on their job—the actual testing.

Due Diligence

I really don't believe it's my job as the PM to inspect every work product my team produces and ensure that it's to an acceptable level of quality. If you do that, then you run perilously close to becoming a mircromanager. That said, I think I'm absolutely on the hook, as the leader of the team, to ensure that due diligence is done.

So what do I mean by *due diligence* in the context of project management? As I see it, it's the PM's responsibility to ensure that the work is done sufficiently to avoid harm to others, the environment, and/or property. This means that enough work and research has gone into producing the project's output that there's a reasonable expectation of safety and performance to specifications.

This sounds pretty straightforward doesn't it? Well, it's not and to demonstrate this, let me tell you a little story. Let's suppose that at one point in my career I worked in an engineering group and ran product development projects for them. This group was somewhat understaffed and certainly didn't manage their project pipeline, so there was always more work than people. I'm sure you can relate. During the course of my first project in this org, I brought up the need for a basic safety review of the design. These projects produced a product that was distributed within the company as well as to external customers. The engineering management team felt *very* strongly that no such review was needed. To be honest, I think the root cause of their opposition was the fact that they perceived an additional design review by an "outside" party as a roadblock that would only slow them down. They believed that what they were producing was a safe product and they didn't need no stinkin' safety engineer to tell them what they already knew. So they had their reasons and I could kinda see their point, but these were products used by people in development labs around the world and I just couldn't reconcile waiving the safety review. Let's just say that it was a long, frustrating battle that I won. Then again, they might have dropped those safety reviews after I left the org. Now I'm not trying to air dirty laundry or anything here, but rather I want to point out that this stuff can get murky and difficult.

Now, how do you as the PM ensure that due diligence is done on your projects? First you have to understand what your organization expects your team do with respect to compliance, safety, legal, design, validation, and so on. You should also understand what's done in your specific industry. A safety review for a new software application is going to be quite different than one for a 300mm physical vapor deposition (PVD) process chamber. Now I'm not saying that you need to be the expert on the specifics of the safety review; rather, I'm saying that you need to understand what makes up the appropriate review and *you* need to ensure that it gets done as part of the project work. One way I do this is to make sure these items are tasks that are tracked within the project—that is, they are line items on the schedule. Further, I use a *release readiness review* checklist for every project. This checklist, which I will talk about in the next section, includes line items for anything I deem a due-diligence requirement. This can span such things as manufacturing approving the project documentation that they will use going forward, to verifying that all quality defects are dispositioned appropriately.

Okay, let's be honest here—this isn't hard and all you really need to do is put some structure in place to ensure due diligence is happening. When the software developers try to beg off of doing a peer review of their code, say no. Pay attention to the disposition of defects and the test coverage. Make sure that the users of project documentation agree that the documents are adequate. Track compliance requirements closely. Yeah, I know you're already doing this stuff…see, I told you it was easy.

In my opinion, my professional reputation is on the line with each project and I have a responsibility to my team, the company, and myself to ensure that any project I lead produces safe and usable products—and that takes due diligence.

Release Readiness

Now let's talk about one of those tricks of the trade every PM should know: how to do a *release readiness review* (RRR) or assessment. When you're at the end of the execution phase, there's a lot going on and your team is most likely getting ramped up to release the project. One of the key tools in a PM's arsenal is a robust RRR. Over the years, I've participated in RRRs as robust as a day-long program review and as loose as a pencil-whipped checklist that forever resides in a bureaucratic black hole. One thing that became clearer as I gained experience was the fact that the better prepared the team was for a release, the smoother it went. One of the best ways to prepare for a project release, in my book, is to do a real readiness review. By *real*, I mean an honest, no-holds-barred team review of the work that's been done and the work that remains before you unleash your project's deliverable(s) on the world.

All RRRs come down to a checklist of some sort. Sadly, most organizations either don't have one, or the checklist they do have isn't very useful for the PM. To be effective, an RRR checklist needs to be specific to your project and its deliverables. It also needs to be specific to your organization and its project lifecycle. When I join a new organization, I usually end up creating a more detailed checklist than is currently on offer. After creating a number of these checklists, I have developed a solid understanding of what they need to contain. So, whether you're trying to assess the usefulness of your org's current checklist or you are trying to create a specific one for your current project, here are the key areas you need to think about when it comes to assessing how ready your project is for release:

- **Development considerations.** Are all of the required design and requirements documents updated to reflect the "as-designed" state of the project deliverables? Was due diligence observed—that is, was a peer review done on the design? Are the known limitations of the design adequately and properly documented? Have all required reviews (safety, OSHA, environmental, and so on) been completed?

- **Testing due diligence.** Are there any open, unresolved, high, or critical bugs? Are there any bugs without *long-term corrective action* (LTCA) plans in place? Are all known defects documented in the appropriate tool of record? Were all of the requirements properly verified? Was the test coverage adequate to ensure a solid design?

- **Release activities.** Are the hardware/software needed for the release available and functioning as expected? Has the release been scheduled? Are the required personnel available on the day(s) of the release? Have the necessary change requests and exit reviews been submitted or scheduled?

- **Operations/manufacturing considerations.** Has adequate training been provided to the end users of the project deliverable(s)? Have the required documents (training, testing, operation, and so on) been reviewed and approved by the end user reps? Does manufacturing have an adequate volume of material in stock to meet anticipated orders? Have all of the operations/manufacturing business process tools been updated? Has the end customer been advised of any changes to order placement or delivery?

Obviously there are other considerations depending on the nature of your project's deliverables. You might need to think about post-release activities or marketing collateral. The point is to do a thorough review, so you should always tailor the checklist for each specific project.

I generally do a RRR a week before the planned release, and it's the primary topic of that week's standing team meeting. There are two other, secondary benefits to doing a RRR beyond making sure that all the ducks are lined up. First, it gives the recipients of the project deliverables one last chance to speak up if the quality of the deliverables is not up to their expectations. I make a point to ask the recipients if they agree that the work is done. This ensures that there are no surprises after the release. The other benefit is that review enhances and drives accountability with the team members. The entire team is accountable for the quality of the release and, more specifically, each team member will have deliverables they are accountable for. This review is the opportunity for each team member to stand up and be held accountable for his or her work.

Finally, for that first pass of the RRR checklist, I don't expect all items to be closed. It's not uncommon for a few things to be lingering, but every item on the checklist should have a clear closure commit date at this point. If you find items on the checklist that have been completely missed, then the team needs to seriously consider pushing out the release. It's worth noting that while it's extremely rare to find such a serious miss, it's not uncommon to have final reviews such as legal and safety still open. At the end of the RRR, you should have a punch list of items that must be closed before the project can release. Everyone on the team has a clear idea of what's open and where to prioritize their time. I do one last review a day or two before the release activities and give everyone on the team one last chance to voice any concerns or reservations about the release...this is the Go/No-Go for the release activity.

The Go/No-Go

Now I'll talk about how to facilitate and conduct a Go/No-Go meeting. Make no mistake: this is where the rubber hits the road when it comes to project management. Orchestrate this meeting poorly and you and your team will spend weeks cleaning up the aftermath. This is one of those inflection points for team dynamics, and PMs would be smart to put their game face on for it.

We'd been working on this product development project since early February. It was a software security application that necessitated a very carefully planned and executed set of release activities. We started bright and early on Thursday and everything went smoothly. The hardware was proven out and the new application was successfully installed. We were ready to rock with the application testing! Things continued to go smoothly and as planned throughout most of Friday. By lunchtime, the team and I smelled the sweet scent of unqualified success. Around 3 PM, things started unraveling. We started finding documentation non-conformances and, while those need to be corrected, they really are not a big problem. Next we found one, two (yikes!), three medium-to-low-priority software bugs. Still no big deal, but it was no longer the unqualified success I'd been envisioning. Then it happened—the fatal showstopper bug. Clearly there was going to be no release that day. By this point in time, everyone was frustrated and my carefully nurtured, constructive team dynamic was balanced on a knife edge.

There comes a point in every project when the PM needs to facilitate a Go/No-Go meeting. Essentially this is the one moment the entire team has been working for. Is the product ready for prime time? If so, then it's a Go.

This is the moment of truth and, unless the data is extremely conclusive, there's likely to be a heated discussion. It's just a fact of life that there will sometimes be No-Gos as well. It's true that you get better at dealing with it as you gain experience as a PM, but facilitating a No-Go decision is never easy.

Part of what makes the Go/No-Go meeting so challenging is the fact that your team has been working on this project for a long time and they justifiably feel some pride in accomplishing their objective and delivering the product. Hearing that No-Go is like being rear-ended on the drive home. It's that frustrating and jarring. Further, you just don't call someone else's baby ugly, so when engineers hear others criticizing their creation they get a tad miffed. So if you're in a situation like I was, you can understand that the meeting is sort of like a sweatin' stick o' dynamite just waiting to go off in your hand. So what do you do? Having danced the No-Go dance a few times, I've figured out some tactics for handling this type of meeting:

- *Set the expectation for the discussions hard and fast.* Begin the meeting by clearly stating that you aren't interested (at that time) in solutions, root causes, potential causes, who may or may not have been slacking, or the like. Follow that by explaining the goal of the meeting, which is to determine if the release is a Go or a No-Go.

- *Ask the technical lead or the test lead to summarize the release activity results.* Here's where you want to keep the discussion focused on data and not speculation. In my experience there's a big difference between hardware and software projects at this point. Hardware projects will have a very clear set of passing criteria that are based on actual measurements; software projects have a set of tests that need to be executed with a predetermined quality level. Hardware exit/release criteria are quantitative, whereas for software projects those criteria are more qualitative.

- *Use a round table approach.* Tell the team that you will go around the table and ask everyone if they believe the release is a Go. Ask those team members whose position is No-Go to state their primary concerns. Go around the table collecting input, but skip the project sponsor and save him or her for the last input.

- *Keep the discussion focused on the two pieces of information requested*—namely, Go/No-Go and primary concerns. You will have to use the rathole card and probably more than once. Remember, as the meeting facilitator your job is to keep the meeting focused and on track.

- *Make the call.* Remember that unless your team has been using the consensus decision-making model, this isn't a democracy and not everyone's vote counts equally. For instance, you should never go against your project sponsor's vote. I always set my teams up to use consultative decision making because I find it to be the most efficient way to keep things going with the highest level of buy-in.

- *Wrap it up decisively and make a solid attempt to bolster the team's spirits in the event of a No-Go.* I always thank everyone for the huge amount of work that has gotten us this far. I also suggest that everyone put it away for the weekend, stating that we'll attack the problem fresh the next week. It's important to remind people of their accomplishments, and it's equally important to give the team a break before tackling whatever caused that No-Go.

- The last thing you have to do, and you must do it right away, is *send out meeting minutes.* You need to do this quickly because, trust me, word is gonna spread like a California wildfire. You need to get the facts out there to dispel any erroneous rumors that may spring up.

Finally, a comment on role modeling and leadership. This meeting is always tense and can resemble that stick of dynamite. It's up to the PM to role-model the behavior expected here. This is not the time to joke around, nor is it the time to multitask. It's a serious decision, so act like it and I promise that your team will follow your lead. It's also not the time to indulge in a witch-hunt or a blamefest. It's time to put your game face on and be the professional PM you are.

Deliver It Late

Have you ever been in this scenario? Your project is now six weeks behind schedule and there's just no way to catch up without ridiculous and heroic efforts from your entire team. Sure, you can deliver part of what was promised for this project, but the writing's on the wall that only divine intervention is going to ensure that all of the committed deliverables are met. By now your team is tired—I mean, really exhausted both mentally and physically. They've got nothing left to give and you think you can motivate them into one final push toward the goal line? Uh huh... are you sure about that? When you get to this point on a project, it's time to retreat and figure out what your next course of action should be.

Okay, hold on to your hats folks, 'cause what I'm about to suggest may sound a tad inflammatory. It's time to consider delivering late. Yep, it just may be time to figure out some damage control. The natural tendency in this scenario is to rally the troops for one more push. Of course, we've all been there, and we already know that there's no such thing as "one final push," 'cause the pushing and shoving just keeps coming. But let me ask you this: have you ever considered the implications of delivering late? Not those implications! Yeah, we all know about ticked-off customers, disgruntled management, and smirking peers. The implications I'm referring to here are things all PMs should consider whenever they are developing recovery plans.

When the situation is already bad, like the one I described previously, the absolute last thing a PM should do is make it worse—but that's often what happens, especially when the team is desperately trying to recover a slipped schedule. All the yelling, cajoling, and bribery in the world will only get you so far, and it's going to hurt your relationship with the entire team. Unfortunately, when you and your team are in a real time crunch, things don't always go as planned. People are tired and they are rushing around, so it's not uncommon for mistakes to be made. Bad mistakes that show up later in some really unpleasant ways. Now's the time to ask yourself what the consequences are for delivering late—and, face it, it might make a lot of sense to do so.

So when would I deliberately deliver a project late? It makes sense to deliver late when the customer can use a subset of the project deliverables immediately. If you partner with your customer, you can often find a partial solution that they can live with while giving your team some breathing room. A year from now, what will folks remember? The fact that your team was four weeks late or the fact that the deliverables are buggy, insufficient, or just generally crappy? Yep, from a long-term perspective, poor quality trumps on-time delivery every time, hands down. Now if my customer can't accept a partial delivery, my team, the key stakeholders, and I must decide what's more important…schedule, scope, or quality.

If it's schedule that dominates the triple constraint, then we go forward with that "one-last-push" strategy, knowingly burning out the team in that heroic effort to deliver something on time. Sometimes quality doesn't come out on top and you're going to knowingly put out a crappy product—which means that your team will have a lot more cleanup to do after the project release, so make sure that you negotiate to hold onto the team members long enough to close everything out. If scope is on the chopping block, then realize that you might need to tee up a second, follow-on project to complete the axed scope at a later date. But don't fool yourselves here; it's called the *triple constraint* for a reason and there's no such thing as a free lunch. You just can't have it all without detrimental impacts to your team members.

So, the bottom line here is that you should consider delivering late, because it just might make sense. I truly believe that you need a deliberate strategy, as opposed to just letting things play out as they will. Take the time necessary to understand your options, including an honest evaluation of all of them. Whatever you decide, it needs to be grounded in the business needs the project is supposed to address. Anything less is a failure to manage the project.

On Time, Under Budget, Delivered as Promised…and Still a Failure?

Call me a cynic, but every time I hear someone spout, "on time, under budget, all requirements met," I mentally roll my eyes. I seriously doubt that there are PMs out there who always deliver "successful" projects on time, under budget and still meet all of the value promised by the project. It's not that I think the PMs are lyin' like rugs; it's that I don't believe "on time" and "under budget" tell the whole story. You see, I know I've delivered projects on time, without spending more money than planned, all while meeting the original requirements…yet those projects were complete failures to my way of thinking.

So, what truly determines whether a project is a success? I think the answer lies in whether the business objectives of the project were met. I'm sure you don't have to think too hard to come up with an example of a project that you and your team executed flawlessly, only to see it never take off in the market or users never adopt it. For me, there was the residual gas analyzer that we developed in conjunction with a vendor. It was a thing of technical beauty with a material cost that was downright seductive…but the effort to get it qualified as a tool of record was an insurmountable hurdle. Conversely, there was a project on which the customer was positively delighted with our work, yet we delivered weeks late and let's just say that the conformance to our internally required processes "could have been better." That one was a runaway success, but you sure couldn't tell it by the project metrics. Go figure.

There's also another component to overall project success, which you rarely hear mentioned, and that's what the project has done to the morale of the organization. We've all worked on projects where the pressure to meet a schedule could best be described as a *meat grinder*. Any PM who's been practicing more than a few years has been in that uncomfortable position of having to motivate a team to work weekends, holidays, and nights to recover a project schedule. This kind of project just kills your team's morale. Worse, this kind of effort can frequently set a precedent for the pace of work or duration of future projects. If you also factor in the poor planning, monitoring, and control that allowed the project to get so far behind as to require a Herculean effort to get it back on track, then you have the MacDaddy of all morale killers on your hands. If you eventually hit the schedule, deliver all of the requirements, and the customer is super-happy, is that a success? I'd say no, and it sure as shootin' isn't going to be repeatable.

So let's say that you're a PM with such a project. On paper it looks good— "on time, under budget, all requirements met"—but you know down in your gut that it was not a success. This obviously doesn't happen all that often, but when it does it's pretty surreal. Everyone is singing your praises and your team has moved on to greater glory on some other project, but you just know it's only a matter of time before the shiny wears off, and it becomes obvious that the business objectives of the project weren't realized. What do you do? Well, this can be tricky, because you want to do due diligence and identify areas where more work is needed, but you don't want to damage your rep or that of your team. First and foremost, you have to raise the flag and point out the issues and gaps with the way the project was released. Don't be surprised if there are certain elements who refuse to see them, though. Do your best to get those gaps and issues fixed, then let it go and move on to your next project. Second, when you deliver the wrap-up review of the project, your story should go something like this: "The team did a stand-up job accomplishing a huge amount of work in a limited time, but there's still more to do." The goal here is to present your team as winners who "did a stand-up job" and some significant work, all while acknowledging that there's more to do. Make sense?

I recently heard a talk at a local PMI event where the speaker pointed out that you need to understand the business drivers for each requirement. Fail to deliver those drivers and you really can't call the project a success. Sometimes I think it's easy to get distracted by a laser-like focus on schedule performance and lose sight completely of the business problem your project needs to solve. Sure, you can pull off the "on time, under budget, all requirements met" hat trick, but whether or not your project was a success really depends on how well the original business needs were met—so stay focused and make sure what you deliver really is a success.

Leading When the Music Stops

Ever been to a *cakewalk*? This was a quaint and rather popular social fundraiser when I was a kid. The idea here is that a table holding a delicious cake is placed in the middle of a circle of chairs. Participants walk around the chairs while some jaunty tune plays. The music is then stopped suddenly and everyone scrambles for a chair. The poor schmuck who's left standing after the scramble loses; a chair is taken away, and the music is played again. This continues until there's only one lucky winner sitting in the last chair and that guy goes home with the cake. In project management, the music stops and your project is the one left without funding or resources or support. What do you do then?

Yet Another Re-Org

Corporations reorganize and shuffle product roadmaps based on changing market conditions, and I'm betting that some of you are managing projects with suspect futures—or at the very least, with a scope of work that is in doubt. This type of ambiguity can really de-focus your team and that can be a very bad thing. For instance, on one of my projects, there's been a lot of discussion as to whether or not a particular functionality will be cut by the customer. The last thing I want to happen is for my team to stop working on developing that functionality, only to find out four weeks later that the customer decided to keep it and now we are month behind schedule. When you are managing a project in this type of environment, you need to consider several things to ensure that your team stays focused and on track:

- **Make sure the *plan of record* (POR) is crystal clear to the entire team**. This sounds simple but, trust me, it's not. There are probably a lot of hallway discussions and plenty of speculation in your team meetings, so it's not surprising that someone would walk away with a different understanding of what the POR is today. To combat this, I make sure I communicate what the POR is in a very clear and succinct manner. I wrap up each team meeting by stating that the "POR has not changed, so let's stay focused on what we need to accomplish right now." Heck, I've even been known to state the POR directly in the meeting minutes if the team seems especially de-focused.

- **Manage your stakeholders so that they are not adding to the general confusion and speculation**. Here I coach the relevant stakeholders not to bring up potential scope changes to the team unless they have a high confidence that this new direction will become POR. Usually there are two stakeholders who are particularly bad about this: the technical lead and the engineering manager. You see, they believe that they are helping the team by giving everyone a head's-up. The unfortunate side effect of this head's-up mentality is that you will have team members who are honestly confused about what to work on or, worse yet, they will de-prioritize POR work since they believe it will be axed at some point in the near future. So, if some of your stakeholders are de-focusing your team, have a friendly chat with them and ask them to stop.

- **Squelch the speculative conversations** and keep the team focused on the schedule and what needs to be done next. It's important to realize that until your POR officially changes, your team is still on the hook for their current customer commits. It's very easy for a team in this environment to get sidetracked by a speculative conversation and totally derail your regular meeting. Do not let this happen!

- Finally, if you aren't already doing this, you need to **enforce stringent change control**. Sometimes if you have a small colocated team you can be, shall we say, "a bit lax" on enforcing change control— but for the most part rigorous change control is very necessary. So whenever there's a large scope change looming on the horizon, make sure that your entire team is actually following its change control process. Now you might think this is a no-brainer, right?

Wrong! What usually happens is that some team members are overachievers and they will inevitably start implementing these scope changes before they are actually approved. Trust me on this one! I've seen this happen over and over again. On the one hand, it's a good thing as it means that the change is implemented very fast. On the other hand, if the end decision is not to implement the change, somebody on your team needs to undo some work they've already finished in anticipation of the change going through. No one likes to tear apart something they've already built, so put the brakes on any work that's not POR.

So there you have it, a few considerations for what you need to do to keep your team focused in an environment where the project or program scope is in flux. As for my team, we finally got clear direction from the higher-ups and I've already submitted a change request for the team to review. Onward toward the newly revised scope of work!

Breaking Up Is Hard to Do

I'm sure I'm not the only PM who's found out a key team member is leaving the company. How we, as PMs, react when we find out one of our team members is leaving has a huge impact on the overall team dynamic. As I see it, there are three basic responses: pout like a three-year-old; pretend it's not happening and/or pay minimal attention to who will pick up the work; or—the best by far—actively help make the teammate's move as smooth as possible for both that person and the rest of the team. Sadly, I see more of the first two than the third. Obviously, this isn't strictly limited to PMs, and it applies to all leaders and managers who interact with the person who's leaving.

First, let's talk about worst possible response—option #1: pout like a three year old. Incredibly I've seen this response more than a rational person would expect. There was the manager who gave the departing employee the silent treatment for two weeks, all while sitting directly across from the guy. Interestingly, the employee had struggled with the decision to leave until he got the cold shoulder from a boss who'd previously been very supportive. Funny how that response from his manager solidified the decision to leave the company. Then there was the program manager who felt personally insulted about my impending job change, even though it was a career move on my part. Again, that person's reaction really helped me see that I was making the right decision. Sure, we all get upset and frustrated when we find out a key resource is leaving. How we handle that frustration is critical to maintaining a solid team dynamic. Do you really want to work on a project or in an organization in which the departing person is subjected to a vicious gauntlet on the way out? I don't, and I refuse to allow that to happen on my teams.

Almost as bad as pouting or open hostility is the second option: to pretend that it's not happening. Burying your head in the proverbial sand will not change the fact that your teammate is leaving. As the PM, your job is to negotiate with the resource owners and work out a reasonable replacement. You're also going to need to reassign some of the work to the rest of the team to make sure everything stays on track while the new person comes up to speed. This is PM 101 and failing to do it is just like the software engineer who neglects to follow coding standards. It's sloppy and someone else will have to clean up your mess. Making sure there's adequate coverage for the work is the absolute minimum you should do as a PM. Do you really want to work on the team that gets so far behind because someone left and work didn't get done? Didn't think so…

Yes, the best possible response is #3: to actively help make the teammate's move as smooth as possible. As you support your teammate's move, you are sending a clear message to your team that you want them to succeed in their careers. What kinds of things can you do to be supportive? Proactively reassign work so that the leaving person has more time to focus on the things they need to do as part of leaving. This is pretty simple to do, and the goodwill this engenders from all involved is priceless. You should also arrange for some sort of team get-together to celebrate this change. It takes about 10 minutes to organize a self-funded happy hour but, trust me, the person leaving will greatly appreciate it. Finally, the most helpful thing you can do is offer to extend your network to help the departing person with his or her transition. Can you recommend SMEs for the new job? How about providing a list of cool restaurants, points of interest, things to do, and so forth in the new location? All of these things are fairly straightforward to do and will be greatly appreciated. Now, why wouldn't you want to work on a team where the departing team member gets all the help she needs to make her next challenge easier?

When someone chooses to leave a team for a better opportunity, it really does matter how you manage that change. This is especially true for PMs because you can mitigate a very bad reaction from a functional manager just by being supportive. This makes a huge difference to the overall team dynamics. You have a choice here. You can send a message to your entire team that you expect unswerving loyalty and traitors will be punished to the full extent of your ability. Or you can send the message that you fully support each team member and their individual career goals. Remember, this isn't personal— these people aren't *your* team, no one is betraying you, and everyone needs to make career-changing decisions from time to time. Take a minute to think about the various job transitions in your own past, and I'm sure you'll find some good examples of how to handle this in a positive way. In the end, it comes down to treating your departing teammates how you'd like to be treated in a similar situation.

How to Lead after the Music Stops

You've just left the program team meeting where it was announced that the funding has evaporated and the program is toast. You're to keep your team focused until the end of the quarter, and then mothball the work. Oh, and while you're at it, don't mention the fact that the project is one of the walking dead to your team… don't want to incite a panic, do we? Ever been there? That nauseated feeling you're experiencing is just the precursor to all those awkward conversations you'll have with your team, your boss, and your customers before the end of the quarter gets here. Been there, done that, don't really want the T-shirt anymore. Or how about this: you've done the Disagree-and-Commit dance, you lost, and now you gotta lead right? What both of these scenarios have in common is a need for you to lead your team through something you disagree with. This is perhaps the most challenging scenario facing PMs. I should know—I've done it more than a few times and have come up with some observations about what does and doesn't work. So here goes with **How to Lead after the Music Stops**:

- *First, get your own head right.* You fought the good fight and you lost. Get over it! Seriously, the last thing your team needs is your ardent soliloquy on why you are right and "Management" is wrong.

- *Don't make it personal.* Sure it sucks and you feel bad but, trust me here, your team doesn't want to hear that. They're expecting leadership from you, not guilt. I once had a manager go on and on about how hard the decision was for him to make. I may be sorry about that fact, but I'm a lot more concerned about my own job stability.

- *Remind yourself and your team what it is that you actually get paid to do.* A former coworker of mine, a veritable RF genius, once told me that he looked at work as a trade-off. He was trading his time and ability for money. What John spent his time doing might or might not make sense to him, but he still benefited from the tradeoff. Sometimes it helps to remember that…just be careful how you remind others of that fact. No one likes to hear the equivalent of, "just be grateful you've got a job."

- *Paint the bigger picture.* Organizations often make strategic decisions that seem half-baked on the surface. You need to help your team understand the strategy in play. Sure, it won't make everyone's concerns go away, but it will provide context and that's a good thing.

- *Help the team get focused on what's expected of them next.* Which tasks need to be completed? When does the work need to be done? Who's going to do it? You get the picture here: drive a course of action rather than endless whine fests.

- *Figure out the "what's-in-it-for-me" equation for yourself and your team.* Even if you don't like the new direction, chances are there's something valuable there for you and your team. I'm talking new skills, contacts, opportunities, and the like.

- *Be real.* It's honestly okay to say things such as, "I don't know the answer to that," "That's a valid concern," or even, "I wish I had a better answer for you on that one." Then follow those comments up with the bigger picture and the "what's-in-it-for-me" perspective.

- Above all else, please *don't abdicate your own accountability.* It honestly turns my stomach to hear a senior person say, "I had nothing to do with that decision." I'd respect them a lot more if they took some ownership of the decision, explained why the decision was made, and provided some insight into what would change going forward.

- In that special case where you know something "bad" is about to go down but you are directed to *keep mum* about it, well that's just what you're supposed to do. That doesn't mean elaborate eye-rolling, grimaces, or other emotive facial expressions. Nor does it mean that you drop subtle (or not so subtle) hints about the impending doom. Rather, you must keep your trap shut. Really! It's a matter of professional integrity.

- *Develop some responses to the questions you expect and dread the most.* Don't forget to figure out a graceful way to say, "I can't comment on that at this time"—because I suspect you're gonna use that one a lot.

So there are my gleanings on how to lead when the music stops. To be honest, I didn't always do these things. In fact, the "not doing" or the "doing it badly" times are how I figured out what works. Here's hoping you can pick up a thing or two so you don't have to struggle so much the next time you find yourself in this position.

You Really Ought to Be Doing This

There are a few things PMs should be doing at the end of a project, but I'd bet my lunch money that many of you don't get to these tasks. The good news is that, while it can have a huge impact on how cleanly a project is wrapped up, none of these tasks is very difficult or time-consuming. Let me show you what you really should be doing at the end of a project.

Formal Project Closure

Project closure is one of those often-neglected areas of project management and that's a shame because it's not hard, doesn't take much time, and it's just good project management. Project teams usually dissolve like sugar stirred into iced tea at the end of a project. After a few swirls of the spoon, you'd never know the sugar was there, but after the ice stops swirling, you see this sugary residue collect at the bottom of the glass. On a project, this means that, although the team has all been reassigned, there are still these niggly things that remain undissolved, if you will. For instance, not all the data gets archived, thereby completely negating the efforts it took to generate it in the first place. There's usually only a token effort made to disposition the hardware used or developed. How many orphaned, dust-catching project remnants are sitting around your cube right now? More than you want, I bet! Worst of all are the cases in which the project just doesn't die for some of the team members.

Ever have to answer questions or provide support for something you finished a year ago? These are the consequences of not formally closing a project.

As the PM, it's your responsibility to perform project closure—just ask PMI if you don't believe me! Unfortunately, a lot of organizations don't document a closure process, so it's often hard to know what to do. Here's what I do, at a minimum, to close a project:

- *Request that all team members review any data they have on their respective hard drives and archive it appropriately.*

Tip If you are doing this via email, provide the link to increase the likelihood that it actually happens.

- *Go through your files and email to ensure that you've archived any critical project decisions, presentations, meeting minutes, and so forth.*

Tip I create a directory on my hard drive specifically to dump all of this stuff into during the project. When I find the time, I just open the file and start uploading. This is a great Friday afternoon activity because it requires very little brainpower!

- *Disposition all of the hardware acquired or generated by the project. If you can't find it a home, then make sure it gets scrapped appropriately.*

- *Perform some sort of lessons-learned or retrospective. While I'm not a fan of the bureaucracy that these processes often entail, I do believe it's worth spending an hour or so as a team discussing what went well, what didn't, and any best practices that should be communicated to others.*

- *Send out a formal project closure announcement. You should do this in addition to a final project presentation.*

Tip Be sure to identify any post-project sustaining support so your team members are off the hook... for the most part!

- *Sincerely thank each team member and coordinate appropriate recognition.*

- Finally, take this opportunity to *ask some (or all) of your team for feedback on your performance.* Everyone is pretty mellow at this point, so it's a good chance to get some thoughtful feedback and identify areas for improvement.

As you can see all of these items are pretty quick to do. Obviously, if your organization has a documented process, you'd follow that—but if not, then I hope this list helps.

How to Throw a Party

As Q4 comes to a screaming finish, PMs should be thinking about organizing a year-end celebration for their teams. December is usually a tough month for project work as there are always big milestones committed at the end of the year. PMs are crazy busy and, for many, taking the time to plan a celebration is just too far down the priority list to matter. I'm here to tell you that you really need to re-prioritize! Holiday or year-end celebrations can be very easy to pull off and they are one of the best ways to show your team your appreciation. Okay, I know what you're thinking: "Very easy to pull off? Is she delusional? I don't have the time for that!" I'm serious and you really can find the time to do this!

First let me break down how to organize a celebration for your team:

1. *Determine what type of event you want to throw.* A lunch is the easiest thing to do and will be the most convenient for the team and anyone else you want to invite.

2. *Determine funding.* Ask anyone in a position to funnel some cash your way to pay for the event—including your project sponsor, manager, and, heck, even your second-level manager.

3. *Determine where to party.* This can be as simple as a conference room in your building, or as extravagant as your budget and good taste allow.

4. *Determine the food.* There's something primal about breaking bread together, and what's a party without food? Be sure you consider silverware, plates, napkins, and so forth, and don't forget to have at least one vegetarian option.

5. *Determine some sort of activity but keep it small.* The best activity I've found is to post some flip charts around the room with questions such as "What was the hardest thing we accomplished this year?" and "What was the funniest thing that happened this year?" Everyone can walk around and jot down their answers and read those already posted.

6. *Ask key sponsors and stakeholders to swing by and say a few words.* Give others the opportunity to thank your team for their hard work, too.

Still not convinced you have the time and brain cells free to do this? Okay, here's what is probably the easiest, cheapest, and fun-est (okay, I know that's not a real word but work with me people!) team celebration I have ever done:

1. Lunch in the large conference room plus a calendar invite—took all of 10 minutes to do.

2. Couldn't drum up official funding but the super managers from my org each coughed up $20. Took about an hour to collect. ☺

3. Ordered takeout pizza, took ruthless advantage of coupons, and picked it up ourselves. We also didn't use any cutlery or plates except for a large stack of napkins raided from the café—about 1 hour total (ordering plus pick up).

4. Did that flip chart thing I mentioned above and it was a hit with the team: about 5 minutes tops.

5. At the lunch I spent about 5 minutes thanking the team for their efforts, recapping what we'd accomplished that year, and thanking the managers for their generosity.

Bottom line? I spent about 3 hours organizing the lunch, resulting in a decent celebration for 50+ people for around $80. Not too shabby, if I do say so myself. See, I told you that you could do this!

There are plenty of nice things that come from taking the time to celebrate with others, but for me the best part is being able to express my gratitude to my coworkers for the many extraordinary things they do all year long. I encourage you to carve out a couple of hours and organize a year-end celebration for your team this year. It's easy, can be done cheaply, and is just one more way to show your appreciation for your team.

Feed 'em Well

Now I'd like to spend some ink on how to organize food for your project teams. You may think you've got this handled and that there's nothing left to learn. You'd be wrong. I know this because each of these dos and don'ts I've figured out the hard way. The hard way to feed a team involves a lot of e-mail, drama, time, and logistical feats that would make FedEx proud. Been there and had the stomachache to prove it! ☺

Don't ...

- *Have a theme,* any theme, any of them at all, especially if it involves decorations, costumes, or cute hats. Trust me, not everyone owns (or wants to own) a Hawaiian shirt, women object to *pirates* referring to them as *wenches,* and no one wants to wear the Birthday Boy hat!

- *Try to organize a formal sit-down dinner.* There are professionals for that and no matter how good you are at Project, this probably isn't your area of expertise. Remember, you have a day job and it's probably not Party Planner Extraordinaire!

- *Plan on doing everything yourself.* A primary reason for feeding the team is to continue to develop a collaborative team dynamic. To do this you need to provide opportunities for the team members to work together. Sharing the work to get the food together is an easy way to do this. Have someone own the beverages and someone else the plates, napkins, and the rest.

- *Offer configurable options.* Want to make a simple lunch run into a major time sink? Take orders for individual sandwiches. Also, consider this: if it's configurable, then the likelihood that someone's order will get jacked up increases. Do you really want to peel the vegan off the wall if their sandwich inadvertently contains cheese? I didn't think so!

Do...

- *Be sure you have offerings for vegetarians, carnivores, and those trying to eat healthy.* You should also know if team members have any special food preferences and try to accommodate them within reason. Despite what the menus say in all the BBQ joints in Texas, not everyone eats meat!

- *Change it up and don't do the same takeout pizza every time.* This is where you can really set yourself apart from the pack. Get creative and try to patronize local businesses. Sandwich trays, burritos, and fajitas are all good options for a group meal.

- *Pizza is by far the easiest way* to go when you need a low hassle, cheap food option. At its easiest is your standard delivery pizza, and you can usually score some discounts if you order more than four or five pies. Another option is a local pizza joint where the pizza is probably better, but you will need to go pick it up. If you want super-cheap, I've yet to find anything cheaper than Costco pizzas, but again someone has to pick them up.

- *Limit the extras.* Food that can be eaten without plates, such as pizza, sandwiches, and burritos are all good choices because you don't need to make arrangements for plates or cutlery. Along the same lines, don't plan on drinks that need individual cups or ice.

- Speaking of *drinks, limit the number of choices* here, too. Frankly, anymore I just pick up cases of cold bottled water. Everyone drinks water, and you don't have to worry about what to do with leftovers.

- If you have a large group to feed, *enlist the admin for help.* Note that this does not mean palming the whole thing off on them. Instead, do the homework and figure out specifically what you want. Talk to the admin (in person is best) and get their agreement to help. Follow that up with a short, succinct email stating what you want them to order, where to order it, and when you need the food hot and available. The goal here is to make it as easy as possible for the admin to help you so that when your next time comes around you can still call on them for help.

I'd be remiss if I didn't discuss the elephant under the rug when organizing food for your team. The reality is that you will need to drum up funding or pay for the food yourself. This is an entirely personal choice and there may be a good reason to open up your own wallet. To be honest, I've never been turned down if I've asked a manager to pay for food. I've also paid for lots of donuts, breakfast burritos, and the like myself. In Chapter 3, I extolled the power of the burrito as a motivational tool and the first time I brought them in, I paid for them myself. Nowadays, my boss tells me to expense them and he gets it that it's not about free food but about motivating the team. You see, for a project manager, sometimes that box of donuts is just a tool, not unlike that book on statistical methods you picked up for your last project.

Finally, when it comes to who pays, it's always best to praise the bosses when they pay and then say nothing when you pay yourself. I've been to more than one lunch where the program manager has a martyr syndrome about buying everyone lunch. Geez, I didn't know that free lunch was gonna cost me an hour of whining. Kinda defeats the whole purpose of feeding the team in the first place, doesn't it?

I hope this has given you some actionable tips on how to feed your team. Breaking bread together is a fundamental bonding moment for humans, and it's a good tool for any PM. Just remember, if you hate dealing with this kind of thing, then maybe you're making it harder than it has to be; hopefully these tips will make it easier. As Julia says, *Bon appétit!*

Recognition 101

So, out of curiosity, how many individuals have you recognized this year? Five? Ten? Twenty? And how did you recognize them? I just submitted nominations for a couple of awards and it occurred to me that I should have submitted more of these bad boys this year. So here's the scoop.

Before we jump into the mechanics of the deal, let's revisit the basics: Recognition 101, if you will. First, it's vitally important to recognize others whenever they contribute significantly to your work, the project, the team, the community, and so on. Besides just thanking someone for help, formal recognition can also be a very effective motivation tool. It needs to be formal, it needs to be sincere, and it needs to be a response to something significant. This is a bit more than a heartfelt "thank you!" you tell someone in response to that fresh cup of coffee right before the 7 AM meeting.

Okay, at this point I have to jump up on my soapbox for a second, so please bear with me (or skip to the next paragraph if you don't want to hear the rant). If you want to genuinely recognize someone and have it mean something, then it needs to be for something significant. Every time I hear about someone being recognized for basically doing their job, a little bit of my belief in the system dies. All those awards for delivering a fix to a system on time just kill me—especially in those instances in which the team fixing the problem actually created it earlier…for which they probably got an award for being on time, too! You see I think those awards for "breathing on the project" take away from the recognition of those doing something truly phenomenal. The way I see it, I get paid every two weeks to do my job. If I spend a bunch of my personal time (yeah, yeah, yeah, I know…I'm salary) working on a project to meet an insane schedule for a critical product, then that's worthy of additional recognition. If I come up with a wildly innovative way to solve a problem that has everyone else stumped, then that's worthy of additional recognition. If I properly implement someone else's design—aka reuse it and deliver that work on time—well then, I'm just doing my job. I shouldn't be recognized as though I came up with an innovative solution. In short, every bit of recognition for "doing my job" just demeans any recognition I might get for the "above and beyond" efforts later. Okay, rant over…back to your regularly scheduled programming!

Now let's talk about the mechanics of recognizing someone. Some folks find it extremely difficult to write up an award nomination. Unfortunately, this is a critical skill for PMs. It really isn't that hard, so let me break it down for you—**Melanie's Tips for Writing Up an Award Nomination** for yours truly:

1. *Set the context.* Your first sentence should provide some sort of background to demonstrate how significant my contribution is. Make this short and sweet 'cause most of the recognition tools severely limit the number of characters you can use to describe the accomplishment.

2. *Be specific.* What exactly are you recognizing me for? You need to be able to write down two-three sentences that articulate what exactly I did that is worthy of recognition.

3. *Say "thank you."* Say something like, "Melanie, your contribution to Planet Blue is invaluable and we just couldn't go on without you!" Oh, and it goes without saying that this part needs to be sincere, too.

4. Somewhere you need to work in the individual's actual name…in short, *make it personal.*

5. *Pick out which of your company values apply* to this recognition. Frankly, you can tie almost anything to one of those values and, if you can't, then you really need to ask yourself if this is worthy of recognition.

There you go, some specific steps for crafting meaningful recognition. Do you know which tool your organization uses for awards and recognition? If not, then I strongly recommend you find it…and start using it! Recognizing your team members for outstanding work should be one of those sharp tools in your PM Toolbox. If you find them difficult to write up, then block out some time and practice writing up awards…and feel free to submit any with my name on them if you need practice using the tools!

So You Wanna Be a Project Manager

Is Project Management Right for You?

I'm often asked about *project management* as a profession and, because I love the work, I tend to gush enthusiastically. However, all that wild enthusiasm can be a bit misleading. Like any profession, project management has its ugly parts, so here I thought I'd share some of the things I wish someone had told me before I started down this road. Oh, I still would have pursued this career…I just would have been a bit more prepared to do so if I'd heard this stuff.

The Difference between a Project Manager and a Program Manager

Are you a *project manager* or a *program manager*? For a lot of people out there, the difference between these two roles is murky at best. To prove my point, take a minute and look at your business card, your e-mail signature, and your official job title. I'm going out on a limb here and guessing that they don't all three match. Further, I'd bet that at least one of them defines your job as a *program manager*. Over the course of my career I've had for official job titles *project manager*, *program manager*, and *operations manager*, but the job has consistently been that of a project manager.

A program is not a project. According to PMBoK, a project is "a temporary endeavor undertaken to create a unique product, service, or result," whereas a program is "a group of related projects managed in a coordinated way to obtain benefits and control not obtained from managing them individually."[1]

I've dabbled in program management enough to know that, while the skills are similar, they aren't exactly the same. A project manager is like the lead roadie for a rock band. That's the person making sure all the equipment is set up correctly so the band can perform. A program manager is the person making sure that Mick actually shows up for the performance, that the venue is booked, that the roadies know what to do when, that the T-shirts have the correct pair of lips on 'em, and so on. Both roles are important but quite different.

When you are the project manager, you have the luxury of being able to pay attention to all the minute details that contribute to the deliverable. You can remember the specific part numbers and due dates and deep dive into all of the technical challenges. You also have the time to develop strong collaborative relationships with all of your team. It's sort of like living on a tropical island and all you have to do is represent your tribe to the greater world.

When you are the program manager, time is at a premium and, frankly, you have to let go of some of your inner control-freak tendencies. There's just no way to do a good job if you're constantly deep-diving into each project under the program's umbrella. Further, it's quite likely that you won't know all of the people working on your program. The program manager has to figure out how to get things done through multiple layers of management and that means that you must excel at influence and motivation to get any particular project team to react the way you'd like. Even small changes at the program level can have huge and unintended consequences if you're not careful. If a project manager is an island chieftain, then the program manager is the senator from Hawaii, representing all of the islands in the archipelago at a much higher level.

So, which one are you? Project manager or program manager? If your job description is wrong, then you should definitely be discussing this with your boss, in preparation for your performance review this year. If your email signature doesn't truly represent the job you're doing, then go change it right now. Do the same for those business cards. Trust me, the people who will notice and care about your job title are definitely going to notice if you've got it wrong. Yes, this is a minor thing, but sometimes it's the minor things that contribute the most to others' perceptions of your competence.

---

[1]Project Management Institute. *A Guide to the Project Management Body of Knowledge*, Fifth Edition (2013).

Stuff No One Tells You Before You Begin

Inevitably, there comes a time when you need to decide if you like project management enough to continue doing it for a while. This is the working stiff's equivalent of, "What do I want to do when I grow up?" Recently, someone at this crossroads sent me an email asking to pick my brain. As I responded to the query, it got me thinking about how I made that decision. I also recalled a few things I wish someone had told me—you know, the things you end up learning the hard way? So, in an attempt to help anyone out there considering whether or not they want to make project management a long-term career, here are a few things to consider:

1. *If you don't deal well with ambiguity, then don't go down the PM path.* Seriously, a good PM has an above average tolerance for ambiguity. She can work in environments in which the requirements, goals, timelines, and so forth are undefined. I mean really undefined, as in, "It's anyone's guess when that stuff will get nailed down." Be brutally honest with yourself because it's not enough to be functional in a highly ambiguous environment; you really need to *love* working that way. If you don't love it, then you will constantly find yourself stressed out and miserable.

2. You've heard it muttered more than once: "*All of the responsibility and none of the authority*" (see the next section). That's the name of the game when it comes to project management. I have yet to run across a program or project team at Intel in which everyone working on the effort directly reports to the PM. It ain't gonna happen, so if you're a person who prefers direct control, think about a career in management, not project management. To be a successful PM, you need to excel at motivation, inspiration, and empathy.

3. *Be a recovering control freak.* A PM needs to have the control-freak tendencies to be a good leader, but also be able to let go and let the teams do the work however best suits the team. I once was a demon control freak and everything had to be done the right way, aka my way. I found myself working crazy hours and essentially doing a lot of work that wasn't PM work. It wasn't until I let go of the control over how the work got done that I was able to work reasonable hours. For me, the number of hours I was putting in had a direct correlation to how much control I could not let go of. If you find yourself redoing another team member's work, then you really need to step back and ask yourself if you truly want to be a PM.

4. *Do you want to lead people but not deal with the HR headaches of managing direct reports?* If so, then project management might be the career for you. I was once on a panel with other PMs talking about the profession. Hands down we all agreed that the best part of being a project manager was not having to address those messy HR issues. You get to have all of the fun while being able to hand off the really nasty work to someone else.

5. This brings us to what I think of as a harsh reality of project management: *You will only rarely get recognized for your own efforts,* but you will constantly recognize others for their contributions. If you need to see your name shining up on the big screen, then this may not be the career for you. I don't think you can do a good job leading others if you're constantly trying to gain recognition for your own personal efforts. Be sure you can live with this reality before fully committing to project management, because if you can't deal with it, you will never be the kind of leader your teams need.

6. *Can you take it on the chin and still grin?* (Euphonious turn of phrase, huh? ☺) As a PM, you will need to admit to "dropping the ball" occasionally. Further, you will need to admit to your team's screw-ups, both real and imagined. To be the kind of PM you want to work with, you absolutely cannot name names or otherwise throw others under the bus. You will have to stand up to that GM and say, "I take full responsibility for that big failure." Can you do that? If not, then do us all a favor and find some other profession to pursue.

7. *Figuring out how people work* and what motivates them is possibly one of the greatest puzzles of all time. If trying to solve that puzzle turns your crank, then you might become a great PM. Personally, I reached a point in my career where I found the technical challenges weren't doing it for me anymore. I needed new puzzles and I found them in understanding, motivating, and leading others.

8. *A serious PM gets certified through PMI.* I'm not saying that a PMP certification will make you a better project manager, but I am saying that if you're serious about this as a profession, then you need to demonstrate that through mastering the recognized best practices.

I hope these items have given you some food for thought. Personally, I find project management to be a career choice that is well suited to my strengths and the types of activities I like doing at work. That may not be the case for you, so spend some time thinking about what you love and hate about being a PM, then make a choice. Remember, work should be something you enjoy, because you spend most of your waking time at it.

The Mirage of Positional Authority

One year at the PMI Global Congress, I picked up a button that said, "All of the RESPONSIBILITY…none of the AUTHORITY." This is so true of project managers and it gets to the heart of why project management is so challenging. You see, you have to lead a team even though you don't have *positional authority* over your teammates. This is something PMs struggle with a lot early in their careers. Most of us are hungry for tips and tricks on how to lead a team without that silver bullet, positional authority.

Now, there are quite a few of those tips and tricks out there to help you manage a team without positional authority, but frankly none of them is going to help you until you get your head right. Yep, proven techniques are all well and good, but until you change your perspective, you're still going to wind up frustrated with that slacker circuit designer who won't get her work done. If you think that the reason you can't get your teammates to do certain tasks is that you lack positional authority, then I think you're missing the point. You're most likely struggling because you are unable to motivate them to do that task. So what am I talking about?

You have to fully internalize the fact that long-term success in getting work done through others is grounded in motivation. Any leader who can't motivate his or her team isn't really leading; they're just playing at being the boss. Further, any leader who uses negative motivation to get work done is doomed to failure sometime in the not-too-distant future—and it won't be "in a galaxy far, far away." So, bottom line? You have to get a lot better at motivation to lead a team. That positional authority you think you need? Well, that's just a crutch. While positional authority could make your life easier in the short term, if you can't motivate a team, then even positional authority won't help you. So, if you're telling yourself that you aren't successful because you don't have the authority, then I suggest you go talk to someone who's a great leader. I'm betting that they'll tell you the same thing I am: it's not the positional authority but the ability to motivate that matters most.

Sure, there's more to great leadership than motivation, such as trust, influence, and sound judgment. But realize that to be successful at motivating others, you need those skills, too—so again, it all circles back to motivation. I've managed projects and programs in which I was the anointed leader and, in the end, that positional power didn't matter much. I figured out real quick that to be successful I had to motivate my teams to do the work and, trust me, that had nothing to do with my positional power. I keep that button from the PMI Global Congress in my cube for one simple reason—to remind me that blaming my lack of effectiveness on a lack of authority is a cop-out. If my team misses a critical deadline, then I know that in some part I wasn't as effective at motivating them as I needed to be, and that's on me, not on my lack of positional authority.

So what do you think? If you really had that silver bullet—positional power—would that make you a better PM? Would it ensure that your projects came in on time and under budget? Would you really be doing anything differently than you do today? Me, I think I'd be managing my projects pretty much the same way I do now without that positional authority.

How Technical Do You Need to Be?

A common question people have about project management is, "Just how technical do you need to be to be considered successful as a project manager?" They are, of course, talking about managing technology projects. Frankly, I believe that being technically competent is only a small part of what it takes.

First, let me clarify what I mean by being considered *technical*. People are considered to be technical if they have worked in an engineering discipline and can talk intelligently about various engineering challenges and best practices. But this is a subjective assessment, completely dependent on who's judging you. I've been told before that I wasn't technical enough, yet I have plenty of professional experience as a practicing engineer and an MS…seems pretty technical to me. ☺

What these people were really telling me was that they didn't think I was technical enough in their specific engineering discipline. For the most part, these people were right. I can't design high-speed electronics or a showerhead for a chemical vapor deposition (CVD) process chamber, but I can understand those unique design challenges. That understanding is at the heart of what makes a good technical PM. You must be able to understand what the scope of work entails, what the challenges are, and how to explain these things to all levels of the organization. Trust me, the GM doesn't want to hear about ground loops and impedance-matching any more than the engineering manager wants to hear a high-level summary highlighting revenue projections for the next ten years. The job of the PM is to accurately deliver the information each person needs to do his or her job, in the appropriate level of detail.

For me, the most important factor for a successful technical PM is communication skills. As the PM, I often feel like I work at the UN, translating what the electrical engineering (EE) expert is saying to the materials expert, and vice versa. It often seems like the two speak completely different languages. The PM needs to understand the languages of each discipline represented on a project team. In addition to understanding all of these languages, you need to be constantly vigilant that everyone involved in the conversation understands each other. Your job as the PM is to be the facilitator of the information flow and not the technical expert.

Does this mean you don't need a technical degree then? No, not really—you see, you really do need the ability to think critically and the concepts a technical degree teaches you. Having that technical degree won't guarantee your success as a technical PM, because the degree alone isn't enough. To be successful you need practical, hands-on experience, just as in any other field. But remember, your field isn't an engineering discipline; it's project management and that's where you need to be most competent. You can still be successful as a project manager in the many non-technical disciplines. If you really like project management but don't have the technical degree, then focus on finding a niche outside the engineering disciplines where you can be successful.

Finally, if you are considered highly technical in one field, are you also technical in another? Again, that's really a subjective measure, but I can say that I've successfully switched engineering disciplines as a PM three times now. At each point, I had to start over and seek out background engineering information. This can be hard, especially if you're not comfortable admitting that you don't know something. The key to these transitions is a solid base of project management skills. I can focus on coming up to speed on the technology, because I can do the PM stuff blindfolded.

Bottom line:

Do you have to be technical to be a good PM? No.

Do you need a technical degree to be a good technical PM? Yes, but it probably doesn't have to be in any specific discipline if you're willing to start over occasionally.

Are You a Professional?

So often PMs fall into the profession and it's only later that they realize that it is in fact a profession. Many fields have global professional organizations that manage certifications and provide numerous resources to members. For PMs this organization is the Project Management Institute (PMI). But simply being a PMI member isn't enough, nor is it enough to hold one of its credentials. No, to be a professional PM requires much more.

What It Means to Be a Professional Project Manager

What constitutes professionalism in a project manager? This question somehow gets lost in the day-to-day hustle and bustle of work, but it's something you should be considering if you've decided to specialize in project management as a career. So, what does it mean to be a *project management professional* (PMP).

In the course of gaining your PMP accreditation (or any other PMI accreditation for that matter), you have to agree to uphold the PMI Code of Ethics and Professional Conduct. In fact, it's a bit stronger than that… you sign on the dotted line indicating that you will adhere to the Code and you will report anyone else who does not. Among other things, the Code requires that we negotiate in good faith, that we "inform ourselves and uphold the policies, rules, regulations, and laws that govern our work," and that we do not engage in behavior that is meant to deceive. These are all straightforward, right? But let me ask you this: how often do you cut corners and not do a gate review? Isn't that an expectation of your organization or local project management office (PMO)? What about negotiating with vendors? Do you actively rein in an overzealous teammate who is no longer negotiating in "good faith"? When I received my PMP certification, this Code was one page, but today it's much longer and much more detailed. If you haven't read it in a while, you should take the time to do so. In my book, anyone who does not fully follow the current Code is not a PMP.

Now let's take this a step further. Are you demonstrating your mastery of project management best practices daily? Do your projects have schedules that were built from network diagrams and leveled resources? What about risk management? Are you actively managing risks on all of your projects? How often do you use established statistical estimation techniques? These are just a couple of examples of applying best practices—not just in special cases, but daily, and not just because you are required to do it, but because it's the best way to manage the project. Sure, foregoing any of these things does not make you a bad PM, but I'd argue that not using best practices is a sign that someone is not a professional. Okay, I do have a caveat here: If you fully understand and normally use the best practice, but for your specific project some other technique works better, then in that case I'd say that was professional behavior.

So what does a PMP look like? One characteristic that's always present in true professionals is a passion for the job and the field of project management. These are the folks who know what's going on in the industry and what the hot new ideas are. They are the people who recommend books, articles, blogs, and so on and always know what other PMs around the company and at other companies are doing. In short, they bring the new ideas and they play with new techniques to see if they can make them work. These are the folks you go bounce ideas off of 'cause you know they've got some ideas of their own to share. I once heard a senior software engineer discussing what professionalism means in his area of expertise. He basically said that if you have no passion for the work, then he isn't going to spend his energy helping you along. Ouch! In a way I agree with him. If you're not willing to understand what's going on in your field, then I know at least ten others who are, and that's where I'll spend my time and energy. If you're just showing up for a paycheck, that's fine—but don't call yourself a professional.

I really do hope you'll take the time to really read and think about the PMI Code of Ethics and Professional Behavior. Are you upholding the Code? Could you do more? When's the last time you hit projectmanagement.com or a meeting of your local PMI chapter? If it's been a while, consider this your wake-up call to get back in the game!

Project Management Professional

I'm often asked about the PMI's PMP certification for project managers. People want to know a variety of things, but the two questions that come up the most are, "Is it worth it? and "Is the test as bad as I've heard?" The answer to the first is "Yes" and "No, not really" to the second. This chapter discusses what you need to do to get ready for the exam and why you should bother in the first place.

Is It Worth It?

Okay, I have to confess that the primary reason I went off and got the PMP certification was that I was out of work at the time and needed the PMP credentials on my resume. Yes, sadly, I did not see the real value of PMI or the PMP until after I'd survived the gauntlet of the certification exam. I was a PMI heretic—a nonbeliever, if you will.

Luckily, with the benefit of the exam in the rearview mirror and a few more years down the road, I can say with high confidence that getting the PMP certification was great for my career and a good thing for my professional development. Today, I'm a big proponent of getting certified, and I have to say that it has opened some very nice doors for me.

- Behind Door #1 you find a little gem I like to call "The Big Picture." Prior to studying for the PMP, I really didn't see how all the project management dots connected. I understood the mechanics of risk management, how to run an effective meeting, how to create a schedule, and so forth. In short, I understood large pieces of each knowledge area, but I couldn't see how intertwined these areas actually are. Post-PMP, I now see how risk management feeds the schedule and how meeting minutes are only one small part of the project's communication plan. Heck, I now know that referring to the *schedule* as the *project plan* is one of those "open-your-mouth-and-remove-all-doubt" comments we should all avoid.

- Step up to Door #2 and you will find a great job offer from a world-class semiconductor company. Let's face it: there are a lot of experienced project managers out there looking for work. One thing I noticed from my own time in Layoffville was that as soon as my resume had those three magic letters, my resume started getting a lot more notice. I firmly believe that I would not be working where I am today without that certification. On any given day, on any job posting site you choose, you will find that the majority of project management jobs either require or prefer the PMP. Having the PMP doesn't guarantee anything, but it's probably going to help your resume get past the first filter and in front of someone who can help you.

- Inside Door #3 you find the real prize. You find a community of people who do what you do in different industries, a huge grab-bag of useful information, and enough career development opportunities to choke a horse. I'm blown away by the resources PMI provides to continue learning. I've found some of my best ideas and strategies while talking to PMs from other companies. In short, you find a networking opportunity like no other with an instant "in."

So here's the bottom line in my opinion: if you want to continue to practice as a PM as your chosen career then you need to get certified. Certification won't necessarily make you a better PM, but it will open those doors to people and opportunities you don't have access to today.

Is the Test As Hard as I've Heard?

Now let's talk about what it takes to get through the test.

It's unfortunate, but there's a lot of fear-mongering going on out there about this test. Years ago, when I was researching taking the test, a lot of people told me that it was horrendously hard and that I'd need at least six months to study for it. Further, the total cost for getting the certification was way more than I'd expected. It seemed that everywhere I turned there were resources that would almost…but not quite… guarantee me a passing grade as long as I forked over some large amount of cash. People in the process of psyching themselves up to take the test would speak in reverential tones in some weird language only the PMP-traumatized could understand. They would allude to "the pembock" and "Rita" as if you should know what they were.[1] Now I ask you, how is someone completely new to PMI supposed to know those? It's terrifying and insane!

My experience preparing for and taking the PMP test was straightforward. Notice that I didn't say that it was easy… that's because it's not! It's tough to squeeze in study time into an already hectic round of personal and professional obligations. Also, let's not forget that, for the most part, this stuff is as dry as my front yard along about July here in Arizona. So not only is it hard to carve out time to study, you have to find prime learning time. Trust me, you don't want

---

[1] "Pembock" is the pronunciation of PMBoK. "Rita" refers to Rita Mulcahy, late lamented author of bestselling PMP exam preparation books.

to try reading a chapter of the PMBoK any time you are the least bit stressed, tired, hungry, or bored. You will either wake up an hour later with the book plastered to your face with your own drool or find that you've scrubbed the entire kitchen floor with your own toothbrush. Not good, not good at all.

So, here are my tips for taking and passing the PMP exam. This is what I tell people when they ask me about the test. Trust me, it's not as bad as you might think, and you can do this:

- Before you attempt the online application for the exam, *build a spreadsheet and document your hours of experience.* This saves a lot of time and frustration later when you are completing the online application.

- *Develop a plan,* or at a minimum, a realistic timeline. This probably won't take you six months, but then again it probably isn't something you can do tomorrow either.

- *Sign up for an exam prep class*—the kind that lasts a week and will pound so much information into your brain you will walk away each day feeling like Johnny Mnemonic.

- *Utilize some software to mimic the computerized test* so that you get a feel for the time constraints and question styles.

- *Memorize the stuff suggested.* Yes, this is tedious, and no, it won't make you a better project manager, but it will make taking the test easier.

- *Get into the PMI mindset*—assimilate into the Borg. Remember, it's only the right answer if PMI thinks it is, so be sure you assimilate before you take the test.

- *Be realistic about what your goal is.* The passing grade for this exam is shockingly low (68% when I took the exam back in 2005). Trust me, once you get the certification no one will ask you what your exam score was. It no longer matters. What does matter is whether or not it was a pass or a fail—so prioritize your time accordingly.

Here are a few warnings that you should bear in mind. I personally know people who have had their applications audited or who have failed the test. These things happen and it's not the end of the world. In the case of the audit, PMI requested additional information and the matter was easily handled. In the case of those who have failed the test, almost all of them walked away with a better understanding of project management and their experience level.

So, if you are contemplating taking on this challenge, I encourage you to go for it. It can't possibly be as bad as everyone tells you it is, and it probably won't take you near as long as you've been told. Also, there's a strong possibility that you can get your company to cough up the coin to pay for it. From my perspective, the time spent getting certified was well worth it. So go ahead—bite the bullet and do it!

I Got It, Now What?

Okay, once you've done the hard work to obtain the PMP certification, just how do you go about keeping it? Well, according to the PMI, you need to accrue 60 hours of Professional Development Units (PDUs) every three years. The challenge comes in figuring out just what kinds of activities rate PDUs, so let's break that down a bit.

In your quest to obtain PDUs, your first stop should be the "Certification" page of PMI's website. But let's be honest shall we? There's a lot of data there and it's not exactly a model of good UX is it? Good thing there's a "Ways to Earn PDUs" hyperlink buried somewhere in there! Okay, so far I'm not telling you anything you couldn't figure out for yourself, right? Let's see if I can do better with **Melanie's Tips for Scoring PDUs:**

- *Training, training, training!* This is what it's about folks: continual learning. There are probably classes offered right through your own company that can help you out here. If you're an experienced PM or your company doesn't have PM-specific training available, then you may need to look further afield for training, but the good news is that those classes are generally of longer duration, which means more PDUs for you! A good source for this kind of training is PMI's Seminars World. They aren't cheap, but every class I've taken through them has been excellent.

- *Attend PMI's Global Congress for your region.* If you do nothing else, this is the fastest way to get your years' worth of PDUs in one fell swoop. It's entirely possible to rack up 15+ PDUs by attending these ginormous conferences. Oh, and did I mention that they will upload your PDUs for you? Talk about a bargain! Okay, there's a downside and it's that these conferences are not cheap. Generally when I go, I expense about $5,000 (travel, lodging, conference registration, meals, and transportation). This means that you need to plan ahead and work with your manager to budget for this.

- *Share some knowledge with your local chapter.* Every month, there are four or five professional development meetings sponsored by your local PMI chapter. Each of those meetings needs speakers…and they have no budget for said speakers! So what does this mean to you? Easy PDUs, my friends! Yep, PMI chapters all over have Professional Development Meetings (PDMs) all the time. You will find that the organizers of these events are always looking for speakers and many of them don't care that you're not a regular on the speaker circuit. What they are looking for are speakers who will work cheap and who have something interesting to share. Oh, and when I say "interesting" I mean "interesting to PMs"! These are your people and they are generally kind and receptive audiences.

- *Share some knowledge with the wider PM community.* Submit abstracts for PM conferences; participate in the various public forums; heck, you could even start a PM-oriented blog!

- *Make sure that you carry over the maximum PDUs allowed (20 in 2013) during each renewal cycle.* You just never know how busy or how traumatic your life is going to be three years from now, so it makes sense to get ahead of the game if you can. Go ahead and make sure you carry over some extras for the next renewal cycle.

- Last, be sure you *claim the "easy money."* Yep, if you're a full-time PM, then you can claim five PDUs a year, so that's 25% of your total needed to maintain your credential already in the bank. You are claiming that, aren't you?

Now you know just how easy it is to rack up those PDUs! What's stopping you now?

I confess that I purely hate logging my PDUs! I loathe the task. I will find any number of things to do to avoid it. I'll put receipts for PDMs in a pile on my desk then promptly forget about them. This means that at least once a year I have a pile of PDUs to claim, and since that process is only slightly less complicated than ordering lunch for 20 from the sandwich shop down the street, it isn't a fun time. Yeah, I know I'm a bad PM. The thing is, no matter how I feel about the method for submitting PDUs, I still have to do it right? I mean, it's not like I'm going to let my certification slide and then have to retake the test, right? So, for those bad PMs like me, here are **Melanie's Tips For Claiming PDUs**:

- *If you attend the PMI Global Congress or any of the Seminar World classes, PMI automatically logs your PDUs!* Yep, there's nothing for you to do except verify that the PDUs are actually logged.

- *Do it as quickly as you can after the event that earned them.* Don't be a bad PM and try to claim them all at one time, once a year. Trust me if you do this you'll be cleaning up the chocolate and BBQ sauce for a month afterwards!

- The first thing you need to do when claiming PDUs is to *figure out which category your PDUs fall into.* Check out PMI's website for the specifics.

  Category A is the most confusing and, sadly, it's the one you will probably use the most. Use Category A for:

  - Training classes that are provided by PMI's Registered Education Providers (REPs). You are able to search on the list of suppliers and select the specific class you need.

  - Eligible events offered through your local PMI chapter, aka a "Component 1-2 PDU Event." (Note: "Component" refers to the PMI chapter or sub-group putting on the shindig.)

- For training classes that are not provided by PMI's REPs, you use PDU *Category B.* (Note: This is the category you use to claim credit for training provided by your employer.)

- *Category F* is the "free money"! This is the category you use to claim your 5 PDUs a year if you're a full-time PM. Do not leave these on the table!

- PMI can and does audit your PDU claims, so be sure that you keep the appropriate documentation. Not sure what constitutes "appropriate documentation"? Check out the *PMP Handbook* for the specific requirements for each category.

- If you have a smartphone or tablet, then consider downloading the MyPMI app. It lets you see your certification status and whether you're a member in good standing—that is, whether your dues are current. You can claim PDUs with it, and the Communities tab connects you to special interest groups with their associated blogs and events.

So there you go! Some tips and tricks for claiming PDUs. Yes, it's a hassle, but that hassle must be dealt with!

Getting Better at It

At some point you start to realize that you really like this project management gig and you want to learn more or you want to figure out how to take it to the next level. Just how do you do that? Many PMs find themselves in a position where they are managing multiple projects simultaneously, so I'm going to give you some proven tricks for doing that. Another challenge for PMs is how to improve your business acumen—and I've got some tricks for you there, too. Where can you go to practice specific skills in a live environment? You volunteer, but volunteer projects are their own special fun—so we'll talk about that too. At some point, you're going to want to attend a professional conference and you need to understand how to write an abstract and then how to get along at that conference. I'd venture to guess that you're not going to find this stuff in your standard Project Management 101 text—so here you go!

What's in Your Toolbox?

Do you have a project manager toolbox? Is it a shiny red tackle-box or a rugged diamond-plate lockbox? What's inside this toolbox, and where does it live?

In this dynamic, chaotic world, information seems to arrive in a deluge, leaving little time to understand and internalize it. Today the information stream looks more like the output from a fire hose than a discrete glass of water: email, IM, phone calls, corporate newsletters, blogs, podcasts, radio, TV, and all kinds of old-school paper publications. Obviously, the challenge is how to capture the relevant information and store it in a manner that allows for efficient retrieval.

I'm constantly looking for fresh ideas on how to continue to improve myself, my work, and my team. The problem is how to accumulate those ideas in a way that actually lets me access them when I need them. For me, this storage system has two critical features: it must be simple to use, and it must cut the search time down to mere minutes, if not seconds.

My system is pretty low-key and low-tech. I created a directory on my hard drive entitled "PM Toolbox." This is where I store all of my generic project management resources and data. In this directory I have a few subfolders for things like material from training classes and the company's PMO. However, the content is mostly individual files with long names so I can identify them easily. Here is where I store templates, checklists, and other assorted files that are generic in nature but useful when kicking off a new project. Here's a quick sample of what's in my Toolbox:

- Course material from a fundamentals class I helped evaluate, which turned out to be a great resource that I share with junior PMs through the mentoring work I do.

- Presentations from several internal project management-related organizations within Intel.

Note: I always download a copy of the presentation then take notes in the "Speaker Notes" section of the PowerPoint file during the talk. This means that not only do I have the speaker's material but also my thoughts at the time, all stored in the same file.)

- A folder for interesting articles or information other people send me that I think will be useful later.

- A folder containing all of the material I've developed for presentations and talks I've done not specifically related to the projects I own.

- Samples of award nominations.

- A folder with any details from past team events I've organized.

- My own templates for meeting minutes, kickoff meetings, schedule checklists, etc.

There's also a side benefit to being organized with your project management resources. They are easy to find so you can share them with colleagues when the topic come up. For instance, I've forwarded the fundamentals class material to several people in the course of mentoring them. The toolbox becomes a treasure chest of ideas that you can use to add value to your personal and professional network.

Why don't you take a few minutes today and set up the folder? Or set up some sort of online system. As you run across data that you think you might want to use later, just store it in your own toolbox and soon you will see the benefits of quick and efficient access to this kind of data.

Tips and Tricks for Managing Multiple Projects

How many projects are you managing today? Are they similar or drastically different? For most of my career I've been assigned three or four projects to manage at any given time. Personally I love the variety and the challenge of keeping all those balls in the air. When these projects span the gamut from, say, new product development and business process improvement to joint development with a supplier, it's a little easier to juggle. However, when those three or four projects are producing the same type of deliverable, keeping these projects straight in your head can get pretty challenging. Make no mistake: it really is a juggling act and PMs with more than two projects need some solid tools to help drown out the circus music.

Here are a few tools I've refined over the years to help keep the lions, tigers, and clowns in their respective cages so that the show can go on:

- First, if you have several projects with similar deliverables, **don't trust your memory!** Print out copies of the schedule, risk register, meeting minutes, and so on and carry these with you all the time. The next time you're put on the spot for an update, you don't have to fumble with your laptop (and don't forget that fun fest when you can't get online); you can whip out your hardcopy schedule and say with confidence, "Yes, we are on track to deliver October 15th." The other cool thing about having the hardcopy is that you can make quick notes right on the document real-time while the discussion is raging hot and heavy. When you do get the time to update the schedule, all of your changes are right there in one place, making it less likely that you will forget to incorporate anyone's update. I am almost never without those hardcopy schedules!

Note   You could do the same thing by saving offline copies of critical project documents. Just make sure that your access to the information is not tied to your ability to be online.

- **Use color ruthlessly**. I color-code my projects so that I can tell at a glance which one I'm working on. How far do I take this color-coding, you might ask? As far as possible! I designate a specific color for each project and then keep a folder of that color on my desk to hold any project-specific content I'm working with. I set up custom flags in Outlook so that I can tag each important email with the project's color. I have even been known to go out and buy color-specific pens so that when I'm taking notes in a central notebook I can quickly skim through to a specific project's notes based on color. One final comment here: I never use red for a project. Red is special and it's got its own meaning: "Holy Guacamole! This must be done ASAP!" Only the truly urgent items get tagged with the color red, regardless of which project they correspond to.

- As long as you are being ruthless, why not **take control of your meeting schedule**? Since you are the PM, you have a lot of flexibility to set up the project-specific meetings you run. I've had success with these two strategies:

  - Set up all of your meetings for one or two days of the week. You will have a very long day or two but your remaining week will be free of meetings for the most part and you will have plenty of flexibility to get work done.

  - Set up all of a specific project's meetings and work time on a specific day of the week. For instance, Monday is Project A's day and that's what you focus on for the entire day. This is a little harder to implement but I have found it to be very effective at allowing me time to focus on strategic activities. If you're struggling with finding time to be strategic, give this one a try.

- Speaking of taking control of your schedule—be sure to **block time on your calendar to work on specific projects**. (Note: This tool is critical! If you find that you have too many meetings and can't find time to work, you need to start blocking off time on your calendar for deskwork.) How much time I block off depends on each project; some need more of my attention than others, depending on what stage they are in. Hey, you can also color-code these calendar items!

- Okay, this last one is probably obvious, but if you are managing multiple projects, then it helps to **institute a common naming convention** across all of them. Name the schedule, risk register, meeting minutes, and so on all the same way, no matter which project it is. If your projects get assigned an identifying number through your org's business process, have all of your file names reference that number. That's how I know the project schedule I'm looking at belongs to SR128583 and not SR131683. Trust me, if you have them both open at the same time and are toggling between them, it can get confusing.

I hope these tools are useful to you, because when you have more than two projects it can get pretty crazy and you'll start to see circus metaphors left and right! I've used all of these concepts and vouch for their effectiveness.

Improve Your Business Acumen

To be effective as a PM, you need to understand the business environment you work in. You need to understand what's going on in your particular market segment, what your customers and competition are up to, and what's going on within your own company. In some cases you even need to understand what's going on at a political level and how that may or may not affect your project. You need to stay on top of these things so that you can be effective at making tradeoff decisions and prioritization calls. Unfortunately there's a lot to keep track of—and, really, who has the time?

Okay, let's address the time issue first, as I suspect that's your biggest concern. How much time do you devote to this activity? How much is reasonable? The answer to those questions really depends on you and the environment you work in. Early in my career I got some advice that has stayed with me. A crusty old-timer told me that it was very important to stay on top of what was going on in the industry. He also pointed out that if you can only squeeze in 15 minutes a day, that's 15 minutes more information you will have than your peers who don't bother to stay in the know. He was very successful, so I took his advice seriously and, since he spun his message as a competitive advantage, I jumped all over it. Fast-forward some unmentionable number of years and I'm still making time to stay in touch with what's going on. Some weeks I can devote an hour to this activity, others it's more like that the 15 minutes he mentioned.

So, if you can find some amount of time to pursue this knowledge, how do you go about it? It turns out that there are more information sources than you have time, so you'll need to check out as many as you can and then filter to the ones that provide the most value to you. Here are a couple of ideas to get you started:

- Google Alerts for your company, competitors, industry associations, and so on.

- Company news outlets. (Most large companies have these now, and they practically spoon-feed you the data—so check these out to save time.)

- Business magazines/websites.

If you are still struggling to find good sources, then ask for recommendations from your boss, your peers, and basically anyone who seems to have a solid understanding of what's going on.

If you participate in the PMI community, then you have probably run across Dr. Harold Kerzner talking about where he sees the future of project management going. He's become something of a futurist for the profession and speaks often on this topic at various PM-related events. One of the things that resonates with me about Dr. Kerzner is his observation that, as the nature of projects continues to evolve, the PM is becoming more of a business manager than a technical expert or a project work coordinator. What this means is that you need to step up your business acumen and increase your understanding of your company's overall business. As project management becomes more about managing projects as businesses, a PM can no longer afford to be uninformed about markets and customers. We PMs need to understand our customer's business strategies to an even greater depth and degree.

The Most Important Meeting You're Not Going to

All companies hold regular meetings by their executives for their employees. Sadly, these meetings can be sparsely attended if they are not mandatory and many see them as low-value corporate spin doctoring. Sure, some companies roll that way, but for the most part, these are critical meetings for PMs to attend. Everyone makes prioritization calls about how to use their time—I get that. I even get it that you're crazy busy and you might find some of these meetings deadly boring, but I'd like to use up a few electrons generating text here to make a case for upping the priority of this type of meeting.

Probably the most common reason for not attending these meetings is the perception that there's no new information conveyed. If you think this way, then you really are missing the point. I rarely go to these types of meetings expecting to hear breaking news. Instead I go to gather context. What is the CEO emphasizing? How do my current projects tie into the organization's objectives? From a project management and a personal career management perspective, I want to be working on the initiatives that are important to the company. The best way to understand this is to understand what's important to the company's leaders, and about the only way to get independent intel on this is to attend these types of meetings and pay attention. What's said? What isn't? Sometimes I learn more about the direction my organization is headed by figuring out what they aren't talking about. It should be noted that to gather this kind of contextual information you have to be actively listening and evaluating everything that's said. You cannot do this while multitasking.

Another common justification for ditching these meetings is the belief that the content is all corporate-speak and doesn't reflect reality. Let's be honest here: no exec is gonna stand up there and say, "Oh, by the way, we're laying off 20% of our headcount next week." If you're looking for that kind of honesty, wake up and smell the coffee. Again, the valuable information in these meetings is contextual, not what's literally said. Let me give you an example of what I mean here. In one such meeting I attended, there was an announcement of the organization's intent to staff up a facility in a non-US location. There were some interesting justifications for this move and even an announcement of the pending opening of quite a few reqs for this new site. Later in the meeting there was some discussion of headcount and the speaker went to some lengths to emphasize that it has become rather challenging to get new reqs approved for positions in the United States. She went on to say that any US attrition would be backfilled in the non-US location. Now it's entirely possible that I misunderstood or misinterpreted some of what was said, but the information I gleaned from that meeting is pretty helpful to me both as a PM and to manage my own career. Again, no exec is going to come right out and say these things, but the meaning is there if you bother to attend the meeting and pay attention.

I think it's obvious to say that paying attention and active participation are the keys to getting anything out of these meetings. It always surprises me how few questions are asked at these types of meetings. As far as networking and expanding your sphere of influence, these meetings are a goldmine of opportunity. It's also easier than you think to ask a question. To get the maximum benefit of asking the question, be sure to introduce yourself and mention where you work before getting to the question. If you have trouble thinking of questions, then take a few minutes beforehand and write some down, that way you'll be prepared when the meeting is opened for questions. Another thing to consider is that your questions need to be answerable from the speaker's perspective. Keep them succinct and try not to put the speaker in a position to reveal information they are uncomfortable revealing. There are some specific things that the CEO is not going to discuss in an open forum, so don't waste his time or ours by asking that type of question. Last, I should mention that as long as the question is succinct and articulate it almost doesn't matter what it is or what the resulting answer may be. The goal here is to participate in the meeting and maybe get some name recognition. If you are uncomfortable with public speaking, try to consider these as opportunities to practice.

It may be nerve-wracking to stand up there in front of a large crowd, but it only lasts 4-5 minutes and then you're done. You can do that!

Finally, there's a really good personal reason I attend these types of meetings, especially the open forum after earnings are announced. You see, I happen to own stock in my company and I'm betting that you do, too. As an investor, this is the only stock I own where I can get such candid and in-depth information about what the CEO is thinking and where the company is headed. If I could get this level of information on every stock I own or am considering, then I'd be a lot better off financially. In short, if you own stock in the company, why wouldn't you actively participate in these meetings?

So, did you attend the most recent all-hands meeting? If not, did you accomplish something significant instead? Or worse, did you schedule a meeting over that timeslot and thereby prevent others from attending? If you aren't in the habit of regularly attending these meetings and actively participating, then I'd like to challenge you to do so. Just try it out for a few months and see if you agree with me. There's a lot of information being conveyed— just not all of it is verbalized or even contained on the slides. As a PM, you need to understand how your project aligns to corporate and organizational objectives. As an employee concerned about your career growth, it's negligent not to pay attention to what's going on in the rest of the company. Finally, as a stockholder, it's an invaluable resource for information about your investment.

Volunteer to Sharpen the Saw

Think you've got game as a PM? Think you're pretty good at influencing and motivating others—heck, you own soft skills, right? Okay, hotshot, it's time to put that to the test and volunteer. Yep, you heard me—go ahead and volunteer to lead a project of volunteers…just get ready for a major reality check!

One of the best ways to improve your influence and motivation skills is to lead a team of volunteers. You see, when you lead volunteer teams there are a few realities you have to live with. First, this is not a top priority for anyone on the team. In fact, volunteer work is often the lowest priority for your teammates, and the work will often get axed if their day jobs get busy. Second, there really are very few consequences to dropping a ball on a volunteer project, especially at work since everyone has a get-out-of-jail-free card and isn't afraid to use it. If I fail to deliver something for a volunteer project, sure my rep gets a little dinged, but my performance review remains intact for the most part. So, if you want to lead a volunteer team you're going to have to excel at motivation through sheer force of will and your own talents.

I've managed a few volunteer projects, both work-related and not, over the years. There are a few things I've learned along the way, which I share here:

- Volunteer projects are much, much, much harder to lead than any other project you've led in the past. They are also a great way to work on your motivation and influence skills.

- You have to invest significant amounts of time to get to know your teammates; there's more social interaction with a volunteer team. Understand going in that you will need to spend more time building relationships on an all-volunteer team.

- In order to influence your team effectively, you need to be able to answer the what's-in-it-for-me question for each team member. This will be different for each person, so make sure you have a great big bunch of motivational tricks up your sleeve. One size won't fit all.

- People view volunteer work as optional and, trust me, they will let you and the rest of the team down occasionally. If you're lucky, they will feel bad about it and try to make amends, but most of the time folks feel justified in dropping volunteer work if it means putting in overtime because their day job got busy.

- To address the reality of the volunteer work being a low priority, I emphasize the team dynamic heavily. I make a point to say things like "The team is counting on you" and even "You let the team down when you didn't complete that work."

- Make sure your team dynamic is supportive of people asking for help on their given tasks if they get busy. It's much less frustrating for the entire team if everyone can pitch in when help is needed, as opposed to getting pissy if someone can't deliver on time.

- The more passionate you are about the project, the easier it will be to influence the team. If you truly believe in the project and can paint a compelling picture of its benefits for the team, then you will be a long way towards motivating your team. On the other hand, if you don't really buy into the project objectives, it's a good bet that most of your team doesn't either and getting all of the work done on time will be an uphill battle for you.

- All PMs know that recognition is an important motivational tool, but for volunteer projects, you're going to want to go above and beyond the norm when it comes to recognition.

- It's always important to role-model the behavior you're expecting from the team, especially when it comes to volunteer projects. If you find yourself stuck with a dog of a project, realize that you're committed for the duration. It's a matter of integrity that you stay the course.

- It's also important to realize that when things start unraveling, you really get to stretch yourself as a PM. Often this is the time when you need to step back and re-examine your influence and motivation approaches. Remember, one of the reasons you probably volunteered for this project was that it provided an opportunity to improve your soft skills. So go figure out how to improve.

- And last, there's nothing that says you can't renegotiate the scope of work down to something more realistic if things start unraveling. Often this is the best way to get out from under a dog project with the team's reputation intact. Not every project has to be a home run, and sometimes crossing the finish line is more important than the final score.

After reading this list, you might think I'm pretty down on volunteer projects, but that's just not the case. I really believe that they are a great way to sharpen your motivation and influence skills. But make no mistake: this type of project is harder to manage. Today I volunteer to lead this type of project only when I feel strongly about the project objectives, but that doesn't mean that I don't "get volunteered" for a few dogs now and then. When you are leading an all-volunteer team, it's important to keep in mind the two realities I mentioned. If you're leading such a team and you find yourself constantly frustrated with your team's lack of commitment to the project, then it's time to reevaluate your motivation tactics and try something new. After all, these projects are great learning opportunities, if you'll just take the time to learn some new tricks.

How to Turn Your Ideas into Reality

So, you have an awesome idea to improve a process…*but* it means someone, somewhere will have to do some work. How do you go about getting your idea implemented? In the High-Tech Circus I work in, we absolutely love, love, love process improvements but, frankly, we don't always have the time to implement them, and—though we're loath to admit it—we frequently don't want to change. The trick to turning your idea into reality is influence.

To influence others, you have to define, refine, and confine the problem your idea will address. You must be able to articulate it clearly. More importantly, you need to make sure that it really is an awesome idea. To do this I sit down and think about some key aspects of my idea. First, what's the problem or challenge my idea addresses? Here I try to be pretty specific, using quantifiable data if possible. I write this stuff down! Next I capture what success, or the end state, should look like. If I can't do this, then the idea hasn't cooked long enough. I also like to do the flip side of that analysis and write down what success isn't. I've found that doing the yin/yang sort of analysis is really helpful in clarifying the "pass criteria" for the solution.

Next, it's time to look at your proposed solution. At this point you probably have a high-level concept you think will solve your problem, but it's worth taking some time to brainstorm other possible solutions as well. Remember, if you sell the right people on your idea, the team that implements the process improvement (and yeah, I know that could be you…your own Team of One!) should do a more thorough review of the solution options. Here you just want to make sure you're not off in the weeds with your idea. Now you need to put pixels to work and document the specifics of your proposed solution, which teams or people will be affected, who the decision makers are, how long you think this will take to implement, how much it will cost vs. the savings it will engender, pros, cons, and so forth. You get the picture.

Now you're ready for some old-school stakeholder management. From your analysis of your idea, you know who could potentially be affected by your proposed process improvement. Now you go talk to them! Make it informal but gather some key intel. Do they agree with you that there's a problem? What do they think it will take to solve the problem? Do they have any interest in partnering with you to solve it? Are they adamantly opposed to your idea? If this all sounds familiar…well it should, for this is Stakeholder Management 101. You got this part, right?

Finally, it's time to pitch your idea to the right folks. You may need to do this in multiple forums to get the right level of buy-in. Oh, and don't be lulled by an autocratic directive from on high for some down-trodden worker bees to go implement your idea—you have to do even more influencing and motivation in that scenario! Pitching an idea is not unlike prepping for a potentially deadly ops review, so basically you use the same tactics. Don't surprise the higher-ups, build consensus before the big presentation, know who the decision makers really are, and so on.

▓ **Caution** Do *not* jump right into pitching the idea without doing the analysis I mention above. If you do, I can pretty much guarantee you that your proposal will sound half-baked, you will get some action items to do that same analysis you should have already done, and there's a strong chance that your idea will die an early death right there in your face.

Last, the hardest part about having an awesome idea is knowing when to step aside and let the baby learn to run. Sure it's your baby, you've nudged it to crawl, and now it's walking on its own, but there always comes a time when you need to move on to your next awesome idea. Too often folks get so attached to their idea, especially if it was a success, that they can't let go. Many times, I'm not the one to implement my "awesome idea" and I've learned over the years that there's just as much value in being the idea generator as there is in being the idea implementer. Unfortunately, the generator doesn't always get the recognition though. ☹ Seriously, as a PM you need to constantly hone your skills to get work done through others. I purely love scoping new projects, but when it's time to hand off a solid project plan to another PM, I kinda wanna cry. Those projects are sort of like the big catfish that got away, if you know what I mean. Luckily for me, there's always another project to plan.

In the end, you get to a point in your career where you're expected to generate ideas for improving processes and designs. Being able to bring creative ideas to the table is important, but you must make sure that your ideas are well-developed and that you've greased the wheels so that your ideas fall on receptive ears. The good news is this is really just an extension of basic problem solving and stakeholder management.

It's a Universal Skill

I had an interesting hallway conversation not long ago while I was carrying a cake. That's what started the conversation, but when I mentioned that I was a PM somehow we ended up talking about managing different types of projects. She wanted to know if I found managing projects from different engineering disciplines easy. I told her that I find it very easy and that changing is a great way to stay excited about being a PM.

Now this is an area where I do think I've got the chops to talk. I've been managing projects for over fifteen years now and have experience managing projects that span mechanical, electrical, materials, and software engineering disciplines. I've also led project work in vendor development, joint product development, and operations. My current job entails managing software projects with a little bit of operations work thrown in to alleviate the boredom. So I know a bit about managing projects in different technical disciplines and I've come to understand that you really can switch disciplines if you've got the

PM skills mastered. I think of project management skills as universal skills you can apply across any discipline.

These universal skills come up all the time in conversations with other PMs when we're talking about the challenges each of us is facing. In fact, I've noticed that these challenges are pretty universal, so it makes sense that the skills you use to deal with them are universal as well. Here's an example: my brother used to manage projects in the construction industry and one of his biggest challenges was managing stakeholders who want to get all up in his business… how many people are working on the project, how well trained are they, why can't they work weekends, and all that. Sound familiar? I bet you don't have to think too long to recall a time when a stakeholder demanded that your team work a weekend to make up some schedule slip. You see, whether you're refurbing a school's climate control system or designing a piece of cutting-edge technology, stakeholders are stakeholders—the good, the bad, and the ugly. Further, once you figure out how to deal with that stakeholder and absolutely delight them, you're golden.

What do I mean when I say "you're golden"? I mean that if you've mastered the necessary project management skills, then you can focus on learning the new technology of a totally different field while still making things happen on the project management front. When I joined a new group within Intel, I had pretty much zero experience with software (SW) design. Sure, I'd worked on programs where the SW PM was a peer and I'd dabbled in SW development in college, but for all intents and purposes I walked in cold when it came to the nuances of SW development. I was able to focus a lot of my energy on learning and understanding those nuances because I already knew how to work with a new team to plan a project, how to manage stakeholders I'd never met before, and how to set up and actually do risk management in a meaningful way. This isn't the first time I've switched engineering disciplines or technical areas and, truthfully, it just gets easier as I get better as a PM.

So if you're getting a bit bored with your current projects and still love project management, then I highly recommend seeking out some PM opportunities in another area. This is one of the easiest ways to re-energize your enthusiasm for project management. Stay in the technical realm if you like, or bounce over to supplier management or even operations. Those universal PM skills you already have? They work there too! And here's a secret… that new team you're working with? The one that can run rings around you technically? They'll think you rock as a PM especially when you pull off a realistic schedule, some actual risk management, and well-facilitated meetings all while learning the technology.

Maximizing Your ROI at Conferences

Have you ever considered attending some professional conferences? Think you don't have the time or that you won't get any value out of the experience? Think again! If you've reached the point in your career where you've got this PM gig figured out, then it's definitely time to start attending professional conferences because, frankly, there's more to learn. As for value? Well, there you get out of it what you put into it. No surprise there, right? Professional conferences offer several advantages that you may not be aware of.

First off, there's the networking. A significant fraction of PMI's 700,000 members attend the annual PMI Global Congresses. PMs from every industry are there and you can bank on meeting someone who's figured out how to overcome the challenge of rolling out risk management to a reluctant audience. These are your people! They talk your language and you will be able to share war stories and solutions with people who've been there too.

The second advantage these big professional conferences have is the availability of training. Often there are back-to-back speakers and, depending on the size of the conference, the topics can range from best practices, to case studies, to emerging techniques. Additionally, PMI's Seminar World offers in-depth, advanced training that runs in parallel with their Global Congresses. Here you can pick up a new skill or figure out how to stand up a new capability from some of the best minds in your profession. You really can't get this kind of specialized training through your corporate training arm.

Another overlooked advantage of professional conferences is the opportunity to build your professional reputation by speaking at them. It's often easier to get an abstract selected at the smaller conferences, and you tend to speak to a smaller audience. These can be a great means to advertise your project, especially if the conference is held within your company or industry association. Speaking at larger conferences establishes you as a senior member of the profession and goes a long way to building a credible professional reputation outside of your association with your employer. In both cases, speaking at a professional conference is going to look great on your performance review and resume. But before you are asked to speak at a conference, you need to submit an abstract.

How to Submit an Abstract

Here's how it generally goes. First, you submit an abstract of your proposed paper. This sounds grander than it actually is, as you can draft and polish a solid abstract in a couple of hours. You will most likely need to provide four to five paragraphs discussing the problem solved, the solution implementation, one or two graphics, and references. Once you submit the abstract, there's nothing to do until you hear whether or not yours was selected for presentation at the conference. If you do get selected, then you will need to generate a paper, poster presentation, a formal presentation, or some combo of the three. I find this to be less than ten hours of total work. Assuming you throw in an hour or two to practice your presentation, at the end of the day you've spent less than twenty hours of effort. In fact, since you are already intimately familiar with the topic, it's likely that you won't even need that much time.

The real payoff for your time comes when you get selected to present at one of these conferences. You, your entire team, and the project will get great visibility at the conference, on the program and other handouts, on the website, and of course by doing the actual presentation. Participation in the conference will also establish your team as thought leaders in its particular area of expertise. Finally, you can repurpose the content of your talk for other professional forums, such as your local PMI chapter meetings and your organization's own newsletter. That's a lot of buzz for less than twenty hours of work!

How to Be a "Conference Commando"

Several years ago I read Keith Ferrazzi's book, *Never Eat Alone*, which is all about networking.[1] In Chapter 14, "Be a Conference Commando," Ferrazzi provides some very actionable ideas for how to make the most of any conference. The primary reason to go to a conference, he avers, is to meet and network with "like-minded people." In a nutshell, he's saying that your focus should be on networking, and he goes on to say that you probably already know most of the material being presented anyway. Think back to the last conference you attended. Did you get more out of listening to the talks or actually talking to and networking with the presenters? Did you even make an effort to meet the presenters? I rest my case.

Okay, so how do you go about becoming a "Conference Commando"? (Catchy sobriquet, isn't it? I can just picture someone in full cammo crawling across the lobby of a ritzy convention center...) Well, the best way would be to pick up Ferrazzi's book and read his ideas for yourself. However, in the interests of sharing knowledge, here's my take on his key ideas.

Do...

- Organize a dinner and/or happy hour one night of the conference to provide a networking forum for "like-minded people."

- Put yourself in position to "bump" into people you want to meet. Figure out where a particular speaker will be before the talk and just happen to be there to bump into.

---

[1]Keith Ferrazzi. *Never Eat Alone: And Other Secrets to Success, One Relationship at a Time.* Crown Business, 2005.

- Figure out ahead of time whom you'd like to meet and do some research on them. What are their interests, hobbies, business challenges, and so on?

- Prepare well thought-out and insightful questions to ask speakers of sessions you're planning to attend. Do this before you get to the conference.

- Be an information source. Have information others attending the conference need, such as directions to meeting rooms, the location of the coffee service, the lowdown on local sightseeing attractions, or even recommendations for local restaurants.

- Work the breaks and introduce people to each other as a way to provide value and facilitate building a deeper professional relationship. Do not "take a break" and just zone out for a few minutes—that's wasting a valuable opportunity.

What's the key takeaway? Prepare ahead of time to get the most out of a conference. Block some time on your calendar now and spend it preparing for the conference. Figure out which sessions you want to attend and develop those insightful questions ahead of time. Google the speakers and see if there are any you should "bump" into. Research the area and figure out how to navigate public transportation. All of these ideas are doable in an hour, and I'm betting the return on your investment of time will be substantial.

According to Ferrazzi, here are the things you should definitely *not* do.

Don't...

- Be a wallflower. Get out there and meet people!

- Be what Ferrazzi calls an *ankle-hugger.* That's someone who gloms onto the first friendly person they meet and won't let go. Try to meet as many new and interesting people as possible and don't stick like glue to just one person.

- Focus all of your efforts on getting introduced to the "celebrities." Instead, focus on meaningful conversations with everyone you run across.

- Continually scan the room for fresh meat. Focus on the person you're talking to and have a genuine conversation with that person. Disengage when it's appropriate and move on to focus on the next person.

Finally, realize that there's no prize for amassing the most business cards. At the end of the day, cards don't mean much unless you've established some common interest on both sides and follow up on the initial meeting. Back at your office, that stack of cards is pretty useless.

There you have it: some actionable ideas to help you make the most of your next conference. I hope I've provided you with some food for thought and motivated you to do some advanced planning next time you head to a conference. If you're interested in improving your networking skills, then I encourage you to pick up Ferrazzi's book, as it's chock full of these kinds of actionable ideas you can start using immediately.

I

Index

Get the eBook for only $10!

Now you can take the weightless companion with you anywhere, anytime. Your purchase of this book entitles you to 3 electronic versions for only $10.

This Apress title will prove so indispensible that you'll want to carry it with you everywhere, which is why we are offering the eBook in 3 formats for only $10 if you have already purchased the print book.

Convenient and fully searchable, the PDF version enables you to easily find and copy code—or perform examples by quickly toggling between instructions and   applications. The MOBI format is ideal for your Kindle, while the ePUB can be utilized on a variety of mobile devices.

Go to www.apress.com/promo/tendollars to purchase your companion eBook.

All Apress eBooks are subject to copyright. All rights are reserved by the Publisher, whether the whole or part of the material is concerned, specifically the rights of translation, reprinting, reuse of illustrations, recitation, broadcasting, reproduction on microfilms or in any other physical way, and transmission or information storage and retrieval, electronic adaptation, computer software, or by similar or dissimilar methodology now known or hereafter developed. Exempted from this legal reservation are brief excerpts in connection with reviews or scholarly analysis or material supplied specifically for the purpose of being entered and executed on a computer system, for exclusive use by the purchaser of the work. Duplication of this publication or parts thereof is permitted only under the provisions of the Copyright Law of the Publisher's location, in its current version, and permission for use must always be obtained from Springer. Permissions for use may be obtained through RightsLink at the Copyright Clearance Center. Violations are liable to prosecution under the respective Copyright Law.

Other Apress Business Titles You Will Find Useful

From Techie to Boss
Cromar
978-1-4302-5932-9

**How to Recruit and Hire
Great Software Engineers**
McCuller
978-1-4302-4917-7

**Managing Humans,
2nd Edition**
Lopp
978-1-4302-4314-4

Common Sense
Tanner
978-1-4302-4152-2

**No Drama Project
Management**
Gerardi
978-1-4302-3990-1

**Preventing Good People
from Doing Bad Things**
Anderson / Mutch
978-1-4302-3921-5

**Technical Support
Essentials**
Sanchez
978-1-4302-2547-8

**How to Secure Your
H-1B Visa**
Bach / Werner
978-1-4302-4728-9

**Tech Job Hunt
Handbook**
Grossman
978-1-4302-4548-3

Available at www.apress.com